I0138092

EULOGY FOR A LOST FRONTIER

The Americanization of Alaska

Dave Harman

ISBN: 978-0-578-01001-4

Dedication

My mother died on August 5, 2007. She was ninety-four years old. We like to think that her departure was not as stressful as it might have been; she was not in pain and her dementia had reached the point where she frequently wasn't aware of who we were or where she was. It's doubtful that she was even fully aware of her own imminent passing. She just sort of went to sleep and didn't wake up.

Regardless of the fact that we all knew it was about to happen, the passing of a loved one is never easy. In this case, it brings a flood of memories to me of when she was younger. I was living at home with her then, and she was the personification of everything that was comfortable and secure. I could not then have conceived of a world without her.

I don't know whether or not this book will be a success, but that doesn't really change the fact that I'd like to dedicate it to her.

Thank you, Mother, for life, for Alaska, for opportunities, for happy memories and, most of all, for just being my mother.

You were a beautiful young lady, a responsible and caring young to middle-aged mother and with time; a pretty good 'ol gal.

David

Artic Ocean
Barrow
Wainwright
Atqasuk
Point Lay
Alaska
Point Hope
Kivalina
Kiana
Ambler
Kotzebue
Selawik
Kobuk
Russia
Shishmaref
Deering
Buckland
Hughes
Huslia
Wales
Brevig Mission
Koyuk
Koyukuk
Nulato
Ruby
White Mountain
Bering Strait
Nome
Elim
Shaktoolik
Kaltag
Gambell
Savoonga
Unalakleet
Stebbins
Saint Michael
St. Lawrence Island
Kotlik
McGrath
Sheldon Point
Anvik
Shageluk
Holy Cross
Saint Mary's
Scammon Bay
Chevak
Hooper Bay
Upper Kalskag
Chuathbaluk
Stony River
Lime Village
Nunapitchuk
Akiak
Bethel
Kashegelok
Toksook Bay
Mekoryuk
Chefornak
Eek
Quinhagak
New Stuyahok
Aleknagik
Togiak
Dillingham
Platinum
Naknek
Egegik
Pilot Point
Saint Paul
Port Heiden
Saint George
Chignik
Bering Sea
Nelson Lagoon
Sand Point
Cold Bay
King Cove
Akutan
Unalaska
Chernofski
Nikolski
Pacific Ocean

Artic Ocean

Deadhorse
Kaktovik
Arctic Village
Chandalar
Fort Yukon
Beaver
Circle
Miller House
Fairbanks
Eagle
Nenana
North Pole
Anderson
Boundary
Healy Lake
Delta Junction
Cantwell
Tanacross
Canada
Paxson
Curry
Mendeltna
Copperville
Wasilla
Palmer
McCarthy
Valdez
Cordova
Seward
Cape
Yakataga
Yakutat
Haines
Juneau
Hoonah
Pelican
Gulf of Alaska
Angoon
Sitka
Kake
Petersburg
Wrangell
Port Alexander
Coffman Cove
Thorne Bay
Craig
Hydaburg
Ketchikan

Acknowledgements

I had no idea that writing a book involved so much work. It doesn't take long after finishing the first draft of the manuscript to realize that the writing is probably the easiest part of the whole effort. After that, it still seems like there's a million things left to do. The whole thing has to be read and re-read, and re-read again for typographical and grammatical errors. Someone who is skilled in such things has to edit everything for syntax, word choices, proper 'construction' and the like. After that, there are all the arrangements for formatting, printing, photographs, illustrations, maps, etc. There was also what seemed like an endless list of such trivia as safeguarding against potential legal complications, written assurances against copyright infringements, chronological verifications, notifications to (and approvals from) named people etc. etc. What happened to the dream of just whipping out a terrifically exciting book off the 'top of one's head', having some influential literary critic stumble upon it and then suddenly becoming a tremendously successful but previously unknown author?

It may seem a little phony to be thanking people for their help with a project that may turn out to be a total flop, at least from a commercial standpoint. However, they were all so generous and sincere with their help and encouragement that it would indicate a selfish lack of appreciation if I didn't acknowledge their effort.

Fortunately, my ever-faithful children were more aware than I was of the need for all the related tasks and, although they are all now grown up with the normal adult duties faced by everyone, they agreed to help. Theresa (my Terry) intended to collect, format, and integrate (into the text) all the relative photographs that we could find, as well as the drawings. The drawings were supposed to be prepared by my granddaughter

Dierdre, Kathleen's (Katy's) daughter. However, her efforts were interrupted by her marriage to a Portland, Oregon boy on June 2, 2007, and I haven't heard from her since regarding any further drawings. I fear that most of her intended drawings will thus not be included in the book. Additionally, I have since been advised that it might be best to present the photographs in several 'blocks' at various locations throughout the book rather than include them individually on separate pages. I didn't really want to present them that way, so even though some of them aren't directly referenced to incidents or specific locations described in the text. Nonetheless, that is where some of them ended up, and they look good there.

My oldest son, Jeffrey (Jeff), started preparing the full-size map of Alaska from scratch because he had all the tools for that kind of work, and because I couldn't find any appropriate maps that weren't already copyrighted. So far, I haven't heard much from him, and I will probably have to seek alternate sources for the Alaska map. There was also the option of buying and including copies of copyrighted commercial maps with a statement excluding them from the overall book copyright. At this writing, I am seeking copies of maps in the public domain that I can annotate and use freely without fear of copyright infringement. All the other kids helped with their own memories. Theresa coordinated all these efforts on the Alaskan end and kept sending me all the information as she collected and dated it.

At first we nurtured hopes that between the kids and me, we could also take care of the proofreading and editing for the entire manuscript. We learned quickly that the demands of such a task far exceeded the literary abilities or talents of any of us. Besides, editing a text that's about 140,000 words long is a daunting task, even for a professional. It soon became evident that the kids and I couldn't have done that and still keep up with normal everyday responsibilities, even if we were professional editors, which (we soon discovered) we definitely were not. Accordingly, we decided to hire a professional outfit by the name of Angel Editing to do the proofreading, editing, and the layout of the book.

I should also acknowledge the help afforded me by Eloise's (my second wife) kids. They all (except Cecile) live in Seattle or its surrounding environs. Whenever I called upon them for help, they unfailingly responded with alacrity, interest, and willingness. They don't appear to share Eloise's early expressed, and perhaps justified, skepticism regarding the entire project. She may yet be proven to have been remarkably prescient in this regard.

In general, I want to express my gratitude to everyone in our big family who was involved in this book effort. I have always been convinced that both mine and Eloise's kids are absolutely the best, most considerate and unselfish people on the planet. I suppose almost everyone with kids feels the same way. My experiences with this book, such as it is, are positive proof that my conviction is well placed. Perhaps the most remarkable aspect of their effort is the fact that they have done all I've asked while still maintaining their customary stellar performance regarding the normal duties of life. It should be particularly noted that Theresa has enthusiastically taken on the coordinating effort for me while also in the process of preparing for and undertaking major moves of her household from Alaska to Arizona and back again. I am immensely proud of her – as I am of all my children.

Of course, the kids were so closely involved with putting this book together that they might be fully familiar with the contents of the final copies before the whole package is finished. I don't have a problem with that. Hopefully, they will read it now and then just for old time's sake, and maybe they'll make sure that our succeeding generations keep reading it, regardless of its questionable literary sophistication. God knows that this is not a work of any significant artistic value. That's OK – it isn't intended to be. If my children enjoy reading it, or even grant it a little bit of space on their bookshelves, that's enough reward for me.

Table of Contents

PART V – EXILE

PREFACE

Before you read this book, I would like to clarify a few things.

The incidents and situations related herein are real and, I'm reasonably sure, pretty accurate. Maybe Mark Twain was correct when he said that memory actually improves with age. He reportedly added that, at his advanced age, his memory was so sharp he could even remember a lot of things that never happened to him. In this case, although the incidents described in the book are factually true as I remember them, most of the descriptions of things such as conclusions, people, professions, the consequences of events, attitudes, apparent opinions and the like that are purely subjective. If you don't agree with some of my conclusions or opinions, that's fine. Everyone is, of course, entitled to their own opinion. If you disagree strongly enough, don't bother to let me know; just write your *own* book in reply.

Why did I decide to undertake this project? Some cynical folks might think that, having a twisted and unrealistic opinion of my own literary talent, I hoped to somehow get the book published and make a bundle of money. Admittedly, I did approach several publishers and agents, but I can truthfully say my pursuit of publication was not all that full-blooded, and although I have nothing against money, my basic purpose is *not* monetary. Then why?

Going into retirement, or the 'golden years' as they are often incorrectly referred to by certain younger people, at first seemed to me like a good opportunity to sleep until noon every day. Fifty years of dragging myself out of bed early most days made that extra sleep look very inviting, initially. Unfortunately, as anyone who is retired will tell you, an agenda like that gets pretty old, pretty fast. Consequently, it is natural to look around for something to do that is both interesting and productive. I think that the psychological folks use the term 'fulfilling', whatever that means. In my case, the urging of my kids for some sort of 'legacy' convinced me that it might be a good idea to write up something that would last longer than I would. That thought matured into the genesis of a book.

The idea of writing this book came from a short questionnaire included in a book my daughter Theresa (Terry) gave me some time ago. The book was called *A Father's Legacy*, and the questionnaire contained a number of generalized questions that I was supposed to answer. The questions were quite stupid – they looked like something from a *Leave it to Beaver* script – and they were largely directed toward supposedly extraordinary things that happened to me during my lifetime. Unfortunately, nothing extraordinary ever happened to me, at least nothing that seemed extraordinary at the time. I left the questionnaire with the idea of returning to it. However, it did start me thinking about what I had seen happen in Alaska over the years, and I realized that witnessing the complete change in a region's culture was in fact quite extraordinary. Therefore, I decided to write it all down and the title *Eulogy for a Lost Frontier* seemed rather appropriate. I hope to tell at least part of the story of how Alaska has changed so deeply over the fifty-plus years that I lived and worked there. Such an effort required some pretty deep excursions into my memory, but so far I have been reasonably capable of extracting the relevant information despite the legitimacy of Mark Twain's remark.

After you have managed to survive the vicissitudes of life for as long as I have, it becomes clear that there truly are some things more important than wealth and material possessions. One of them is the recognition of, and familiarity with, *home* and what the word really means. Another is a feeling of worth, some assurance that your ideas and opinions are valued out of respect for your knowledge and experience. A third is the self-confidence that comes from knowing you are among friends and can count on support if needed; or put more succinctly, the ambiance that although unseen, constantly surrounds you.

Growing up in Alaska, I always felt a sense of security vis-à-vis where I was. It was always a familiar world anywhere in Alaska, and there was sort of a subconscious assurance that it would always stay that way. Unfortunately, it didn't, and when the changes came, they were profound.

On January 3, 1959, Alaska was granted statehood, and in 1968, the discovery of vast oil resources on the North Slope was announced. After those events, and in many respects before, everything about the Alaskan lifestyle began to seriously deteriorate.

Not the least of the changes was the effect of the northward immigration of all the stateside opportunists coming up to 'stake a claim' for what they saw as their share of the oil money, or the new bureaucratic and political mini-empires that they knew they could create. It was a little strange because many of these newcomers seemed to adopt the attitude that they were as much Alaskan as the old-timers. A lot of the longtime residents resented that attitude, and the resentment occasionally surfaced in the form of mild violence. Nevertheless, the 'managers' slithered into the workplace, and it wasn't long before they were chairing the staff meetings and making the decisions, despite their deplorable ignorance of technical matters in general, and the effects of the natural parameters affecting northern construction operations in particular. These are the 'dragons' referred to throughout the book.

I wasn't the only Alaskan engineer who resented this

particular development. In effect, we were being told that our experience and knowledge was only good for advising some technically inept manager who, we were given to understand, could marshal more wisdom, reach wiser conclusions, and make better decisions than we could. It was a slap in the face, besides being unmitigated nonsense.

For the Alaskans who have lived there for many years, the general change in Alaskan attitude and ambience was the most noticed and disagreeable of all the outside influences. Most of the real old-timers began to disappear, although no one seems to know exactly where they went. The old feeling of closeness and warm friendliness has eroded to the point of extinction in many places throughout the state and is being slowly eaten away everywhere else. It's hard to describe this in words, but any *real* Alaskan knows exactly what I mean – check it out and ask one.

The recent unsuccessful candidacy of Alaska's governor Sarah Palin for the vice-presidency of the United States has unfortunately focused a lot of political attention on Alaska. Indications are that this notoriety will open further opportunities for Ms. Palin within the national Republican Party, and that she intends to advance on the national political stage. Although this may help fuel a minor economic surge for the state and may generate more interest in Alaskan business and tourism, many long-time Alaskans do not see this as a favorable outcome from a societal standpoint, fearing even further deterioration of their traditional lifestyle. In any case, sheer worldwide population growth and the increasing availability of leisure time will undoubtedly improve the fortunes of the tourist industry. However, anyone with the romantic idea of visiting Alaska and experiencing some sort of 'Last Frontier' adventure should think again.

Due largely to the travel agencies and the tourism promoters, many outsiders still see Alaska as a land fraught with both danger and opportunity. There's no question that Alaskan scenery and the majesty of our innumerable vistas and coastal fjords is unequalled almost anywhere in the world. That alone is easily worth a visit to the state, but don't go north looking for grizzled old sourdoughs, gold mines, dancing halls or frontier shootouts. All that stuff is gone forever. Starting with statehood and continuing with the influx of 'management' from the Lower 48, the Alaska of the past has disappeared, and along with it so have the people and traditions that made it America's 'Last Frontier'.

Now that the opportunists have moved in, Alaskan taxpayers should be made aware of how their money is being squandered by the managers and bureaucrats who have, by and large, taken over the Alaskan workplace. There is absolutely no need for the endless meetings, memoranda, and useless, irrelevant regulations that are the fodder these fat cats feed and fatten themselves on. Someone needs to sweep house, so to speak, and kick out the administrative freeloaders.

The reader will note that at times I indulge in a fair amount of discussion regarding people and professions I interacted with in connection to my work throughout the years. Although I have rarely used any last names, there are occasions where the references are obvious, and sometimes the comments are decidedly acerbic, if not downright insulting. I want to emphasize that the opinions expressed or implied in such cases are just that – *opinions*. Be aware that the people or professions in question may or may not be as bad or as self-serving as I characterize them. My descriptions are applicable only from my own viewpoint and within my own frame of reference. If anyone is insulted, please accept my apologies; if anyone is pleased, I'm glad; and for those who don't care, neither do I.

I want to emphasize that this is not a work of fiction; there is no plot and not even a storyline – it's just the way things happened. There is no moral to the story, and it doesn't pretend to carry any deep messages about right or wrong. Those sorts of things are the intellectual fodder of psychiatrists and philosophers, not engineers.

If there is a central protagonist, it is just one man – me – who, like the vast majority of all men, has lived a fairly ordinary life with pretty ordinary loves, losses, joys, and sadness. Maybe, in a sense, it *is* the story of most average men; starting out starry-eyed, watching their world mature around them and finally surrendering to reality and the great equalizers – physical decline and death. The story here does not, of course, end in death, only in the awareness that death is not as far off as it used to seem. As age and wisdom overcome us, we finally recognize that life itself, with all its diversions, confusions and convolutions, is really nothing more than a slowly developing but inexorable terminal illness. Thankfully, in most cases, the symptoms are mercifully mild.

What then of ambitions and dreams, goals and objectives? Don't these comprise young men's incentives for future success and, we hope, old men's memories of past accomplishment? Whether or not such things are worth writing about, the story here is largely meant to illustrate the societal changes that were taking place while these ambitions and dreams were developing. The personal aspects of what was happening naturally color the descriptions throughout the book. I hope the reader will indulge me when I describe a few of them in relative detail.

I'm an engineer, and my previous literary efforts have been largely confined to technical or semi-technical reports that hardly anyone was interested in or, for that matter, even read at the time. Indeed, it was certainly not unheard of for the conclusions or recommendations in the reports to be completely ignored. I was never particularly concerned about such cavalier treatment as long as the report recipient paid my bill (salary or fee) and didn't want to argue about or endlessly discuss the outcome. That's the way I'm going to write this book. Everything will be true to the best of my recollections. I'll include appropriate personal memories and thoughts with occasional anecdotes about people and/or events that caught my attention at the time. If my writing style isn't dramatic enough to suit you, then try to conjure up some more romantic images of your own. Drama is for fiction, and I don't do fiction I'm afraid.

A Short Story Before I Begin

Sometimes a big bald eagle apparently starts thinking that he's a lot bigger and stronger than he really is. Thinking that way, he may hook his talons into the back of a big salmon that's perhaps even bigger and stronger than him. Eagles aren't able to release their talons until the weight is off them, so the eagle will be pulled under the surface of the water by the fish. He can't get loose until the upward lift of the water relieves the weight, or the fish quits pulling downward, and allows him to let go. I suppose there must be a few who drown during this ordeal, but those who don't will go flopping to shore using their wings in a sort of eagle-style, awkward-looking butterfly stroke. After they get up on the beach, they crawl up on a big rock or something and, all wet and bedraggled with their dignity stripped away, look piercingly both ways up and down the beach. It appears that they're looking to make sure no was watching their failed fishing fiasco. I've seen this happen five times during my fifty years as an Alaskan: once near the mouth of the Taku Inlet south of Juneau, on the east side of Wrangell Narrows just outside Petersburg, on the east shore of Kodiak Island a few miles north of the city, on the west side of Lynn Canal a few miles south of Skagway/Dyea, and near the mouth of the Chilkat River during the early fall salmon run just north of Haines. Each and every time the eagle acted exactly the same way following his futile effort.

There's a lesson here I feel.

Don't get overconfident like the eagle and hook into something (in my case this book) that you're not equipped to handle – you may be 'pulled under'. I don't want to look up and down the beach at my family and colleagues to find that I've failed in full view of those who matter most to me.

PART I
BECOMING ALASKAN

Chapter 1: Introduction

It's gone now, the Alaska we grew up with. It's almost surreal – like a sad, nostalgic dream of something once remembered.

Nobody actually came and stole it away. It just sort of sank into a sea of compromise and conformity and slowly disappeared. It's hard to even recall when it all started. With statehood? With the Oil boom? Maybe the changes started coming sooner than we realized and, being young, we were too busy to notice or to see what was on the horizon. Is someone to blame? Was it the politicians? The 'managers'? The bureaucratic carpetbaggers coming north right after statehood to exploit the political vacuum? Or was it the Oklahoma oilfield workers who came to tear up the tundra and raise up the derricks? They left their pointy-toed boots, big hats, huge fancy belt buckles and an unnatural Eskimo taste for country and western music as lasting mementos of their passing. Was it the tourists who flocked up in their big RV's, or rode in on the luxurious cruise ships? They keep coming even now. They keep coming in their thousands to see some safe and sanitized version of the 'last frontier' from the window of a tour bus. They don't realize that it's no longer there – and who's to tell them, or paint a verbal picture of the way it used to be? Surely it wasn't the tourists who did this to us.

Aren't they just welcome visitors, seeing our home as the world's largest wilderness amusement park, furnished and financed by the travel industry? Maybe a huge wildlife refuge? Maybe a massive national park or a monument like Yellowstone? Could it have been the fault of all of us because we didn't see it coming in time to stop it? I think no one knows the true answers to those questions; I certainly don't, *and **I** watched it happening.* Anyway, the old Alaska is no longer there, except at a few locations in the high arctic where the oil industry has not yet invaded or in the remote mountains where access is limited to bush plane fly-ins. It can no more be brought back than a rising tide can be pumped back into the sea.

My own profession has been deeply affected by all the fundamental advances in technology, and the changing administrative procedures.

In the field, where hands-on abilities and basic knowledge have traditionally proven essential, electronic gadgetry has turned quite a few promising young surveyors into little more than computer technicians and 'gadgeteers'. They may know which buttons to push and how to read the impressive displays presented by the new equipment, but the ultimate purpose of what they're doing, why they're doing it, and the hands-on methods and skills used in the absence of electronics are often only vaguely understood. The once essential and indescribable surveyor's instincts for 'reading' the terrain and topography seem to be fading away.

Worse, the engineering office workplace is quickly falling prey to the idiotic concept of 'generic management' – the bizarre theory that someone fully trained in just 'Management' (upper case 'M') is capable of managing anything and everything with no knowledge of the specific or technical details of what they're actually managing. The result has been a grotesque proliferation of meetings, memoranda, and endless codification of needless, irrelevant, time-wasting and pointless bureaucratic regulations. The eventual goal has changed from *product* to *process*. I refer to this shift in emphasis many times throughout the book because it is the most damaging of all the production-negative concepts so far introduced to the engineering construction discipline by the 'generic management' advocates.

Most long-time Alaskans will agree that the state (territory) is, for better or worse, nothing like it was. However, the problem is that few of us seem to know why, or exactly when, all these changes took place. In many cases, although we can viscerally feel that many things are different, we can't specifically identify or describe what they are. I'm afraid I fell into that latter category, and my curiosity and confusion got worse as I got older. I thought maybe if I tried writing it all down, it might be possible to come up with better descriptions of, reasons for and effects of all these changes, as well as when and how they started to show up.

I will support the effort by writing about a few of my own Alaskan experiences and impressions over the last fifty years or so. I'll also make comparisons of how things were then and how they are now, and how I remember them then, and as I see them today. Maybe it will be possible to identify the points in time when the changes in policies and procedures began to germinate and take root.

Chapter 2: Memories and Miracles

When we were younger and my first wife and I were having each of our eight children, she did all the work, and I did all the worrying. I used to say half-jokingly, "The miracle of birth strikes again." I didn't fully realize it then, but we were indeed witnessing a true miracle in each birth. The real beauty in each of these miracles is that they keep reinventing themselves as time goes by. Isn't that a real bonus? There are eight children from my first marriage, and the gifts of their births will enrich my life until I die, and I hope the lives of others even beyond that. I continue to give thanks for them, and I regard each of them with awe. This is who they are and when they arrived:

Laura RoseAnn – November 7, 1955
Theresa Claire – January 8, 1957
Denise Jay – July 31, 1958
Kathleen Louise – October 10, 1959
David Jeffrey – September 2, 1961
Richard Austin – February 2, 1963
Jacqueline Carol – January 13, 1964
Thomas Joseph – June 1, 1967

We decided to not use any names like 'Gentle Breeze', 'Babbling Brook', 'Love' or any of the names that seemed to be gaining popularity at one time in certain sectors of society. Anyway, these are our true miracles, far outweighing anything else that has ever happened to me.

Additionally, when I married Eloise, my second wife, I was honored to become the stepfather of five more beautiful people: Theresa, Luis (Rey), Delana, Cecile and Karen. This book, however it turns out, is written with thanks to those eight cherished people for being born to me, and to Eloise's five for accepting me. I hope to have at least thirteen readers.

Wedding Day for Eloise and I

Chapter 3: Pre-Career Background

I wasn't born an Alaskan. In fact, I wasn't even born an American. I've been told that Maidenhead in the County of Berkshire, England was, at the time of my birth there on May 30, 1935, pretty much a self-contained town about twenty miles west of London on the Thames River. Since then, my uncle John told me it has become just a 'bedroom community' for Greater London.

Eloise and I traveled there in 1973 to take my inheritance and spend it back in England. We met Uncle John (Harman), who gave us sort of a driving tour of the town and its environs. He's dead now (God rest him), but when we were there he was the typical Englishman that everyone thinks of when picturing the home counties of England. He very much reminded me of Edmund Gwenn, the actor who portrayed Kris Kringle in Miracle on 34th Street. He was reserved and very conscious of the family image. When we were discussing some of the Harman relatives he told us of Uncle Horace who, he said, was "in transportation". We found out later from my mother that Uncle Horace, although capable and hardworking, was not the

Meeting a friend from Kodiak in Trafalgar Square, London, UK.

"brightest bulb in the box." She explained that he was indeed "in transportation", having worked for thirty or forty years as a janitor for the Thames Valley Bus Line.

Uncle John took me to my father's grave, where I 'meditated' briefly, laid down some flowers and said a couple of prayers on his behalf. I concluded that, although death in itself may be the final and inevitable tragedy for everyone, especially those left behind, my father was essentially a stranger to me. I'm sorry that he died at just fifty-eight – a short life – but I'm also sorry that so many others have died younger than expected, especially in the numerous wars that we seem determined to continuously inflict upon ourselves. I really didn't know my father any better than I knew those strangers.

About three or four years after my sister and I were born, my mother and father were divorced. I realize that married couples always have differences of opinions and sometimes pretty extended arguments, and I'm sure that my parents were no exception. I have a suspicion that, in this case, my Grandmother Hornby had a lot to do with it. Granny told me repeatedly that my father drank too much and sometimes didn't make it home for dinner. Apparently, he frequently preferred the camaraderie of his favorite pub. I imagine that Granny spent a lot of time at their home, and that she was almost always hanging around ready to harangue on my father about his arguments with my mother and his drinking whenever he eventually did get home.

Anyway, after her divorce my mother took me and my grandmother took Janet, my sister, and we all went to the United States.

I don't remember many of the details of where we were living and what we were doing before about 1940. My mother told me that we lived in Hillsboro or Corvallis, Oregon (I can't remember which). After that, we lived with our Aunt Kathleen in Oakland, California for a brief time before going to

McMinnville, Oregon and moving in with my mother's parents.

I was six years old when the Japanese bombed Pearl Harbor. The lady who lived across the highway from my grandparents ran over and broke the news of the attack to us. It was, of course, on Sunday, December 7, 1941. At the time it was considered a 'sneak' attack, unprovoked and despicable. Since then, long-range preemptive strikes as initial acts of war seem to have become accepted as legitimate and sometimes brilliant strategic actions on the part of a weaker combatant faced with what they consider to be an unavoidable war.

Unfortunately for the Japanese, the Pearl Harbor attack accomplished exactly the opposite of what they hoped for. Instead of rolling over and suing for peace, the U.S. and our allies got incredibly pissed off at Japan and in the end kicked their ass all over and out of the Pacific Islands and mainland Asia. When I heard the news of the attack, I asked where Pearl Harbor was, and when told it was far to the west I rushed outside and searched the western horizon for smoke from the exploding bombs.

Not even the adults, much less a six-year-old kid, were then truly aware of the long-term implications of the Japanese attack. Apart from the impending horrors and devastation of WWII, American life would never be the same again. The country had now been unwillingly dragged into a new awareness, and we were soon forced to become a full and contributing member of the worldwide community of nations. In a very real sense, it was, in the words of Arthur C. Clark, *Childhood's End.* America's insularity was over and my own life would also be affected – indirectly but permanently – as would the lives of my children and grandchildren yet to come.

Just after the war, when I was ten years old, my mother took a job in the Alaskan Headquarters of the Office of Price Administration in Juneau. This organization was better known as the 'OPA' – the age of acronyms was arriving. I remember that my mother traveled ahead to take care of the preliminaries prior to going to work and to find a place for us to stay. Popeye, my nickname for my grandfather, traveled there with me two or three weeks later. Janet stayed with Granny and did so all the way through college until she got married to some dork from California and moved away. I'm sure the parting was tearful and no doubt very dramatic.

I think Popeye and I departed from Portland, or perhaps we took a train to Seattle and left from there. I don't remember which, and it doesn't matter anyway. In either case, we flew to Juneau in a Pan American DC-4 with a stop on Annette Island for the passengers going to Ketchikan. At that time there was no onshore runway at Ketchikan, so those wishing to go there by air had to get off the plane from 'stateside' (or 'outside') on Annette and transfer to an Ellis Airlines or Alaska Coastal float plane[1] for the shuttle flight to Ketchikan.

It's ironic that Annette Island was both the first Alaskan soil I ever stood on and that the location, design and construction of the new Ketchikan Airport on nearby Gravina Island was the first project I was involved with as Director of Aviation for the eight-year-old State of Alaska twenty-two years later. For a long time, the City of Ketchikan funded and operated a little passenger ferry from downtown to the new Gravina Airport. Now, however, there is a bridge from the city to the airport island.

Popeye and I flew on to Juneau after spending about an hour or two at Annette while the airline picked up a few passengers who were leaving Ketchikan; we finally arrived in Juneau unscathed and landed without incident. Now began what was, for me, a totally new way of life.

Of course, I couldn't know it at the time, but during the next

[1] Usually a Grumman Goose or sometimes a PBY.

fifty years of my life, I was to witness the home I grew to love change into a place depressingly like everywhere else.

Downtown Juneau – During the southern approach to Juneau Airport

Chapter 4: Alaskan Simplicity

It was cloudy the day we got to Juneau, but somehow it didn't seem like the cloudy days I was familiar with in McMinnville. It wasn't cold, but the air smelled like fresh ice water with just a touch of the scent of fir trees. Even the clouds, which always looked so gloomy 'at home', seemed like raincoats that the surrounding mountains had put on. I was fascinated by the way the edges of the fogbanks dispersed into the trees as though they were retreating to where they had come from. I've never forgotten those impressions from that first day; nor have I forgotten the disappointment I felt upon finding after a long absence that those memories had become nothing more than ghosts of the past. It's still a little surprising, even to me, that such things would so profoundly impress a ten-year-old kid in that way.

The Alaska, and the Juneau, where I arrived that year were vastly different from what they are today. Statehood was still more than twelve years away, and although it was the territorial capital, Juneau still had the pleasant ambiance of a small town. The Mendenhall Valley just north of the city was almost entirely unpopulated, and the city itself seemed much less crowded than it does today. Of course, I was only a child, but even at that age I could sense that this was a town with the emphasis on working and producing. Politics must have only been a secondary concern at that time, and there were no doubt more fishermen than politicians – more 'halibut shirts' than suit jackets. As we will see, these conditions in Juneau were going to change, and in many respects the changes have been so pervasive and so all-consuming that when one examines them it's impossible not to wonder how and when it all happened.

There was no scheduled car ferry service then, and after living there a few months one could identify the owner of every car in town just by looking at it parked on the street. There were, of course, barge services as well as Alaska Steamship Lines going both north and south providing irregular auto transport. However, the ease of intercity travel provided by today's ferry system was a long way off as were the effects, both good and bad, of such convenient access.

I entered the local education system in the old grade school just east of the old high school. The school building was one block uphill and one block east from what is now the Alaska Legislative Office Building but was then the Federal Building. All the kids had a sort of informal inside gathering space around the northeast corner bottom floor entrance to the Federal Building, where most of the post office boxes were located. By the time I got to high school, the area had become an increasingly popular spot for many students from all grades who wanted to postpone the inevitable and prepare for the school day ahead. I'm sure the post office patrons didn't appreciate our gatherings, but I can't remember any big fuss about it. My subsequent (much later) experience with the 'new' Juneau administration showed me that such casual gatherings would be strictly forbidden today, largely because of the fear of a bad impression on visiting politicians. Sadly, perception has largely replaced necessity as the driving force behind most of the politically motivated 'improvements' in today's Alaska.

At that time there was little or no residential or commercial development in the Mendenhall Valley, so we didn't go out there much. There were several swimming holes (mostly abandoned gravel pits) hidden in the brush out there with barely passable haul roads leading to them. We held many, many parties at all these places, and I attended almost all of them, as well as class picnics for all the classes – freshman to senior – even though I wasn't a class member for most of them. All the old gravel pits are filled in now, and the little access roads are all blocked off. I suppose it was a good thing to be so well protected, even from ourselves.

The Mendenhall Valley is now completely filled with suburban development, just like any city residential neighborhood anywhere in the United States. I didn't see it at first, but the rapidly encroaching housing developments in the Mendenhall Valley after about 1955 were probably harbingers of things to come.

During this period, I became particularly fond of South Franklin Street. It was considered a sort of 'skid road' at the time – I think the term comes from the name used for the old logging town waterfront roads once used to 'skid' logs down to the waterfront. A lot of parents forbade their high school age children from going down there. I don't know what they imagined would happen to their kids on South Franklin, or what they thought was going on there, but I'm sure the perception was far worse than the reality. There *were* things that I suppose some of today's more 'upstanding citizens' might consider objectionable, although I don't recall anything nearly as dishonorable as what routinely goes on in many lawyers' offices and legislative conference rooms these days. There were frequently a certain number of drunks (nowadays known as alcoholics and/or homeless) asleep in the various doorways during the summer, but they were almost always harmless, unlike in most of today's larger cities in the 'lower 48'.

The City of Juneau had ordinances against this sort of

behavior at that time – people who got drunk and staggered around the street or laid down and fell asleep in doorways could be taken to jail to sober up. They could be charged with 'Vagrancy', a rather nebulous term that has since been supplanted by the non-criminal designation of 'homelessness' – one of our newer professions.

In many cases getting jailed was the best thing that could happen to them. Nowadays the ubiquitous psychologists/sociologists analyze the hell out of such people and either send them to some place for 'the cure' or turn them loose to think about it before going out and doing the same thing all over again.

This was not really a problem on the South Franklin of the late 1940's and early 1950's. It seemed that nobody who was in that kind of shape was ever aggressive like they are in many cities (including Seattle) in the 'lower 48', and they almost always fell asleep in such places as doorways so that they didn't block the sidewalks. If they *were* blocking the pedestrians, either the police (walking foot patrols at the time) would take them to jail to sober up, or some concerned denizens of this allegedly infamous area would move them to protected locations.

Front Street – Downtown Juneau

There may have been plenty of social outcasts on that street, but one thing is for sure, we had no phony big shots or conniving, self-serving do-gooders out to use as many people as necessary for whatever political notoriety they could get while feigning community concern. On the South Franklin of that time there were, believe it or not, strong convictions about honor and ethics – instances of cheating or stealing were rare or nonexistent. Nothing even close to that can be said of the so-called 'respectable' world of business or, even more emphatically, about the falsely admired legal profession. I'll discuss the tragedy of the modernization of South Franklin in a later chapter.

There *was* the occasional street and bar fight, but it was almost always limited to spur-of-the-moment disagreements between only two, three or maybe four opponents, and it happened all over town, not just along South Franklin. There were no gang fights or drive-by shootings that seem to characterize the semi-slum urban streets of today. Although often discussed by people who knew less than nothing about South Franklin, knifings or shootings were *extremely* rare, certainly much less frequent than in most of the big lower 48 cities today – even per capita. What fights there were hardly ever lasted more than two or three minutes and grudges were almost never held afterwards. I can't remember a single fight that resulted in anything more serious than black eyes, broken teeth, or (rarely) a dislocated jawbone. I don't think there was ever any murderous intent in any of the fights that I personally witnessed. Indeed, it seemed like the combatants would often forget the reasons for the disagreement even before all the scuffling was over. In such cases, the pushing, shoving, and swinging would slowly die out and the two or three fighters would usually have a few beers together before leaving the bar. Such things and such people have probably disappeared from South Franklin by now. The reasons for their disappearance may become obvious as my story develops.

In those days, the actual physical appearance of the waterfront as well as South Franklin Street was a lot different than it is now. The new, fancy downtown Marine Park along the city waterfront wasn't there then. Alaska Coastal and Ellis Airlines had their tie-up floats at the north end and the rest of the dock frontage was lined with fish/shrimp canneries except for a couple of industrial loading platforms and the downtown small boat harbor located just south of where the library/parking garage is today. The boat Harbor is still there but there aren't nearly as many resident boats using it as there once were.

Today's South Franklin is only a shadow of its former self. Its character, atmosphere and general ambiance have been stolen and can never be brought back. The bars, cheap hotels, steam baths, warm family run Filipino restaurants and simple, rain-soaked boarding houses are gone now. The houses of 'ill-repute' with their white lights are gone too. I suppose the lady practitioners have been forced onto the streets so that the phony politicians and the 'upstanding' city officials can point to a 'sinless city'. The tourists, the lawyers and the 'Managers' (uppercase 'M', if you please) have taken over. The enemy occupation is complete. Today's South Franklin is so obviously given over to the tourist industry that it's truly sickening.

Juneau – Marine Park

Could we have seen all these changes coming even then? It wasn't obvious to us. Of course we could note the burgeoning tourist trade, and some of us even sensed the ominous and awful growth of government with its attendant spread of the management and bureaucratic malignancy. Anyway, we were still kids and who listens to kids? We obviously couldn't have predicted the changes that would come with statehood, and the political opportunists who crowded in behind it.

About the end of 1950, my mother took me back to McMinnville. I guess her employment agreement had expired. She didn't mind going back down there, but I hated the idea. She never gave Juneau a chance; she disliked it from the time we got there until we left. Personally, I had now grown to love it and felt strongly opposed to going back 'outside'. Besides, I had a more personal and sentimental reason for wanting to stay.

I had met and become much attached to a Juneau girl named Irene, and we had, by now, grown to be quite fond of one another. The separation was very painful. I promised her I'd be back soon, and I knew that I would, although I didn't know how I would manage it. This time, when I kissed her goodbye, with my eyes closed, I actually saw those stars and flashes that everyone talks about. It was the most amazing thing (of all the delightful things up to that time) that had ever happened to me. Irene was to become my first wife in 1955, and we stayed married for seventeen years, but that's another story all by itself and not really germane to the message I'm trying to convey here. Besides, it's still a little painful to talk about.

While we were in McMinnville this time, I was totally preoccupied with finding ways to get back to Alaska. At one point I hitchhiked to Seattle hoping to catch a fishing boat heading back to Juneau, and I almost did, missing one departure by only a day or two. You might say I ran away from home except that nobody came looking for me – slightly deflating for one's ego. I think being searched for is one of the requirements for classification as a 'runaway'.

I was unaware that right after I left a boyfriend of my mother's named Hubert "Jack" Thatcher from Alaska arrived in McMinnville and urged her to go back up north and get married, presumably to him. I had met Jack previously in Juneau and was favorably impressed, although it was probably doubtful that he cared about my opinion one way or the other. I was delighted to find that she had accepted his invitation, and, I guess, what amounted to a proposal of marriage after his divorce from his first wife became final, if it wasn't already so. This was not the last time Jack would prove a welcome benefactor. He was also instrumental in steering me into an engineering career, a choice that I never regretted.

For some reason, we took one of the Alaska Steamship coastal passenger vessels out of Seattle rather than flying. At that time they offered passenger service to all the key towns that served as distribution hubs along the southeast and southwest coasts of Alaska. The Alaska Steamship Company went out of business in 1971 as the airlines took over.

We were ticketed on Alaska Steamship from Seattle to Valdez (pronounced Valdeez) with only a two or three-day stop in Juneau. In those days the Alaska Steamship vessels made Seattle-Seattle round trips with stops in Ketchikan, Wrangell, Petersburg, Sitka, Juneau, Seward, Valdez, and Cordova in that order. I don't know if there was any backhaul from any of those ports, and I don't think that Kodiak was included every time.

There are no longer any passenger ships, except for the state ferries and the cruise ships, serving Alaska's coast, and that's a shame. It was a delightful way to travel. The unhurried atmosphere aboard the ships, the opportunity (particularly in winter) to meet other Alaskans from throughout the territory, the good food with waiters to serve it, and the unparalleled scenery all combined to make those trips another unforgettable Alaskan experience. That's another example of an opportunity now gone

Alaska State Ferry

forever but not forgotten, at least not by the old-time real Alaskans.

Our trip back up north was in the spring and the school at Mt. Edgecumbe, near Sitka, was just ending its school year. Edgecumbe was a BIA (Federal Bureau of Indian Affairs[2]) high school. Incidentally, although the BIA was indeed badly choked with bureaucratic bullshit even then, it was nothing compared to what the Alaska State Government has now become – but more on that later.

There were a lot of Indian guys (and two girls – one very pretty, and of course I developed an immediate crush on her) from Edgecumbe who boarded the ship at Sitka to return home from the school there. They were very genuine, delightful, and friendly kids about my age, and I made some friendships that have lasted to this day. In fact, when Roy (one of the guys) came to Anchorage several years ago to answer a DWI charge, he stopped in to see Eloise and me, and we had a *very* enjoyable visit. He was by then a big shot – the chairman of an Indian organization whose name I can't spell or pronounce.

I suggested that, being such a public figure, he would probably only be subjected to the minimum penalty under the law, and I asked if this was his first moving traffic violation. He showed us that astonishingly charming and remarkably broad smile of his (probably a factor in getting the chairmanship) and said it was his fifth DWI. Incidentally, many of the Indian folks jokingly refer to this particular violation as 'Drinking With Indians'. I hoped that his engaging personality and social skills were sufficient to charm the court into holding his penalty to the absolute minimum.

At this point I must acknowledge that there has been one *very* positive change in the attitude of many Alaskans. When I first moved there, most bars and many restaurants would not

[2] Also known as 'Boss Indians Around' or 'Bureaucracy In Action'.

serve Indian folks. Not being inclined then or now to think much about or even notice such things I simply went wherever we *could* go when I was with an Indian friend and never developed an opinion about it one way or the other. Now, however, both the more liberal attitudes of the younger generation, and the fact that many of the Indian groups (or tribes, or whatever) have been awarded very large sums of money from land claims, Indian people can go anyplace they like. In fact, they *own* a lot of the bars, restaurants, hotels, etc. Good on 'em, as they say in Australia.

When we arrived in Valdez in early 1950, the downtown area and much of the residential section were still located in a little bay that ended at what was essentially a glacial out-wash fan from Valdez Glacier. It was glacial till, and the folly of building on such material, especially in the presence of subsurface water under any artesian pressure, became evident during and after the Alaskan earthquake of Good Friday, 1964. Nonetheless, the town had been there in that spot without incident since the middle to late nineteenth century. It served as the farthest north ice-free salt-water access for the trails/wagon roads to the Fairbanks area gold fields, including Pedro Creek and Livengood.[3] After the oil discoveries on the North Slope and the construction of the trans-Alaska pipeline, Valdez was to gain more prominence and suffer a more profound change than almost any other town in the state.

When we got to Valdez I had no car of my own so hitchhiking was my primary means of travel if I wanted to go very far. These days everyone knows that hitchhiking is a very dangerous way to get around, both for the hiker and the drivers. It's been that way for some time in the lower 48, but it was actually pretty safe in Alaska until just before statehood when so many opportunists and carpetbaggers began moving north. It

[3] Yes – it's spelled correctly and pronounced Lie-ven-good, not Living-good.

was another precursor of the changes to come that slipped by unnoticed by so many of us.

Valdez Episcopal Church – 1950

I made a number of short excursions around the territory during that time, and I made one major expedition through Anchorage, Seward, Fairbanks, and back to Valdez in the company of a guy recently up from Washington, D.C.

When I got back to Jack and my mother's trailer in Valdez in the spring of 1951, I found that Jack had just returned from Haines, where he was coordinating several survey crews working in British Columbia, Canada. The goal was to improve the Haines Highway alignment where it crosses the coast range summit, fittingly named for the overwhelming presence of the adjacent peaks called the 'Three Guardsmen'.

I asked him if he would consider hiring me into the lowest position on the crew. We discussed several issues that made such a thing very difficult, among which were the following: I would not even be sixteen until the end of the month, and that being his stepson might raise questions about the appearance of nepotism.

I managed to confront and resolve most of his concerns, and

after noting the sincerity and intensity of my request for the job, and wanting to please my mother, he relented.

In those days, it was a little easier to circumvent some of the peripheral regulations such as those governing age limits because there weren't so many bureaucratic managers running around looking for something to do. Additionally, there weren't really enough ironclad restrictions to furnish them with the self-assumed importance with which they love to cloak themselves. This, of course, would change, but at the time we were blissfully ignorant of the pending administrative entanglements and nightmares.

We left for Haines on May 16, 1951 at 5:45 a.m. I remember it well because it was exactly two weeks before my sixteenth birthday.

PART II
STIRRINGS

Chapter 1: An Age of Innocence

The job on the Haines survey crew wasn't my first working experience, but it *was* the first of any substance. Before my mother married Jack I had worked at several different part-time jobs such as inventorying and stocking for a few Juneau merchants and washing windows all over town. I even spent three non-freezing months working for the U.S. Forest Service. We were supposed to be clearing, brushing and cutting away wind-fallen trees over trails in the Juneau area, but we actually spent all but one month carrying materials halfway up a mountain for building a Ranger's residence. Now I was going to begin a *real* job. Even though I was still just a kid, I could sense that thanks to Jack I was now about to enter a line of work that promised a genuine future.

The Haines job was the beginning of what was to be a life-long career in engineering. There were good times and tough times to come, just as in the careers of almost everyone. All things considered, this job was a major turning point in my life. What I wasn't aware of at the time was my opportunity to witness the profound changes in Alaska that would gradually swallow us over the following fifty years. However, all that was in the unforeseen future; our job was immediate.

Coming north out of Haines toward the Haines Highway

Junction with the Alaska Highway, the Canadian border is at about milepost 42. The beginning of our project was at about milepost 55 on the existing road, and the end was at about milepost 70 at the Three Guardsmen summit of the Coast Range Mountains.

Three Guardsmen Summit, approximately sixty-five miles northwest of Haines.

Our campsite was on a tributary of the Klahini River called Seltat Creek, where we brought in four eight-by-thirty-foot trailers. One was a mess trailer, one was a sort of office trailer where the chief of parties or an occasional visitor stayed, and the two others were sleeping trailers. We had a canvas-shielded outhouse built rather precariously out over an eighty-foot bluff along the Klahini River about a hundred feet downstream from Seltat Creek. We drew our domestic water from the Creek, but the location was far enough upstream from the Klahini to prevent contamination.

I have described our campsite in some detail to show that we were capable of setting up something like that without the continuous oversight of the environmental zealots, health department experts, saviors of the fish populations and so on.

They were on the horizon though, and they would descend on all those delightfully remote projects soon enough. When they arrived we would face the turnaround from concern about project progress to ridiculously overdone environmental regulations, which severely impacted both remote surveys and construction projects with no commensurate benefit to either the environment or the taxpayers. At the time, I doubt if any of us foresaw the unnecessary and ineffective regulations of today, so we just kept on making progress – we were happy in our ignorance.

On rare occasions official visitors either from the sub-district office in Haines or even from Juneau conducted inspection trips throughout Southeast Alaska. I think such trips were largely a means of escaping the confines of the office because the visiting officials never told us what to do and never tried to look or act 'official'. It's different these days. The opportunity for such posturing is not lost on the upward-thrusting young MBA's of today. It's one of the chief administrative mechanisms through which many of them can pursue supervisory positions without really having to know or learn anything requiring a modicum of mental exertion.

One of these rare visits that I specifically remember was quite late in the season and involved a small group from Juneau. They were conducting on-site inspections of all the field projects in Southeast Alaska. They had a couple of jobs close to Haines, so I guess they decided to come visit ours while they were in the neighborhood, so to speak. There happened to be a rather attractive young lady along who was a member of one of the committees, or groups, or panels, or whatever they were.

At some point, she asked if she could use our restroom. The whole group including our boss, Robbie, had been up to the summit and back, walking along the line relocation with the 'inspectors', and she had apparently been holding her urges for some time. After looking over our facilities, she said she could wait till she got back down the road to a more 'suitable' restroom.

We weren't insulted, but we *did* remind her that it was late in the day and the customs office would probably be closed by now. At that time, the customs station kept regular working hours and was usually closed at night. If she insisted on a traditional toilet, she would most likely have to wait all the way to Haines, or very nearly so.

Nonetheless, she still insisted on declining our well-meant offer of hospitality and gambling on her chances of making it to Haines.

In the years since, I've often wondered if she made it. If not, I've speculated about how she contended with the necessity of using just the roadside woods, without even the shelter of a facility as primitive as ours. If she did make it, it occurs to me that she must have been facing a medical near emergency before she got there.

It's worth noting here that all the people on such rare inspection trips were engineers and/or professional road builders in those days. There were no management or administrative folks represented at all; they began showing up later in droves, or herds, or flocks, or whatever such dragons run in.

Sometime around 1960, the agency lawyers began showing up on these survey inspection trips, as well as going out to look over construction projects. Ostensibly, they were there to make sure the engineers and surveyors didn't do anything that, in the effect on future construction practices or on the finished facility, could create any sort of liability and the subsequent potential of paying damages in the event of road-related collisions. That might make sense in principle, but it soon became obvious that most lawyers couldn't even keep their feet under them in the woods while walking over survey cut-lines. On construction jobs they were almost always so pathetically ignorant about what was going on that they didn't have a clue regarding what the work would produce. I once suggested to one of them that we avoid all liability by simply not doing the project; it was a joke, but he didn't even smile.

I know there are lawyers who have some engineering and construction knowledge, but I never met any of them on those inspection trips. In fact, that may have been the birth of my life-long disregard for the legal profession. I don't really disrespect or dislike lawyers as individuals; it's just that I see what they do as self-serving and opportunistic more often than not. Despite my attempts to contain my feelings, I also resent their usual know-it-all attitude, particularly about matters and disciplines they had hardly even heard of until they picked up a few words of the professional jargon.

Our mission on the Haines job was to locate and stake a new 'P' (Preliminary) roadway centerline from which we could (and did) gather field data for the design of a final construction route up to and over the summit. We hoped to eliminate several switchback curves which some larger trucks couldn't negotiate without backing and maneuvering and to generally improve the alignment and gradient coming up out of the Klahini River Valley – we succeeded.

I loved the work, the living conditions, the food and generally everything about the job. This was truly Alaska; the air was clear, the rivers and creeks were clean, the lush green forest was undisturbed and the nostalgia-producing smell of wet fir and spruce was all around us.

Still today, every time that smell reaches me my emotions are flooded with memories of things long past, including the Haines job. We were alone on that job, and we were happy to be alone. Sadly, there are no more jobs like this, but I was still in time to experience a few more of them before such 'pioneer' projects faded away forever.

As I noted above, we had very few visitors to the job from the headquarters office in Juneau, or even from the sub-district office in Haines. In those days, before the management or administrative 'movers and shakers' began to smother us, project decisions and staffing requirements were the exclusive responsibility of the project engineer or chief of parties on the job. The headquarters offices, and the administrators who worked there, served only in a supporting role.

At that time, such things were of no concern to me. In the years that followed, however, I watched the proliferating managers and administrators increasingly interfere with the project supervisors and insinuate themselves into positions for which they were and are woefully unqualified.

Non-electronic surveyor – circa 1950

There were no electronic survey instruments available then. Accordingly, we had to use real hands-on skills with the traditional tools and instruments and to note the *character* of the terrain over which we were working. I've always felt that these requirements taught us, as it did all surveyors of that time, to 'read' the topography visually and thus obtain the ground measurements truly necessary and relevant for accurately preparing design and construction drawings and performing the related calculations.

Sometimes it appears that today's surveyors simply go out, set up their electronic 'data collector' and saturate the whole area with as many random readings as possible. There is apparently no attempt to make sure that the relative locations of the data points 'paint' a numerical (quantitative) picture of the terrain. Additionally, it's still true that unless the office reviewer of the field notes is also a surveyor or has some surveying experience, the resulting analyses of the field data will probably be bogus regardless of the sophistication of the tools.

The data taken from today's electronic *field* gadgets are usually taken to the office and fed to an electronic *office* gadget. Except for punching a few keys, a living knowledgeable office *person* often never even sees, much less evaluates, the data until they are presented in the form of a completed drawing, or in extreme cases even a design.

I never learned to operate those electronic survey tools. Maybe that's why I tend toward saying that today's crews often consist more of computer technicians than surveyors. They often lack the traditional surveyor's instincts that were usually as indispensable as precise measurements in reaching logical conclusions and making on-site decisions.

We never saw much game on the Haines job except for an

occasional moose or black bear, and none of them took much notice of us. We did see lots of goats on the mountain north of the first switchback curve at the bottom of the steep grade leading to the summit. The subject of game on the road reminds me of an incident that I've always remembered as very humorous. In fact, considering who it happened to, it was hilarious. If the reader will indulge me, I'd like to relate the story here.

One day at about dusk we were halfway down the steep section of the road from the summit heading back to camp for the day. Coming around one of the switchback curves, we suddenly encountered a large black bear sitting right in the middle of the road. As soon as he saw us, he stood up on all four feet and ambled off into the brush on the downhill side. The bear didn't seem frightened, probably because in those days the hunting pressure at that location wasn't nearly as intense as it is today. Many of the wild animals there had not yet come to recognize the vicious and murderous nature of mankind.

Anyway, one of the guys on the crew was the type that one hates to encounter in any situation where it's necessary to have a conversation. His name was Doug, and he was a complete bore; always bragging about his exploits at one endeavor or another. Besides that, his language was usually vulgar and more often obscene, regardless of who was within earshot. He was particularly verbose about his role in WWII, claiming to have won a battlefield commission at Kasserine Pass in Tunisia and about his prowess as a woodsman, hunter, experienced guide, etc.

When he saw the aforementioned bear, he ordered the driver to stop. He then jumped out of the truck unarmed and for some reason began throwing rocks into the brush at the point where the animal had left the road. He must have thought the bear would have kept going after entering the brush and been long gone by the time the rocks landed, and he (the rock-thrower) would emerge as some kind of hero having faced down, as he apparently imagined it, and chased away this vicious bear.

Not so, the bear popped up out of the underbrush at considerable speed because of the additional effort needed to climb the steep roadway side-slope.

Doug stumbled all over himself; he actually fell on his face at least twice, getting scratched up on the gravel trying to get back to the truck. In the meantime, the bear was so puzzled by this bizarre human behavior that it took off in the opposite direction like one of those streakers we used to see occasionally at sporting events. We all enjoyed a good and lasting laugh at Doug's expense. In fact, we didn't stop needling him about it for a long time afterward.

Maybe partly because of this treatment, he left the crew well before we finished the work. To make sure that his well-deserved comeuppance wouldn't be overlooked, we told several other people outside the crew. I'm sure the story followed him back to Juneau.

Since I've related one story at this point, perhaps I'll tell another story about how one of my visits to town was concluded.

One weekend in the fall there were several major washouts on the highway back to camp. No one knew or wanted to predict when the road might be repaired, or at least made passable.

Being in excellent physical condition and anxious to get back to camp, I decided it would be a good idea to walk the approximately fifty miles. I picked up a flashlight and an extra level tripod for making noise in case any critters got too curious, then gathered up the camp mail and a bunch of sandwiches with a thermos of coffee, loaded up a pack-board and started up the road at about midmorning.

The walk took all the rest of the first day as well the following night. Fortunately, the sky was mostly clear and the moon was almost full, so I didn't even need my flashlight to see things not obscured by vegetation. I stopped to rest, have a smoke and a cup of coffee three or four times (maybe more), and I ate most of the sandwiches while I was walking, although there was at least one or two left when I got back to camp.

I was a little concerned because the salmon were running heavily in the Chilkat River, which was very close to the road for the first twenty miles or so. I knew all those fish would attract a lot of brown bears, and that it was a good idea to be prepared. Although I have never experienced the slightest sign of aggression from any bear, I felt that walking so close to them while they were feeding might cause a little more anxiety than normal.

"What kind of critter are you?"

As it turned out, I only saw one adult brown bear. She was a sow with two cubs on a river sandbar about twelve miles out of town and only about 200 feet off the road. This is pretty close considering the potential danger, which by the way I have since found to be very highly exaggerated. In most cases involving any bear/human interaction I have come to wonder who is in the greatest danger – us or the bear. There are definitely cases of bear attacks on humans but they are rare, and more often than not in response to some foolish action on the part of the human. I protected myself by banging the tripod legs together when I saw her and she turned briefly to look at me. She seemed to ignore the banging, my principal means of defense, and almost immediately turned back toward her cubs, continuing to teach them how to catch fish I suppose. She probably thought I was just another goofy human with some of those crazy human noises. I kept turning to look back at her as I walked until I could no longer see her. As nearly as I could tell she was not impressed by my tripod banging and apparently gave me no further thought.

As I mentioned previously there was a pretty full moon that night and I could easily see the road for walking. At one point I met the Canadian Customs Officer snagging and netting salmon on the American side of the border. I couldn't see him clearly so I banged my tripod legs at him, and he responded by saying hello. I noted that he was carrying a very large handgun in a holster on his belt.

The moonlight, although pretty bright, was not sufficient to allow me to see into the brush along the river. As a back-up precaution I therefore banged the tripod legs together randomly from time to time just to prove to whatever critters were lurking out there that I really meant business.

Discretion is the better part of valor

Evidently, they took the warning to heart because I neither saw nor heard any further animal life.

I have since been told that while they are fishing may be the safest time to encounter or approach brown bears. Although they will often put up a big show of fierceness their fishing activity at such times seems to be all-consuming and very competitive. Apparently the show they put up is primarily intended to frighten intruders away from their fishing spot. I can't speak for anyone else, but I know it would certainly work on me. I've never asked a bear about it, but the experts tell me that fishing bears are very reluctant to stop eating or to give up their riverside location to any competing bear, or any human either. I'm sure the fish they get constitutes a very large portion of the food they need to generate fat for their sleep(s) during the coming winter. Thankfully, it seems that even the temptation of a juicy surveyor is usually insufficient to lure them away from the river; particularly if the surveyor is banging tripod legs together. There were no real incidents of any kind during my walk and I arrived back in camp just after noon the following day.

In those days, Haines was more of a 'destination' town than it is today. As I recall, the car ferry service at that time consisted of just two or three old military landing barges that were often delayed for long periods due to inclement weather, and I don't think they were bound to a regular schedule. This meant that a significant proportion of the folks on the street were townspeople rather than just travelers passing through. It was a very friendly little city and most of the people one met in the restaurants, bars, stores or even just walking

Fort Chilkoot in Haines, overlooking Lynn Canal

around were long-time residents; willing, and often even eager to talk about their town and to point out places of interest. Even for someone raised in Southeast Alaska, where only one or two of the towns are connected to the outside world by road, Haines always carried an indefinable air of its own. There was a vague feeling of being able to just drive away if one wished to do so that wasn't present in the other coastal settlements.

Today Haines residents, like those in many other Alaskan towns, have become more reticent in their dealings with strangers or even just visitors they don't know. I guess that's part of the price we pay for the privilege of being integrated into mainstream American society. What an honor!

The largest aggregation of bald eagles in North America, or maybe in the whole world, is located just north of town along the Chilkat River, within easy viewing distance of the highway. During the fall salmon spawning periods, the birds are so numerous that they used to occasionally disrupt traffic by flying into (and smashing) the windshields of passing travelers. Unlike ravens, eagles aren't very bright, but perhaps even they have by now learned to stay away from the traffic as such incidents are apparently no longer as common as they once were.

White Fang movie set in Haines

I think the travel industry has promoted bald eagle tourist excursions as cruise ship on-shore tours to the extent that Haines has become a regular stop. If so, the town can be added to that long sad list of Alaskan towns that the tourist industry has turned into, or is trying to turn into, a reflection of their imagined version of what they want the visitors to believe is the 'real' Alaska. Apparently it is now desirable in the interest of money, that those paying enough can see 'Alaska' as the promoters would like them to see it, and thus be prompted to pay a lot of money to experience this sanitized and comfortable version.

There was another notable event that occurred while we were on the Haines job. I call it the 'Goat hunt from Hell.' It left me with a very uncomfortable memory I'd like to share here.

For some reason Robbie, our chief of parties/location engineer, decided that we needed some wild meat to supplement our dwindling supplies. The road was again closed due to washouts at the time, and though it could be fixed easily enough and quite soon, it could quickly get that way again after any significant rainstorm.

Perhaps Robbie thought that the current road closure would last a lot longer than it actually did, or maybe he just felt that if the customs agent could take fish on the American side of the border, we could take one of the queen's goats. In any case, at the insistence of Robbie, who at that time would rather hunt than eat, we loaded up with minimum gear and trail food, tied the pack sacks on the pack-boards, cleaned and loaded the rifles and headed out.

It wasn't long before we spotted a large group of goats grazing on the mountain at the headwaters of the Klahini River. The goats must have spotted us even before we got off the road and started up the trail. They started moving higher up the mountain as soon as we got out of our pickups. Once we got above the timberline, it was much easier to keep the goats in sight, and Robbie finally cornered a big ram.

Two young 'Spikehorn' mountain goats up close

The ram knew he was sighted, and he continued climbing up

to the point at the summit where there was no more 'up'. Robbie fired the fatal shot with an old 30/40 Krag, a WWI vintage weapon but good enough in the hands of the right person. I never fired a shot, and in fact I think Robbie's shot was the only one fired by anyone that day; it was the one that ended the goat's life. I swear the following is true.

Upon suffering what he apparently knew was the fatal wound, the goat climbed with great effort – at one point falling to his front knees – to the top of a gigantic cliff. It started at the summit, and dropping at least 300-400 feet almost vertically, faced a magnificent view of the Klahini Valley to the south. When he finally got up there, he stood on a rock ledge, looked around in all directions for almost five minutes and then jumped off the cliff. He didn't fall accidentally; he deliberately committed suicide. I saw it with my own eyes but I still find it difficult to believe. Robbie didn't fire a shot during this moving display of goat emotion and courage. Maybe he was just as impressed as I was. He later told me that this was not the first time he'd seen such behavior by a mountain goat and that mountain (Dall) sheep sometimes do the same thing in similar situations.

I think that this may have been the first time in my career that I began to see some things from the animal's point of view. This was something I hadn't previously thought about, but this event and my many subsequent hunting experiences definitely changed my perspective. They finally led to my personal renouncement of hunting, trapping and all the other so-called 'sporting' activities (atrocities) in the pursuit of which we inflict such suffering, terror and pain on our fellow creatures.

We butchered the goat under Robbie's supervision and hung up the pieces in the cooler, which was really a structurally supported cache (not pronounced 'cashay' as it so often irritatingly is, but just 'cash') set about twelve feet off the ground to protect it from scavengers. We usually placed some stainless steel or aluminum around each leg to keep the little woodland critters from climbing up and robbing or trashing the cache.

Robbie cooked most of the meat – it was terrible. It had a strong gamy flavor and was obviously damaged by the goat's suicide leap. Maybe that was his sort of partial revenge. It led us to revive that ancient, maybe even Homeric, question about the necessity of accepting, appreciating and understanding the gifts of nature. It comes down to us in the form of a deeply searching verse:

Why reeks the goat
on yonder hill
Who seems to dote
on chlorophyll?
Anon

I almost became ill while we were butchering the goat, not because of the blood and guts, but because I was beginning to feel like we had just violated some very basic rule of nature. Are we any more important to nature than any other creature? Do we have a right to kill other animals when it isn't necessary for our survival? Some people actually enjoy it, although modern weapons have really taken the 'sport' out of it. It would be good if we could somehow equip the hunted critters with weapons equivalent to ours, teach them to use them and to hunt for pleasure without the actual driving force of immediate hunger.

We could add a lot of excitement with such a life

or death game. The critters would learn to recognize humans as fair targets; then we would have a *real sport* of hunting with equal risk on either side. Well, those are my views on hunting. I avoid arguing about it or even discussing the matter; particularly with those people who point out to me that animals are slaughtered every day on a commercial basis. Typically, such people then perform a remarkable leap of logic, saying that such production-line slaughter for commercial purposes is necessary to provide meat for our population, and that this is somehow the same as killing animals for sport. Nonsense! Any airhead can see that taking the lives of wild animals, ripping them away from mates and young and depriving them of a God-given right to enjoy the life and environment that they were born into is not the same as commercial meat production and distribution. More often than not, such arguments are presented by desk-bound weekend woodsmen who wouldn't be brave enough to face an enraged squirrel without a high-powered weapon. Actually, I don't really like the commercialized killing of domestic critters either, but I recognize the necessity of it in today's society, and I don't get all exercised when the subject comes up.

I have especially fond memories of Seltat Creek, probably because it was my first wilderness survey camp, and for that matter my first experience of any survey camp.

Our project ended and we closed up the camp around November 1, 1951. I hoped I was only temporarily out of work, but just in case I did have the confidence of youth and a little reserve money set aside. The winter was to prove a bit trying at times, but on balance it was enjoyable. After all, I was finally returning to Juneau.

At that time in Alaska there was a lot of mutual concern between people, and no one went hungry or was forced to sleep on the street, so I wasn't really worried. Even the drunks on South Franklin were taken care of. It was the Alaskan way of doing things in those days. Sadly, things have changed a lot since then; the mutual sincere concern for others seems to have largely disappeared.

On an early frosty November morning in 1951, I boarded the old WWII landing barge that served as one of the two or three providing driver-attended vehicle transport between Haines and Juneau. There were no fancy ferries in those days with snack bars and dining halls, reading rooms, staterooms and such, just those old barges with their entire deck being a weather deck except for a little iron shack with a table (legs welded to the deck), a few benches and a coffeepot. As I recall, something between thirty-five and fifty cars could be accommodated on the vessel, and when she was fully loaded, the little iron coffee shack was crowded to its limit.

Passengers were allowed to sit in their cars at that time, so they could get some coffee and go back to drink it in the car. I don't refer to the little iron shack as a coffee 'shop' because the coffee drinkers were just expected to drop some change in a small Styrofoam cup that was left on the table next to the coffeepot. If anyone had elected to skip payment, I doubt if they would have been challenged. In those days, all the Alaskans pretty much trusted each other. If someone stole everything in the cup, they could probably have gotten away with that too.

The trip from Haines to Juneau usually took four to five hours, except when it was stormy and/or they were running against the tide, in which case it might take six hours or more. What money I had put aside from my summertime wages wasn't anywhere near enough to buy a car, much less one that would run, so I rode the little landing barge ferry as a foot passenger. My distaste for, and fear of flying were already becoming part of my phobia collection, and I was much more comfortable riding the ferry than flying. Besides, for a foot passenger, it was a lot cheaper.

I believe the ferry landed at Auke Bay, near where the state ferries come in today. I can't remember for sure but I do know that it was maybe fifteen to twenty miles northwest of town and I had to catch a ride in after we got there. There was a ferry landing downtown, but for some reason we didn't go there.

Auke Bay Ferry Terminal (wife & grandchildren included)

I checked in at the Bergman Hotel in Juneau – cheap, but warm and comfortable. The Bergman didn't have a restaurant at that time, although it does now, and the food is pretty good. At that time I had to seek out various low-cost eating establishments around town to keep the expenses down, and I couldn't be too picky about taste. Percy's Café on Front Street wasn't too bad price wise, although the food certainly wasn't gourmet quality. Actually, I can only speak for the cheaper sandwiches, French fries and milkshakes because I usually couldn't afford anything beyond that. The little Filipino restaurants[4] were outstanding and I patronized them at least two or three times a week. I always got full meals there when I could because they tasted so good, and because they gave me a feeling of being well nourished.

Downtown Juneau – Front St. (Left), N. Franklin St. (Right), and sister-in-law in front.

Unfortunately, I couldn't afford those full meals every

[4] I think there were three or four of them, including the City Café that wasn't Filipino owned but had a Filipino cook.

day. Even though they were more reasonable than most meals elsewhere, they were still more expensive than such things as ketchup with crackers and coffee or some second-rate soup at some of the other places. Some of the bars, in particular I remember Sweeney's, the Triangle and the New York Tavern, offered some pretty good 'free lunch' sandwiches with two or three beers on specified days of the week.

There are no more free lunches and the little Filipino restaurants have all disappeared to make room for the ubiquitous gift shops peddling 'Alaskan' gift items to the tens of thousands of tourists debouching from the many cruise ships from April/May through September.

As I recall, the sandwich makings at the free lunch tables were usually spread out on a big platter, and you could make your own – as Spartan or as fancy as the supplies allowed. The advantages of a setup like that included the chance to get more than one sandwich if the makings held out; you could use other patrons to sort of screen your surreptitious actions if necessary. There was also always the possibility of a small enough crowd so that there would be plenty for two sandwiches without depriving anyone else. Additionally, if you could muster up a certain amount of sneakiness, you might go home with a little 'take-out' to eat later and maybe give the cockroach and her babies (more about that later) a few bites. I recall that the best spread and the tastiest ingredients were usually at the New York Tavern, where I had also sold the daily *Juneau Empire* newspaper with good results not so many years before. The Red Dog Saloon also had a free lunch two or three times a week which, although plentiful, was not quite as tasty as it might have been. However, beggars can't be choosers as they say.

In retrospect, it's hard for me to believe, now being an adult, that we freeloaders, a sort of informal social class for whom the free-lunch scene was a scheduled routine event, were actually getting away with as much as we thought we were. In those long ago wintertimes the bartenders and waiters were usually Alaskans with the concern for fellow permanent residents that was so common in those days. Many of them had spent some time of their own on the free-lunch circuit and they knew what it was all about. They were more likely to 'look the other way' than to make a fuss about our foraging. Such pilfering as ours would not be tolerated these days. We would surely be charged with some degree of larceny, harangued on by a prosecuting attorney, defended by a twenty-five-year-old public defender and generally subjected to a demonstration of our wondrous and convoluted legal system – an exaggeration obviously but generally true of the system.

In those days, the Red Dog was at what I believe was its original location on the east side of Franklin about a block south of the Front Street intersection. Five or so years later it moved across the street and a little bit more south to where there is a gift shop today. I think that they stayed there for maybe five or six years and then moved even further south to the intersection of Egan and Franklin where it is located today. I don't think there was an Egan Street at the time. I seem to recall that it was constructed later as a southern extension of Egan Drive, which replaced the old Glacier Highway running from the east end of the Juneau-Douglas Bridge out beyond the airport. It's not very complicated, but it sounds like it is so I won't say any more on the subject.

Juneau – View of downtown Egan Drive from the office of the engineering director

After the 'old' Red Dog (1940's – 1950's) moved to the Egan Street location, they went to great lengths to dress up as a nineteenth century old west saloon, like the ones in all the John Wayne movies. They put sawdust all over the floor and hung all sorts of authentic looking western paraphernalia on the walls behind the bar, including what the sign says is one of Wyatt Earp's guns that he left with the city clerk or some official like that. It may be truly authentic, but I, for one, sort of doubt it – it's a pretty shoddy-looking revolver. The handle has been taped up with cheap black tape, and it's just generally decrepit looking. It doesn't even have a trigger guard, and it looks like it was made that way. It seems likely that a man with the reputation Earp needed would certainly equip himself with a more presentable weapon than that.

Wyatt Earp himself did *not* leave his gun in the *original* Red Dog, as the bartender would let you believe, because it didn't even exist at that time. I'm not sure that he ever even came to Juneau either, although I could be wrong about that. I was told that Earp actually did serve briefly as a marshal, sheriff, Wal-Mart security guard or something similar in Nome. Given his historical reputation, I suppose he did a good bit of gambling there as well.

I guess that these days it's important to have some sort of gimmick to attract and amuse the tourists – God knows there are plenty of both, tourists and gimmicks.

There *was* considerable action in Nome after someone found placer gold on the beach, which precipitated a brief but intense rush around the turn of the twentieth century and maybe a little earlier. Nome was relatively easy to get to by steamer and retrieving that kind of gold, compared to hard rock or hydraulic mining, required much less equipment and a lot less work. At least that's the way I've been told it happened.

Such events bring a lot of undesirable people to town as well as a lot of crimes like assault and battery and things normally associated with violence. The local governments in such situations were reportedly often willing to hire someone with a strong reputation like Wyatt Earp and pay him a little more than usual. I think that's how Earp got to Nome, but I'm not a western historian so I can't be sure.

Anyway, the current Red Dog is definitely not a gold rush era saloon, nor were its predecessors. I believe it was opened in its original location on the east side of Franklin Street by a man called Gordy Kanouse and a partner sometime in the early or mid-1940's, long, long after the famous gold rush.

The latter-day tourism boom has spawned a lot of Red Dog wannabes and gift shops selling everything from 'authentic' Alaskan gold pans to 'pioneer' computer parts up and down South Franklin Street.

I became something of an authority on Alaska bars and saloons in Juneau, as I spent a lot of my time in them when I was younger, and maybe that's why I'm using up so much space on them.

The Bergman Hotel deserves a few more words here. I don't know when it was built, and I don't know that it's even there anymore, but I'm pretty sure that it is. If it isn't, it ought to be. It's almost a Juneau institution and shouldn't be allowed to disappear. It may not have been as fancy as people today are accustomed to, but it provided everything you could ever need; it was clean and it didn't take a small fortune to stay there. There were in-room washbasins, but I don't think the hotel had any rooms with showers – that sort of amenity was almost non-existent in those days, at least in Alaskan hotels in the Bergman price range. The shower wasn't really a problem because there were almost always showers on each floor just a few doors down from most rooms.

Now please read the following carefully because no matter what you think, it's absolutely true, and if you're a bug person you may find it interesting.

When I stayed there, I had a little family of cockroaches living between the back of the in-room sink and the wall. At first only a single roach crawled up from her hidey-hole. I don't know much about the physiology of cockroaches. For all I know, both the male and female critter might be wrapped up in the same body, but subsequent events convinced me that if possible, she was a lady roach.

At first all she did was walk back and forth along the back of the sink several times every day and then duck back down into what was apparently her nest. Strangely, she didn't seem at all spooked by my presence; maybe cockroaches are blind, poor things. Initially, I thought maybe I should squash her, but that seemed so gruesome, and I realized that he/she/it had a purpose and a right to live too just as I did, and besides, she wasn't bothering me at all.

Alaskan cockroaches are small, only about half an inch long, and they only stand about an eighth of an inch or less high. They certainly aren't threatening like those monsters in Hawaii that are about the size of a small rat. When those Hawaiians dash out across the floor, they look like they're charging with malicious intent. Alaskan roaches like my little friends don't bite; at least none of them ever bit me. All they really do is to eat up scraps of things like breadcrumbs, popcorn pieces, etc. Actually, compared to such horrors as spiders, scorpions or some beetles they could be called rather handsome little critters.

After disappearing and being gone for about two or three days, and causing me a little concern for her welfare, she showed up from between the sink and the wall one night with six little ones following along behind her in a tiny cockroach column. At the risk of disturbing the bug haters, I have to say that she actually seemed proud of her well-behaved little ones and that they were cute in their own way.

I began leaving out breadcrumbs for them on a regular basis, and she seemed to appreciate it. They would always finish up every crumb that I left. You may think that I was either drunk or on dope or both when I saw them, but that wasn't the case. Moreover, what I'm describing here may be virtually unheard of among people who really know a lot about cockroach behavior. All I know is that I saw what I saw. I swear that however uncharacteristic her behavior in taking care of her young may seem, the whole episode is absolutely true regardless of what the bug 'experts' may say. In my view, she was a mighty fine little lady.

There was another, sort of surreal, thing about the Bergman that deserves mention. The hotel staff included a lady who collected and replaced towels, changed bedding, and I assume took care of other housekeeping duties. She was in many respects one of the most unusual ladies I ever met, or more accurately, passed by. For starters she was always in the hallways; never emerging from a room, never sitting behind the desk or in the lobby, never coming in or going out of the front, back or side doors – just in the hallways. She also seemed to be constantly changing floors, but I never saw her on any of the stairways. She only appeared in the hallways pushing one of those housekeeping supply carts or packing some sheets, blankets, pillowcases, towels, etc. Additionally, she could never be seen coming from or going to work, or on any of the nearby streets; she just seemed to appear there very early every morning and disappear very late at night every day; never resting, eating or drinking.

I must say that although I never actually saw her working I was very favorably impressed by the fact that the linens were always replaced on schedule, and they always had that pleasant smell of cleanliness. There was one more thing about her – her coloring. She was very, very light skinned. Perhaps her coloring could best be described as translucent. It almost seemed like one could look *into* her skin although it wasn't possible to tell how deep.

She rarely responded to a greeting like, "Good morning," or "Good evening," and if she did, it was just a sort of squeak. I'm probably being unreasonably critical here. I know she was efficient and hardworking because the results of her work offered evidence of that every day. No doubt she was very shy, thereby explaining her meek responses. Her skin color may well have been the result of some sort of disorder over which she had no control. It's just that taken together all these characteristics created a rather extraordinary picture of both her and the hotel.

Sadly, a hotel such as the Bergman was then could not exist today, at least not as a competitive business enterprise. If they've done anything to modernize the Bergman, the building may still be there, but it's soul is probably gone

One of the major hotel chains might well move in someday if they haven't done so already. They would surely send a young, snappily dressed and well-spoken executive schooled in hotel management to run things 'right'. The lobby would be re-done, probably with period 'Alaskan' furniture, a shiny marble and chrome reception desk, elevators and a bunch of neatly costumed young men to run out to your taxi, carry in your baggage and show you to your room. Just the thought is quite horrid.

About three or four months after arriving back in Juneau, I took a rodman/chainman job with the Bureau of Public Roads (BPR). We were working on a grading and drainage project covering about ten or twelve miles of existing highway leading into the Auke Bay Recreation Area and a mile or two beyond.

The BPR survey crew on that project wasn't unusual at that time for that agency. Such a crew today, however, might be unique. Each member of the crew was a professional at whatever he did; the head chainman was a Head Chainman, the rear chainman was a Rear Chainman and the instrument man/party chief was an Instrument Man/Party Chief. What I mean by that is that they didn't really care about moving up to the next career step, or what was considered to be the next step *up*. This particular crew had been together for a long time, which was pretty much a standard for the BPR at that time. They traveled together and when out of town they stayed and ate together. They usually didn't frequent first-rate hotels featuring gourmet dining, but they were definitely together. With that agency in those days it wasn't customary to break up such a crew and ship them individually from job to job.

Non-electronic survey crew – circa 1952

I'm sure that a policy like that is easier for a federal agency to follow than for a state or local agency because they have so many more projects to choose from. The result from my standpoint was both good and bad. Because of the work practices and ethics of these crewmembers, they became very, very good at what they did, and in this respect they naturally set a good example for any neophyte working man. I was still functioning as a stake artist, axeman, etc., albeit rated as a rodman/chainman and still just as anxious to learn all I could and move up within the crew.

A less desirable result (at least for me) of this specialization was that no one in such fixed positions wanted to allow anyone below their own 'rank' to learn the next step up. I suppose they feared that if they taught someone all about their own job, they could be easily replaced on the crew. Despite this factor I was learning a little more every day just by watching and asking questions; almost to the point of sometimes annoying people. I would occasionally even get someone not on the crew to teach me things after hours. However, because of the job protectiveness attitude it was noticeably more difficult to learn on this job than on most others.

I didn't know about such things as 'job jealousy' then, but thinking back on it I can see the ogre of 'my turf', the federal job curse, rearing its ugly head. This attitude has stifled incentive, destroyed potentially fruitful and innovative new federal programs, and generally rendered any improvement to federal agency efficiency, productivity or service almost impossible for many years. Sadly, the federal government agencies sort of transferred much of this attitude to the Alaska government administrations during the mercifully brief 'mentoring' period immediately after statehood.

Actually, I started the preceding paragraphs intending to point out how good this crew was and how proficient each member was at his own job having completely mastered it over long years of practice. All this was true and regardless of the effect on me personally, I could only admire their crew skills and efficiency. I still remember them that way; maybe even more so as I note the questionable work ethics and limited skills of some of today's survey crews.

I don't know if it means anything, but the Bureau of Public Roads had always been, at least since the Stone Age, an agency of the Department of Agriculture. I believe that since then the agency has become part of a National Transportation Department. In the 1950's and before, they were responsible for road design and construction of all roads on federal property such as parks, Indian land and (after statehood) such lands as had not yet been deeded to the state. After settlement of the Indian land claims, Tribal government lands became pretty much the same as private holdings in effect and were also exempt from Bureau of Public Roads authority – I guess they still are.

The BPR is a big agency. As is the case with all big federal agencies they are also what's known as 'hidebound'. There were still active policies regarding regulations, procedures, standards, administrative codes, etc. controlling the facilities to be provided for horses and buggies.[5] Most of these written documents do not have the force of law, they are really just the way some government functionary *interprets* the law, and therefore at best they can only have the 'color of law', if I understand what that term means. The dedicated bureaucrats, managers and administrators will try to convince us that these rules, regulations, codes, etc. are legally binding.

I always try to remember that the only document that's binding in law is the document accepted and approved by the congress elected by the people, bureaucratic interpretation notwithstanding. The bureaucrats do not make law, they only interpret it, and their interpretation could be totally at odds with the original intent of the actual lawmakers. Most politicians and bureaucrats want you to believe that they have more authority than they actually do, and they usually have a flock of lawyers paid to believe that and to follow them around helping to give everyone that impression. I, for one, am not impressed by this. I am afflicted with a complete lack of interest in the details of such subjective and simplistic things. Unfortunately, arguing with the bureaucrats over such things would be counterproductive because, while the argument was going on, project funding would almost certainly be delayed. Prevailing in such an argument would be a Pyrrhic victory at best.

---

[5] I may be exaggerating, but not much.

However, the bureaus, commissions, agencies, etc. do exercise a lot of de facto control over projects. The elected representatives have, in their wisdom, surrendered control of much of the funding to such little intra-agency groups which, in effect, provide the bureaucrats with artificial legitimacy and the opportunity to build their little 'empires'. It is an unhappy fact that right after statehood, many of the excess former federal managers and administrators moved into various non-technical positions with the new Alaska state agencies and brought a lot of their bureaucratic baggage with them. In many cases, they behaved like 'strangers in paradise' as whole new fields of opportunity opened up before them. They lost no time in building multitudes of new, and unnecessary little intra-agency empires with ostentatious titles, staff, new regulations, meeting schedules, memoranda, written procedures and all the trappings that are the life's blood of today's 'Manager' with whom we have now all become sickeningly familiar.

The phenomenon started just prior to statehood; it has grown like an infectious fungus under the guidance of a surplus of overeducated, under-experienced management and/or political people with *no* practical knowledge and little or no common sense. Unless someone sees this condition for what it truly is, it will continue to consume time and resources at greater and greater rates. It will reach deeper and deeper into the pockets of the taxpayer while offering no commensurate value of its own. It can't go on indefinitely; the agencies must ultimately choke on their own increasingly complex administrative structure.

Such organizational malignancies do not cure themselves. Like any other cancer, they will continue to grow, consuming the operational juices of the agencies in increasing amounts until the organization ceases to function productively, or until someone bypasses some typically useless committee meetings about the subject and simply excises the malignancy. It can be done. It *must* be done to assure the long-term survival of many of the otherwise essential organizations.

Being back in Juneau, and more or less around old high school friends turned the winter of 51/52 into a sort of enchanted season. It was easy to get around the downtown area on foot, and if I wanted to go further, there were always friends that I could get rides with or borrow cars from. Happily, I was also without any debt to amount to anything, and in general it was so pleasant it was almost unreal. I don't think I've ever experienced anything more soul satisfying and enjoyable than spending a warm and dry winter evening in Juneau sitting on a stool and watching the street through the front window of the Triangle Bar, hearing the passing traffic crunching on the new snow or hissing along the rain-soaked street.

Juneau: Looking west on Front Street – the Triangle bar is on the left.

While I was still working for the BPR, I applied to the Alaska Road Commission (ARC) to go back to work in the spring. In those days the BPR and the ARC were, although both federal agencies, not at all alike – neither in bureaucratic structure nor in their approach to projects. Finally, after continual and persistent phone calls, I was hired to a permanent position by the Juneau office of the ARC. I was then assigned for the season to a reconstruction project from about milepost 45 to milepost 92 or so on the Richardson Highway – Alaska's first highway, although Anchorageites may claim otherwise.

Those milepost numbers may be inaccurate, but give me a break. I'm an old man and I'm just hoping to finish this while I can still remember who I am, where I am, and what I'm trying to do.

Chapter 2: The Unseen Dragon

The Alaska Road Commission started out as a 'Commission', organized and then authorized originally by the U.S. War Department. The War Department has since become the Department of Defense, probably because that makes it sound less like we're waiting to pounce on some other nation(s) and make war.

Unlike the BPR, the ARC's responsibility covered roads and transportation facilities only within Alaska that were not on federal or Indian-owned land or otherwise privately owned. In Alaska, that covers an immense amount of property, much of which was and is urgently in need of modern roads. At least ten to fifteen years prior to statehood, the ARC was re-commissioned under the Department of the Interior and stayed that way until being phased out of existence following statehood.

The original Richardson Highway runs from Valdez to the gold fields north of the Alaska Range, including the rich finds around Fairbanks and north and east of there. It was the first destination-to-destination highway constructed in Alaska and should be designated Highway No. 1. However, the loudmouth claims of many of the transplanted outsiders in Anchorage may have succeeded in usurping that number for some Anchorage area route that didn't even exist when the Richardson was first built – for that matter, Anchorage didn't exist then either.

The project to which I was assigned pretty much followed the Tonsina River from about milepost 52 to milepost 85. Through the southern section the route crossed a number of smaller creeks/rivers and wound through a short and shallow canyon. That's about as many routing details as I can recall, but that's OK because I can still remember most of the construction operations well enough to describe and explain the job. This particular section of the existing Richardson turned West (or rather began turning West) at about milepost 70, climbing out of the Tonsina Valley and then continuing northward before rejoining the existing road just over half a mile north of the Tonsina Lodge.

The administrative structure of this project may have been one of the earlier precursors of what was to come. We all assumed that the project engineer, Hal, was an engineer, but we were doubtful of his competence in the discipline of road construction because he was always so indecisive. Many of us, me included, believed that one purpose of Hal's frequent trips to Valdez, besides brown-nosing the district officials, was to get collective opinions and instructions about what to do next on 'his' project. It may have been an early example of 'consensus management', the foundation of the 'Management' methods that have now permeated the supervision of virtually every project in Alaska, from conception through design to construction. If Hal was actually down there looking for instructions on how to run the project, the men comprising his group of advisors were probably knowledgeable about highway engineering because at the time it was customary to seek advice from people who knew what they were talking about. However, this process was soon to begin creating opportunities for the burgeoning ranks of the non-technical MBA's to become involved, and for the nonsensical concept of 'generic management' to take root and flourish. As just a working crewmember then, I was not really concerned, or ever consulted, about such things, although the seeds of skepticism may have first been sown in my mind on this project.

At the time, there were a number of lodges along the highway with bars, pool tables and dance floors. Of course, we frequently dropped in at some of our favorite ones for a few drinks or pool games whenever we had the time. Everyone in such places was very friendly in those days, even the people who worked there and the Alaskans who were just passing through.

I've stopped at a couple of these lodges once or twice over the years just to check them out and see if any of the old-timers are still hanging around – they're all gone now. The places that are still there are nothing like they used to be. None of the customers in the barrooms seem to know each other. They mostly sit alone or in small groups, keeping to themselves as though they are in some sophisticated cocktail lounge in the states. Some of the old lodges that used to be there probably faded out of existence as the highway system improved to the point that travelers could significantly increase their daily mileage; another casualty of almighty ‘progress’.

I was told that most of the oldest lodges/roadhouses along the Richardson had originally been built there to serve as way stations for the horse-drawn stages stopping in during their trip from Valdez to Fairbanks or back. They were nominally spaced ten to fifteen miles apart for some reason having something to do with the horses. I never did understand it, but then I never did really understand horses either except that they tend to bite and to step on your feet. Most of the proprietors of those old lodges were there before dirt, and they had some really good stories to tell. Our project construction crew (Morrison-Knudsen) left one of them with an experience that he probably related for a good many years after we left. The story goes as follows.

The old man who owned the lodge at 52-Mile found a deteriorated box of dynamite partially submerged in the creek about a hundred feet behind his main building. Apparently, it had been inadvertently left there after some past construction job in the area.

A group of about five or six of us stopped there for a beer one Sunday night on the way back from Valdez. One of our group members was a powder ‘monkey’, so after hearing this, the old man asked him what the best way to get rid of the box of dynamite would be. The powder monkey guy jokingly told him to leave it in the creek and shoot at it with his 30-06 rifle.

I was told that the old man didn’t realize the remark wasn’t serious. He reportedly followed the ‘advice’ and the blast knocked over his outhouse, blew all the windows out of the lodge and seriously scared the hell out of both him and his wife.

Nobody sued anybody, as would be the case today, but although the whole thing had been the result of a misunderstanding, we did take up a collection and we paid for all the repairs to the lodge and the outhouse. As I recall we also had enough money left over to pay the lodge owner something for his inconvenience. I guess it wasn't really a very funny gag, but the whole thing was settled pretty amicably, which wouldn't be the case nowadays with all the lawyers hiding in the bushes looking for fee opportunities.

We did quite a lot of boozing and partying at the roadhouse lodges in those days, probably much more than we should have. There was one drinking party incident that I can still remember as if it were yesterday.

Unless we stayed in camp all the time like hermits, we were bound to meet a lot of people who lived along the Richardson, as well as both the Glenn and Alaska Highways at distances of a hundred miles or more apart. The area was like a very small community in terms of population, but covering many thousands of acres with residents living great distances from each other.

Over the last fifty years, I've sensed a distinct erosion of this long-distance camaraderie that once characterized the sparse populations living up and down the long roads and highways that crisscross interior Alaska.

Anyway, one night when we were drinking at Copper Center, we met a group of friends from Glennallen who were similarly engaged. One member of their group, a man named Johnny who was an outstandingly skilled dozer operator, decided to join us as we kept drinking, laughing and telling lousy jokes. At some point, Johnny told us that he was heading for the toilet. Have you ever noticed that when drinking with a group and having reached a state of semi-inebriation, whoever wants to go to the toilet always feels compelled to announce it to the whole table? Why is that?

After he didn't return for about half an hour we began to worry about Johnny. So, thinking that he may have wandered off into the woods since he was as drunk as we were, a couple of us went looking for him. We found him at the bottom of an outhouse pit near the lodge.

It was an old outhouse, the seat had evidently broken, and he was standing a little over waist deep in the pit. We asked him why he hadn't shouted for help, and he replied that he had done so, but apparently nobody heard him, so he decided to save his breath and just wait till someone else showed up. I don't think it was particularly cold down there; at least he wasn't complaining about it.

We helped him out of the hole, and he wanted to return to the bar immediately, but after some discussion he was finally persuaded not to go back in right away – he still had some solids stuck to his clothing. Someone went to get a hose and Johnny was thoroughly hosed off. After that, he really didn't smell bad at all. I can't say he smelled good but not too bad either, maybe a little musty.

We all then returned to the bar more or less like nothing had happened. Johnny was, of course pretty wet, but it didn't seem to affect his enthusiasm for drinking and bullshitting and by the time we left he was almost dry.

The main lodge and lounge (bar) was equipped with modern plumbing by this time, although when leaving the bar one had to pass through the lobby on the way to the indoor toilet. Perhaps Johnny felt that passing through the lobby when drunk would be too embarrassing, as did many of the lounge customers. He had therefore taken the side door, which placed him next to the old building that had once served as an annex to the main lodge. This building was where he found the adjacent outhouse that was only used occasionally and was apparently in pretty bad shape, structurally speaking. Outhouses were very much a part of life in those places and at that time. Some of our best stories, true or false, involved them.

I once knew a man who claimed he had installed a speaker

just under one of the holes in a lady's outhouse. He said he would wait for a lady to go in, give her a few minutes and then say into the speaker, "Would you mind being careful, ma'am – we're working down here." He told me he got a lot of different reactions.

Many, if not most, of the old family lodges along the Richardson Highway have been replaced with new, fancy, hundred-dollar-a-night (or more) hotels or else abandoned – often torn down. The new facilities are almost always set up to cater to the tourist trade with dead animal heads or skins hung on the wall, old unidentified pictures nailed up and so on. In general, the local people who've lived around there for years avoid those places like the plague unless they're drinking and there's no place else to go.

There was one other surveyor on the Tonsina job who deserves a mention before moving on chronologically. His name was Ralph, and he was a very capable guy, although his goal was decidedly not the completion of the project. He liked it in Glennallen and he meant to stay there. He was a very short man; He wasn't a dwarf or anything like that, he was just short like Danny DeVito. In fact, he was so short that even after spreading the legs of the transit tripod as far as possible and pulling in the extensions by some reasonable amount in accordance with the circumstances, he still had to stand on a stake bag (twelve to eighteen inches high) to reach the telescope and look through it.

I always liked Ralph because he was ambitious, and he intended to become the best at whatever he decided to do – unless it was surveying, which he really didn't like too much. I could understand that, considering the fact that he probably wouldn't even be able to see over any really tall grass if he was ever so challenged. Ralph was also a very practical man. For his wife's last birthday before we left he bought her a crosscut saw. Now that's a *real* man. I heard that he now owns a successful retail hardware store and lumberyard in Glennallen, or at least he did about twenty-five years ago. Good for you, Ralph.

By late in the season we had a new party chief named Gordon. I think he had graduated from some fairly prestigious university in civil engineering, and he felt that he was automatically more qualified to do anything related to civil engineering than anyone else in sight, or maybe even on the whole job. Admittedly, Gordon had an outstanding ability to look at maps and drawings, relate them to what was actually on the ground, and to see what actions needed to be taken. His problem was that he didn't have a clue how to do them. However, he refused to admit that he didn't know about the tools and methods of real surveying, and he kept meddling in the hands-on survey work. We always just went ahead with the work, did what was necessary to get the job done, and let him take credit for the results, which he probably would have done anyway.

Gordon may have been another harbinger of the ubiquitous overeducated and under-experienced engineers of today. We were unfortunate enough to meet several of them on the Tonsina job. These days, the graduate engineer who can supervise a survey crew or, for that matter even perform to an acceptable level in any crew position, is a rarity. It's not very pleasant to work with people like that because most of them have, during their years in college, developed a very bloated opinion of their own importance and knowledge. Gordon was like that, but even with the frustration of working for a technical (surveying) nincompoop, we still found places and time for fun. Here again, I'm going to tell a story about I guy I met at one of them.

The 42-Mile Roadhouse was just a few miles down the highway from our camp at 47-Mile where we spent the last third or so of the project. We used to spend a fair amount of time there because it was only five miles away, it was very informal, and people there were always friendly and never confrontational. They were Alaskan construction people – a disappearing type even at that time and by now completely gone.

I met a man there named 'Pigshit', which is the only name I ever knew him by. Pigshit was a powder monkey and one of his legs had been replaced by a prosthetic device from the knee down. No doubt the loss of that part of his leg had been the result of some kind of blasting accident while he was doing his work. Whatever it was that had caused the accident, the partial loss of Pigshit's leg didn't slow him down at all, according to his friends who knew him both before and after the accident.

I happened to see Pigshit in action at 42-Mile many times, and I was impressed by his dancing ability; which was a lot better than mine with two good legs. Despite his artificial leg, he apparently never thought of himself as handicapped. I was even more impressed watching him perform after he had a few drinks. He liked to take off the artificial portion of his leg, put it on backward and ask the ladies (especially the ones who didn't know him) to dance. His requests met with a wide variety of reactions. Some of them would scream or express disgust and refuse to get up – especially some of the tourist ladies just passing through. Some would get up and dance through the whole number without saying a word about Pigshit's backward foot or asking any questions at all, probably afraid of hurting his feelings, which it definitely would not have done.

Regardless of how they reacted, Pigshit always got a tremendous kick out of it and loved to spend a lot of time telling the café patrons and us all about it after the bar floor closed. He never mentioned if the leg was uncomfortable or painful when on backward, but if it was, it apparently wasn't bad enough to discourage him.

I didn't really know Pigshit well, in fact I hardly knew him at all beyond introductions and conversations; I mostly just watched and listened to him, but I profoundly admired his attitude. I really think he enjoyed being who he was, peg leg and all. We could all do with a bit of that kind of outlook on life. I imagine there are a lot of psychological issues involved here, especially nowadays when nobody can do anything without supposedly being driven by some deep and maybe even sinister, hidden psychological motivation.

I think Pigshit stayed on as lead powder-man for the company at least through the next year. I found out later that he was widely known for his skills and abilities and was always in demand. Among powder-men with many years of experience, being a bit busted up wasn't really uncommon at that time. As far as I know, Pigshit is still alive, still setting charges and probably still teasing the ladies. Maybe not though, he'd be pretty old by now.

These days everyone on these jobs takes themselves so seriously that it keeps the whole project crew sort of gloomy all the time. Where have all the Pigshits gone?

The atmosphere and attitudes that prevailed at the 42-Mile roadhouse and others were pretty much the standard in those days, but now they have become largely just treasured memories. Walking into one of the roadside cafés or roadhouses along most of Alaska's well-traveled highways is now little different than entering similar establishments anywhere in the lower 48. There are exceptions; some of the unadvertised or little-known places in the arctic or along a few of the shorter and lightly trafficked dead-end or looped roads in the coastal areas still offer some of the sense of being welcomed around the kitchen table of a friendly neighbor. I fear, however, that this can't last either; just the increasing pressure of population growth will force change.

On all of the interior road projects of those days, part of the

ARC crew came out of the district office,[6] and part from the Juneau territorial headquarters. Since I was dispatched from the Juneau office on a job-by-job basis, I went back there every fall. Juneau was, and still is, my home of choice, and I was always happy to get back there.

During part of the winter after the Tonsina job, I sat across a drafting table from a man of about sixty or more, which seemed almost unimaginably old to me at the time, named Frank Metcalf. He had served as territorial engineer for a few years. As I was to find out for myself much later, a job like that is very political and actually has little to do with real skill or technical ability. If your administrator, manager, or political backer, if you have one, doesn't have the guts (and most of them don't, particularly these days) to shield you from the political winds, you are bound to be used as a scapegoat sooner or later. Whoever the political mouth behind your job is, he must save his own ass when necessary so you have to be prepared to be thrown to the wolves so to speak, and you're doomed from the day you start. This was as true, although not as pervasive, then as it is now.

Frank, of course, knew nothing of the electronic tidal wave that would soon be engulfing the profession. He was truly one of the 'good ol' boys' in the Engineering profession. He owned two or three calculators, including a couple of Curtas[7], and at least one each of all the drafting tools that were ever marketed. Not only that, he knew how to use them all, an ability that is truly rare these days among the 'new-age' engineers. He was an outstanding engineer, designer and draftsman, not the typical political appointee. He was not at all bitter about losing his job with the territory. When asked why he left the job he simply replied, "I got fired." It was the sort of honest answer one rarely

[6] For this project it was Valdez, now a sub-district attached to Fairbanks.
[7] Now a defunct company.

hears these days. He said that he went into it knowing it was a political position and didn't really expect it to last as long as it did. I got the impression that he hadn't liked the job very well anyway.

The chief design engineer, a man named Dan, was (as the title implies) in charge of the design crew and the office. He was a world-class drinker, frequently allowing this avocation to interfere seriously with both his judgment and his professional responsibilities.

Almost all of Dan's subordinates liked hunting and would indulge their desire to murder things whenever possible during the summer field season. An adult moose is a very large animal and when dead, it provides a lot of meat for those who like to eat it. It was, therefore, customary for those members of the field crews who had been successful in murdering a moose during the fall to bring some of the meat back and share it with their friends and/or co-workers in the office. In the fall of 1952, someone brought a sizable hunk of moose meat back to Juneau, took it to the office, and gave it to Dan.

It was on a Friday, one of those 'long lunch' Fridays, and when Dan went to lunch he locked his office door, leaving the moose meat inside. He got caught in a saloon someplace and didn't show up again for about two weeks, or maybe even a little longer. One of the worst aspects of the whole scenario was that he had left the meat on a shelf mounted right on top of the radiator.

After a few days, the meat began to smell, a few days later it began to stink, and then it began to get rapidly worse and worse until the whole building was permeated with the unbelievably sickening smell of rotting meat.

The building was owned by a pioneer lady named Belle, and I'm sure she was less than pleased about Dan's oversight vis-à-vis the moose meat. I guess that, for some reason, she didn't have a passkey for Dan's office. I can't remember how we got in and disposed of the rotten meat, but we must have because it would have been impossible to work there otherwise. As I recall, the whole building had to be fumigated as a result of Dan's negligence. I don't remember hearing that Belle took any punitive action.

When I came back to Juneau from the interior this time, I had a lot more money than I did before, but I moved back into the Bergman Hotel anyway. It seemed a little more like home than any of the so-called classier places, especially since I was able to get my old room back. The 'Translucent Lady' was still there, but alas my little cockroach family was gone – perhaps victims of the common but erroneous belief that cockroaches are somehow 'dirty'. This, of course, is nonsense. In fact, they spend most of their time cleaning up after us.

Since I had spent a long working season in the interior of the territory, I now began to feel and, unwisely, to talk as though I was a seasoned Alaskan traveler. The season that was to follow began to open my eyes to the vastness of the territory and to introduce me to some of the wide variety of personalities we were populated with at the time. I was also to witness the first rumblings of the profound changes with which we were to be confronted in the coming years. The dragons were starting to gather.

In the spring of 1953 I returned to the 47-Mile camp, even though the project was about 99.5% completed. In a couple of locations, the contractor was tight-grading the finished surface to final grade, dressing up cut and fill slopes and just sort of 'bull-cooking' all up and down the project to satisfy the ARC inspectors, all 500 of them, or so it seemed.

The project was seriously overstaffed, but in fairness to Hal, it should be noted that overloading projects and surveys with apprentice-type people was unwritten policy with the agency at that time. It was an effort to allow deserving students to earn college money, and at the same time to encourage their interest in engineering. The concept was, in my opinion, a good one. However, the problems generated by such things as agency mismanagement, abuse by field supervisors and political pressure from influential parents probably caused numerous detail problems for the program in addition to giving these students the wrong ideas about how things should be run. The practice gradually faded away prior to statehood.

About the middle of July I was transferred to Anchorage as a rodman/chainman, which I didn't mind too much because Valdez, 47-Mile et al. were getting pretty boring with not much work to do. However, having more or less grown up in Alaska during my formative years, I wasn't really prepared for what I was about to see.

Anchorage – Fourth Avenue circa 1953

It had been just a little over two years since I last visited Anchorage, and that visit had been brief, hurried and limited to downtown and the industrial areas before leaving on a railroad lumber flat-car headed for Fairbanks. The commercial changes in the downtown area and the doubled volume of traffic were astonishing to me. Just the almost frantic activity and the obvious rush to accelerate development in the outlying business and residential areas were enough to clearly demonstrate, even to a youngster like me, that Anchorage was in the process of separating itself from the rest of the territory, even if unconsciously. Already most of the population knew nothing, or very little, of the territory outside the immediate Anchorage area. They seemed already deeply into an attempt to turn this part of Alaska into a place just like the one they had left in appearance, activity, and ambience. Unfortunately, they have now largely succeeded.

The place was a new experience for me, and during my stay there I had a very unusual encounter in a movie theatre that, for some reason, still sticks in my mind.

At that time, it was customary to play the national anthem at the beginning of movies, at least at the beginning of this particular one. It was expected that, when it was played, everyone would stand up and display some sign of patriotism such as the right hand over the heart or a military salute. When the anthem started, I stood up and placed my right hand over the left side of my chest and suddenly felt a little tug on my right shirtsleeve. The man next to me was still sitting and was apparently trying to attract my attention. I asked him if he had a problem, intending to offer help if necessary. He told me that he didn't have to stand up. I should have said right then that it was OK with me if he stood on his head as long as he didn't fall on me, but I didn't say anything; I just turned my attention back to the screen.

Again he attracted my attention in the same way and asked if I knew *why* he didn't have to stand up. This was beginning to get annoying, distracting and, who knew, maybe a little dangerous, but I said that no, I didn't know why he didn't have to stand up. He said that he was a Jehovah's Witness, and I guess their religion tells them that they don't have to show that kind of devotion or whatever to anything not biblically ordained (according to them of course), or something like that.

I didn't reply this time, but I did move to another row as far away as possible, and I was prepared to leave the theatre altogether if he followed me.

You never know about people like that, they may suddenly leap up and start running all over, jumping around and shrieking like a banshee or maybe whip out a revolver and start shooting at everybody they regard as a non-believer or a heretic, acting like an Islamic radical. In any case, if they make a fuss and you're sitting next to them, you become involved whether you want to or not. It was only a day or two later, in late August, that I left Anchorage for Palmer.

I was then assigned to a survey crew working north out of Palmer setting out the first survey line for what would eventually become the Parks Highway. The 'Parks' route is now the most heavily traveled highway between Anchorage and Fairbanks, following the Alaska Railroad corridor in large part. It is by far the shortest route between the two cities and has probably been disastrous for the businesses along the Richardson between Big Timber and Delta Junction. Big Timber is (or was) the name attached to the junction between the Richardson and the portion of the Glenn Highway sometimes called the Tok Cutoff, running from the Richardson to the Alaska Highway at Tok (pronounced 'Toke') Junction.

Because of some uncertainties regarding the part of the route from Palmer to Wassila, we left Palmer and moved to cabins that the agency had rented from the owner of the Willow Lodge. They were very Spartan but had reasonably comfortable beds and plenty of washbasins. If we wanted warm water to wash up with in the morning before going to breakfast, it was necessary to fill the basins before going to bed and leave them on the table near the heater till morning. The heaters were not really capable of keeping the cabins comfortably heated, but they sure tried, running at their maximum output all the time. At that time no one complained about such things because we had all experienced camp living conditions that were much worse.

These days there are employee complaints about everything from the food to the unscented toilet paper to the type of hand soap supplied. I think the ascendancy of the unions to the point of almost complete takeover of the workplace is largely to blame for such things in both Alaska and the lower 48. It's disgusting, and the union demands for full salaries even for those just beginning in a particular position have virtually destroyed the concept of an apprenticeship. It discourages supervisors from advancing untrained people to the next step up for training, and it deprives many promising young technicians of the opportunity to learn. Such are the restraints of today's Alaskan workplace, and apparently nothing can be done about it because the supervisors no longer have any say in such matters.

Early in the work from our Willow base, we came abreast of Nancy Lake – the northernmost of two deep lakes in the area. One day, when we were out there stumbling over trees that Ken (our clearing dozer operator) had pushed down, an old Russian guy named Mikhail came blasting up onto our line from Nancy Lake driving a big 'swamp buggy' – a converted Dodge Power Wagon fitted with great big airplane tires. Of course he was known locally as 'Russian Mike'. He told us that he really appreciated the road we had just built, and that he now planned to set up a fishing lodge and bring in people from all over the world to enjoy it, at reasonable rates of course.

We tried to explain that this was not a road, not even an access road, only a cut line for our survey, but he would have none of it. This is a lake that, with its well-drained uplands and lack of swampy ground, is more suited to recreational use than Big Lake, the other lake to the south, which is now overrun with

Anchorage folks, often seeking what they think is wilderness solitude. I hope that Mike was successful with his fishing lodge, and that he got rich from it, although we all knew that getting rich was not at the root of his desire for a fishing lodge.

We're running out (or have run out) of the 'Russian Mikes', the 'Robbies', the 'Pigshits' and others who helped give the Alaska that I grew up in its unique character. They actually began to slowly fade away into the shadows of entrepreneurial and political sophistication around the time of statehood. It seems like they finally just disappeared like one of those morning mists that gradually retreats into the woods until it breaks up and you can't see it anymore. They won't really be missed much because, sadly, most of today's neo-Alaskans won't remember them or their contributions to the now vanished ambiance of the territory. *I'll* remember them, and I'll miss them.

We kept pulling the alignment and profiles northward on the job, planning to tie off the line about five miles north of Willow, when we were treated to a demonstration of military arrogance in excess of anything I for one had ever seen.

We were out on the line working as usual, Ken was clearing line with the dozer and rear chaining when necessary, I was head chaining, Don, the new party chief, was bossing (or whatever), and Fred was peering through the transit – though I don't think he could see very much since he was damn near blind. Suddenly, we heard a mighty roaring behind us and after about five minutes two D8 dozers (ours was a little D6 with lots of experience) roared up behind us in tandem, grading and dressing up a drivable road as they went.

It turned out that this was the U.S. Army building access for some planned maneuvers north and east of Willow. They sure didn't waste any time; they didn't even stop to talk, but I heard that some Army guys came into Willow later to talk to Don and explain what was going on. I guess they hadn't told anyone except their own superior officers about their progress. I suspect that they called all this a security matter and wouldn't admit that the failure to inform anyone was simply just an administrative bungle. In the end, the Army operation destroyed about three or four miles of our staked alignment, but it was well referenced and easily reestablished.

Such things happened more often in those days than they do now. However, since there weren't yet today's flocks of administrative dragons to run around making profound statements and trying to demonstrate their own importance, the problems were almost always cleared up with very little fuss. Despite what seemed to us an arrogant attitude, the Army road builders at least provided Russian Mike with much better road access than our cleared line did.

One clear memory I have from the Willow area is of an incident that may have been a confrontational wildlife encounter, or perhaps that was just my imagination. Fred was still with us at that time and had just set up the instrument on an angle point near the north end of Nancy Lake, and he was ready for back-sights and fore-sights. I had a range-pole on the forward P.I. (point of intersection) waiting for Fred to wind up the angle when a big cow moose emerged from the brush less than a hundred feet in front of me. She must have had a calf somewhere nearby because she started getting really jumpy; not actually charging but glowering and sort of snorting at me, scratching at the ground with a front hoof and making on and off partial advances toward me.

Acting in accordance with my lifelong belief that discretion is without doubt the better part of valor, I turned around and climbed a tree directly behind me. After Fred kept trying to get a forward sight from me without success, he finally realized what was going on, so he and two other guys (including Ken with his dozer) came to my rescue. However, the old cow was long gone before they got there.

Since then I've often wondered if she actually had any hostile intent or if she was just hanging around to protect her unseen calf. The guys who came to 'rescue' me wouldn't stop laughing and teasing me about it, so I just ignored the subject and they finally stopped calling me things like 'moose-bait' and so on. In all the years I've spent around or in the wilderness, that's the *only* time I ever even came close to a confrontation with any wild critter unless you count mosquitoes, bees, or other such pests.

In the case of this Palmer/Willow survey, there really isn't much to describe about the technical aspects of the job because they didn't offer much challenge even to a neophyte like me, much less to the more experienced guys on the crew. As it got later in the season and living in those cabins at the lodge got more and more uncomfortable, Don and the deciders in Anchorage started thinking seriously about shutting us down for the winter. We were already scraping ice off the wash water every morning, and whatever our feelings about the job might have been, we were ready to leave. It was close to the end of September, and I was unknowingly about to start working on what turned out to be my favorite remote job of all those I have worked on throughout the years – the Taku River.

Chapter 3: Dragon-in-Waiting

When I got to the Taku, the job had already begun, and in fact had been in progress for about two months. Apparently, I wasn't all that important to the project, as evidenced by the fact that they had begun without me! The political implications of the Taku project are probably as important as the technical considerations, and as much as I despise politics and politicians, the subject probably deserves some discussion before recalling any memories of the project itself.

The Taku project had its roots in the Alaskan political arena with pressure from *Anchorage Times* publisher Robert 'Bob' Atwood et al., and a few self-appointed Anchorage mover and shaker cronies. I'm sure there were others before them, but they had the biggest and loudest mouths I heard during my entire fifty years living up there. They were desperately trying to get the seat of the Alaskan Government moved from Juneau to Anchorage.

Atwood was a genuine Alaskan product, although for his own reasons he seemed consumed with a passion to turn the Anchorage area into a copy of the lower 48 states. He kept pushing the capital move issue up under the noses of the Alaskan legislators, and if he was still alive and as greedy as ever, he would no doubt still be at it. He was so obviously motivated by selfish personal interest that it would have been almost comical except for the potentially devastating affect on the then territory and later the state, not to mention the city of Juneau. His efforts were, of course, effective in gaining political substance because all but a very, very few politicians are much more concerned with maintaining a positive public image than in actually serving the public good. Atwood's control of the Anchorage press, Alaska's largest newspaper at the time was naturally very influential in the creation and preservation of his own self-made image, and the power of the press, however provincial, is something that all politicians fear.

Had we been more politically astute in those days, we might have seen these events as one of the first stirrings of the political maelstrom that would, in a few short years, overwhelm and alter the lifestyles of so many of us. The ominous implications not only surrounded the serious enough issue of moving the seat of government, but also upsetting the Southeast Alaskan economy and plunging us into the enormous financial indebtedness that would have been incurred just to cover the expenses of physically making such a move. We should also have foreseen the coming of an age of political maneuvering that would tragically overshadow the real world needs of a young, naïve and hopeful Alaskan electorate. Although seemingly stripped of its urgency since the death of Robert 'Bob' Atwood, the capital move issue still looms as a selfish legacy of his pro-Anchorage (Alaska be damned) political skullduggery. What follows is, I believe, an examination of the issue from a more statewide-oriented viewpoint.

The Anchorage pseudo-Alaskans cloaked their intent by insisting that their only motive was to make the capital city more accessible to all Alaskans (read 'Anchorageites') and by suggesting that the move not be to Anchorage, but to some nearby wilderness location – bullshit. There is *no location* in our state that would (or will in the foreseeable future) be easily accessible to all, or even most, *real* Alaskans, and just the cost of implementing these idiotic ideas of a new 'Brasilia-style' capitol complex would be damnable.

The whole nonsensical idea has taken on a political life of its own. It has become a periodic phony cause for numerous opportunistic politicians from the Anchorage area. They are, more often than not, seeking to advance an otherwise pallid career resulting from misguided convictions, inadequate understanding of statewide Alaska/Alaskans, or just plain stupidity. Like all politicians, they, their motives, and their transparent phony blab about what the 'people' want make me sick. The vast majority of them don't even associate with any real 'people'.

All this pursuit of such an impractical and totally unrealistic objective probably still persists, even in the face of the fact that the idea of moving the capital has been placed before the Alaskan electorate at least twice and has been roundly defeated both times. These defeats at the polls have served to clearly demonstrate the selfish absurdity of Atwood's perennial cry of "Let's put the issue before the voters and decide it once and for all." Obviously what he and his cronies have always really meant was something like "Let's *keep* putting the issue before the voters until the result comes out the way we think it should." Atwood is dead now, and I realize that it's not proper to speak ill of the deceased. My negative remarks are, however, directed more at his goals regarding this particular issue than at him personally.

Many of Atwood's supporters in this greed-motivated capital move issue are probably still around and still pushing their idiotic ideas. This was pre-statehood political influence in action. They thought they were pretty good at such things, but when the *real* professional high rollers came in to fill the political vacuum opened by statehood, the locals were made to look like a bunch of bumbling hicks.

Naturally all the squawking about the possibility of a capital move aroused some concern, both among Juneau officials and the members of the territorial legislature who opposed Atwood and his screwy ideas. As a result, they managed to put enough pressure on whomever it was necessary to put pressure on to buy feasibility studies aimed at finding the best highway route out of Juneau.

At the risk of losing some readers' attention, I'm going to describe the three possible options explored in the expensive, and ultimately futile, search for an economically justifiable land access route to Juneau.

One of Atwood's main points was that there was no road into Juneau. As a result of other political pressures from both the Juneau advocates and the Anchorage 'furniture movers', the ARC and subsequently the Alaska State Department of Transportation & Public Facilities (DOT-PF) began and has continued looking at several possibilities for gaining access to the capital city from the existing highway network. I don't think the BPR got involved, probably because they knew the whole business was wacky and driven by nothing more substantial than internecine politics.

The intent of the program was to make cost predictions, construction feasibility studies, and such things that could satisfy the need for supporting arguments and that would be flexible enough to twist to the satisfaction of whichever political advocate was requesting the information. There were three possible access corridors considered.

One option was the extension of the Glacier Highway from Eagle Beach north of Juneau up Lynn Canal to a point opposite Haines, then a ferry across the canal to Haines providing access to the Alaska Highway via the existing 165-mile Haines Highway, at the time known as the Haines 'Cutoff'. The cutoff was the road for which our 1951 survey had sought solutions to some substandard alignment and gradient conditions. A corollary to this routing would include bridging Lynn Canal from east to west somewhere between Eagle Beach and Haines. The consensus among the planners was that bridging any of the tidal basins between Eagle Beach and Haines, or even north of Haines at a narrower spot, would be cost-prohibitive. The expense of construction and maintenance for such a bridge exposed to occasional extreme environmental stress would pay for a lot of ferries, especially if a crossing toll was imposed for each ferry trip.

A second possibility was a similar extension up the east side of Lynn Canal to Skagway and connection to the Alaska Highway via the 100-mile southern portion of the Klondike Highway. The Chilkat mountain pass over the Coast Range Mountains and the high elevation plateaus along this route had already been shown to impose very heavy winter maintenance costs on the existing road, supporting a strong argument against this route choice. It would also make the Anchorage-Juneau driving distance almost fifty miles longer than the Haines cutoff route.

The third proposed routing ran from Juneau (actually from Thane – about ten miles south of Juneau by road) south to the Taku Inlet and then up the inlet to the Taku River, across the river west of the Taku Glacier and up the south side of the Taku Glacier flats to the Canadian border. There would supposedly be a subsequent road built from the border to Atlin, Y.T. from where there was an existing connection to the Alaska Highway. This was the route survey that the crew I was on were assigned to pursue.

There had been reconnaissance surveys along similar routes near the Taku alternate, but ours was to be the first to gather definitive and extensive field data over at least the southern portion. I was assigned to one of the crews working from Juneau

(Thane) toward the border. There were also crews stationed at Taku Lodge, who would be starting at the other end and working toward us from the Canadian border.

Incidentally, the word Taku (tah – koo) sounds very poetic, doesn't it? It's a Tlingit Indian word, and as we all know from innumerable films about Indians, those ancient folks always spoke the way Moses did when he parted the Red Sea with sweeping gestures, grandiose language and the whole act. We would thus expect the word to translate to English, which in ancient times they had never heard of, as something like 'South Wind Bringing Us the Magic Gift of Life From Our Great Spirit', or similar. Actually, it translates to 'Goose Down', disappointing, isn't it? Or 'place where the geese leave down.' I guess the migrating geese make extensive stops at the small ponds and lakes up there and take care of doing whatever geese do during stops; maybe just scratching off some winter itches. During such visits, they reportedly released a lot of down from their bellies.

"This was a pond last year!"

I'm told that the nearby residents would travel up the Taku Inlet/River to gather the down, probably for the same purposes it's used today: pillows, coat padding, mattresses, etc. I guess the genuine stuff is really expensive nowadays if you can even find it, so maybe all these 'home hobby' enthusiasts we have around us should also head up the Taku and see what they can find.

Our first survey camp on the job was set up along a short, sheltered beach just under Point Bishop at the northwest corner of the entrance to the Taku ('Goose Down' – I love it) Inlet.

Original planning had informally envisioned the survey project in four phases as follows: 1) Thane to Point Bishop; 2) Point Bishop to Strawberry Cove, about two miles west of the Telegraph Creek powerhouse; 3) Strawberry Cove to Turner Creek, including extensive ferry slip topographic surveys as well as soundings on both sides of the Taku River/Inlet at Strawberry Cove; and 4) Turner Creek to a connection at some point with the westbound survey crew on the Taku Glacier Flats. They would be coming south from the Canadian border near the Taku Lodge.

In those days, it was considered important that the supervisor know more, or at least as much, about the details of the work and how to do it as the subordinate members of the crew. In this day of generic managers, overeducated but under-trained engineers, and decision-by-committee, such abilities on the part of the technical supervisors are apparently not required as long as they are good at 'Managing', whatever that means.

Such deterioration of the necessity for supervisory technical ability was particularly damaging in Alaska. We usually had relatively small survey and design crews, and as the technical abilities of the supervisors (party chief, chief of parties or design engineer) became secondary, we were effectively deprived of a producing member of the crew. This was an early, but at the time unnoticed, casualty of the creeping age of 'Management' as a profession that would soon begin to overtake us. Even as we began to feel the early effects of this insidious encroachment into our professional prerogatives, we still failed to recognize the phenomenon for the dangerous and debilitating workplace nonsense it was to become. Had we known then what all this 'Management' business was leading to, we could have stood up and shouted (figuratively), "The emperor has no clothes," in places where it might have done some good, e.g., the floor of the Alaska legislature. Head it off 'at the pass' as they say.

During the second or third week of October, we turned the corner at Point Bishop and started east-northeast up the Taku Inlet over some increasingly rough terrain, much of it standing on edge, so to speak.

By the third week in November we had advanced probably two miles from Point Bishop toward Strawberry Cove and the budding 'Managers', most of whom never came near the job, decided that it was about time to shut down the project for the winter and return to the Juneau office. These weren't the worthless MBA 'Managers' that we unfortunately know so well today, but in their increasingly common tendencies to make long-distance, uninformed decisions, they were beginning to look that way. I suspect that perhaps a few of the latter-day types with such high opinions of themselves had already begun to creep in 'under the tent flap' as it were.

It wasn't really all that cold, but it was wet, *really wet,* with off and on wet snow flurries. However, we all had nice warm and dry quarters where the clothes could be dried out every night, and from a personal standpoint we felt that we could keep going up the Taku Inlet all winter. However, the decision to move back into town was made for us – a procedure that I learned much later was largely standard practice in the lower 48 and one that would soon enough become all too familiar to us. The MBA dragons of generic management *would* take over; it was just a matter of time.

The job was shut down during the last week in November and we took our two boats into town for storage along with the remainder of our perishable supplies, our instruments and tools and the more expensive cook-shack appliances.

I think that today our move back to town would be largely driven by the fact that the fall storms would be becoming more and more frequent so that access to the project would often be impossible for the 'Managers' (the MBA's) or their informers.

They wouldn't be readily able to keep track of what was going on, and they are desperate to convince everyone that their input is essential for a successful job. As most astute observers know, then as now, MBA's almost go nuts if it begins to appear that a project is moving ahead successfully without their 'Management' (read 'interference'). In this case, the basic decision to move back to town was left to Robbie, our chief of parties.

These days, leaving a livable tent unoccupied and unattended, not to mention tools etc., over the winter in a location as close to Juneau as we were would be an act of utter and unforgivable irresponsibility. Destruction or theft of anything like bunks, shelves, or even the tent itself would be a virtual certainty. Disrespect for personal property has migrated northward to Alaska along with the hordes of politicians, lawyers, and bureaucrats lured by the political opportunities that opened up immediately following statehood, and the increasingly litigious business climate. Later we would see the population swell even further as the oil boomers migrated north.

I don't want to sound bigoted against our newly arrived southern neighbors, but before most of them arrived property such as tents, and even portable goods, regardless of value, were almost always safe when left unguarded in the woods. In fact, notices were often left inviting anyone stranded, or in need of shelter, or even just a particular tool temporarily, to come in and feel free to use whatever they needed. It was assumed that anyone availing themselves of such remote hospitality would, if the occasion ever arose, behave in a

Refuge

reciprocal manner toward others. Such consideration toward others in need is no longer characteristic of Alaskans (even the soon-to-be-extinct *real* Alaskans) except in the remote arctic or the very inaccessible mountainous areas. These self-serving attitudes of unconcern for the property rights of others were not yet in evidence in the 1950's, but they were on the near horizon; perhaps nearer than we in our naivety could realize. We have been forced to grow up and it's a damn shame.

There was one particular incident from that period of the Taku job that bears mentioning.

About two days after one of our chief design engineer's (Dan – from Juneau) marathon drinking expeditions, he showed up on the project for what he called a 'Field Design Review' – an unprecedented event. He brought a man named Charlie with him. Charlie was about thirty-five to forty years of age, but he looked about sixty or more because of what we heard was nearly a lifetime of extremely dissolute behavior.

They had come out on a special boat trip ordered by Dan because, although there was a good trail from Thane to Point Bishop, there was no way that either of them could have made such a hike – drunk or sober. I guess that Dan had met Charlie at one of his many stops during his latest alcoholic tour and had been impressed by what Charlie had described as his impeccable qualifications. As any drinker or former drinker knows, alcohol has the almost unique property of making things look and sound either *very* good or *very* bad.

Anyway, Dan promised Charlie a job, and apparently a surveying assignment on our relatively remote yet reasonably accessible project was how he intended to honor that promise. Maybe even Dan had regained enough discretion, after a sober look at Charlie, to realize that hiring him was not such a brilliant move after all, and that the Taku might a good place for him (Charlie) to avoid excess public scrutiny.

Dan brought Charlie to us at about noon on a Friday, and Charlie walked up to the office tent where Robbie assigned him the extra bunk and immediately fell asleep. He slept almost continuously – awakening periodically and briefly to use the outhouse or get some coffee – all the way to our 5:30 a.m. breakfast call on Monday. He refused breakfast and nursed a couple of cups of coffee until we left for work at about 7:00 a.m. with Charlie in tow.

At that time, I was still working as head chainman on the transit crew, and Charlie was supposed to start work as an axeman/rear chainman/stake artist, the standard entry-level survey crew position at that time. The survey line was about a quarter mile or less up the hill from the camp; a fairly steep hill, but certainly not as demanding as most of those we had to climb every day in staking the survey line. When we got to the line location, we looked back for Charlie, but he was nowhere in sight. We began setting out the chain and preparing the set-up area, after which the instrument man started setting up the transit. After a few minutes Charlie slowly crawled up onto the narrow natural bench where that portion of the line was located. Gasping and coughing, he rolled onto his back and struggled for breath while spitting up big globs of mucus. He was obviously not prepared to help with any kind of survey task, so we helped him back to his bunk to let him sleep for a while longer.

Watching him lay there on the trail in that condition, I swore to myself that if I ever got like that, I'd ask someone to shoot me. However, my attitude has moderated somewhat over the years.

I think that Robbie finally found some office work for Charlie. He wasn't stupid, just terribly out of shape, so maybe he learned how to calculate the field information and plot data or something. Anyway, the work didn't seem to agree with him and within two weeks he was gone. I wonder if he's still alive – I very much doubt it considering the lifestyle he reportedly resumed at his earliest opportunity.

Alaska was, as they used to say, the 'Last Frontier'." Even a cursory glance at an Alaskan map makes it obvious to the observer that, like a true frontier, most of the greatest (if not *the greatest*) of the state's needs are transportation related. Although railroads have traditionally been shown to offer the lowest nationwide point-to-point cost per mile, I think the figures must be based only on the mileage within the railroad corridors. Actually, Alaska's problems result not so much from major point-to-point transport as from bulk unloading locations to supply points. Unfortunately, distribution difficulties from the points of unloading such as airports or barge landings, to supply or consumer access locations are vital, and the difficulties have gone largely unaddressed. Shamefully, this may well be because of the relatively minor political influence of the bush areas.

Early transportation – Hotel to airport?

Individual deadhead railroad extensions to each of these supply points would be prohibitively expensive and of questionable value considering the remaining need for loading and unloading capabilities and small quantity 'bush' deliveries. The answer of course is roads – they're cheaper to build because of far less rigorous design and construction standards than railroads regarding grades and curve radii, and they provide much greater physical/economic flexibility for area-wide supply distribution.

Alaska is a far-flung 'country' and its population and supply needs clearly reflect this characteristic. All the foregoing may help explain to the interested reader why, when I was a young, healthy and hungry surveyor, most of the jobs I worked on and enjoyed were in remote road locations or on pioneer road construction surveys. I don't mean to imply that I sought out such jobs only because I liked that kind of work. I needed to make a living, and at that point surveying was the only reasonably lucrative and saleable skill that I knew, however minimally. In any case, although I didn't even think about such things then, I was soon to become a witness to the most profound changes in the Alaskan lifestyle since the gold rush.

This was a period of Alaskan expansion for some political and/or economic reasons that I didn't really understand or care much about at the time. I have a suspicion that some of the more perceptive and farsighted politicians of the day knew even then that statehood was coming, albeit at some distance, and that if we had a number of road projects (even just the surveys) in progress, the federal folks would take over and help get the jobs funded, contracted and finished when we became a state. On the face of it, this in itself was a very good idea because there were a number of federal aid programs in existence at the time that offered substantial road-building assistance to the states, but not the territories.

Regrettably, helping the state and its people was frequently not the primary priority of these politicians, bureaucrats and lawyers – the waiting dragons. More often than not, they were actually angling for influential and lucrative positions for themselves, using the road construction issue as one publicly visible vehicle toward that end. If it came to a showdown between their personal political or financial interests and the projects and/or the people, it's no great mystery where they would direct their efforts. I guess most of our Alaskan population in those days was still naïve enough to believe that these conniving schemes of the lurking dragons were sincere. The awakening was just over the horizon.

While all these deliberations, and perhaps surreptitious statehood planning sessions, were going on, I was merely a happy fledgling surveyor entertaining few, if any, thoughts about statehood or its implications. I *did* realize, accept or assume, that at that time all of the defining project decisions were made by engineers, or at least by people who were familiar with the technical aspects of the proposed jobs.

Today it's different. Regardless of the obvious absurdity, many of the critical decisions regarding road locations and geometric standards are often, and ridiculously, made by committee or under the 'guidance' of one or more MBA dragons. The membership of these committees is frequently drawn from the political, and technically ignorant, segment of the public or from agency supervisors such as accountants, personnel directors, and so on. Naturally, such modern ad hoc project committees are almost always headed or guided by one of the now ubiquitous MBA-type 'Managers'.

At the time I retired, there were fortunately still a few old construction hands and dirt engineers around most of the contracted projects to see that many of the stupid decisions arising out of these ludicrous committee deliberations were ignored or sensibly modified. A measure of the suitability of today's management high rollers for guiding road construction or design is the fact they can rarely tell if their irrelevant and clearly nonsensical decisions are being ignored or not. All this is adding to and accelerating the demise of the engineering and construction professionals as leaders in the technical aspects of the public works disciplines – at least that's the case in today's Alaska.

A survey crew returning from the field to the office faced, and still faces, a myriad of tasks that vary widely. The survey methods used in response to the topographic challenges certainly affect the design approach, as do other parameters evidenced during most of the field season. The specific natural parameters as well as many other factors governing each separate project make it difficult or impossible to formulate a set of protocols or standards which can be applied to all projects. Most of today's 'Managers', and even some of the younger engineers, are constantly coming up with drawings and specifications that they publish, label as 'Standard', and circulate as what they insist are solutions to most design questions.

These are examples of *solutions preceding the problems*, and the approach is both technically and logically stupid. Regardless of this typically persistent approach of most of today's so-called leaders (the MBA's), one size does *not* fit all. In the early 1950's, we approached each job as a separate and unique project, with its own parameters and problems. Of course, we had standard drawings and specifications, but these were treated as only suggestions, and the individual project engineer/designer was expected to tailor them to his or her own project needs.

The problem became glaringly obvious immediately prior to and after statehood when the BPR assumed temporary responsibility for Alaska's roads while the new state was setting up agencies of its own. These were the beginnings – the labor pains if you will – preceding the ultimately pervasive 'Day of the Dragon'.

Now I think it's time to go back to the Taku project and the winter of 1953/54 for further illustrations of the 'good old days' and the first stirrings of the changes that were yet to come.

This was another of those delightful winters I spent in Juneau. I can never really explain my reasons for always being so pleased to get back to Juneau except to say that getting there always makes me feel like I'm coming home. I've always felt that Juneau is my home. Not only was I coming home again, but the winter of 53/54 was to prove a very meaningful one for me in my on-the-job training for this and for many other jobs to come.

We got back into town permanently from the Taku ('Goose Down') some time around the end of November. I immediately reported for work at the design office on the second floor of the Simpson Building. Dan was there and he was sober – a periodic and productive interlude. These days Dan would be fired immediately after the first time he took off on one of his boozy excursions. No consideration would be given to his abilities, drunk or sober; just the fact that he had broken some regulation included in the sacred *Book of Management*, if there is such a thing.

Contrary to what many of the workplace psychologists of today would insist, we didn't look to Dan as any kind of role model. It's doubtful if any of us even knew what a role model was. He was the boss, drunk or sober, he knew more about road location and design than any of us did and *that* was why he was the boss, not because he knew the right people or had some influential political connections. We didn't consider his personal behavior to be any of our business – we just worked around it.

The process of analysis and utilization of the field data leading to the final plan preparation for highway construction involves many progressive calculations, reductions and adjustments. This series of steps is highly susceptible to the 'law of diminishing returns'. That is, each calculation 'step' will, regardless of effort, skill, and dedication unavoidably introduce a certain amount of error, even if only from the rounding of decimals – and the errors will accumulate. Of course, an error introduced during such a process is not an isolated error; it carries into any subsequent calculations and magnifies itself with each repetition, particularly in cases of exponential relationships. The more the numbers are finessed, the more pronounced the effect of the 'law'. The end result must thus be a final set of drawings (plans) less precise than the initial calculations and design sketches. This is not a result of any incompetence or anything like that; it is a natural consequence of any series of calculations directed toward the same end goal. An experienced engineer could, in the 'old days', recognize such things and tailor or guide the precision of each step to achieve the desired result with the finished product.

We're now told that such judgmental step-by-step supervision is no longer necessary because, say the 'electronic engineers', their devices do not suffer accuracy deterioration from one design step to another; I doubt that they have any *feeling* about it either. Most of these minor and unavoidable errors entering the chain of technical production today are the result of faulty entries or misinterpretation of existing conditions just as they always were. They are identical in effect to many factors that are central to the 'law of diminishing Returns'. A certain amount of intuitive survey ability or engineering experience is still necessary to control the introduction of error and to recognize illogical data, regardless of how minor they may be. The electronic 'eye' cannot (thank God) do it without human intervention because such a tool has no surveying intuition (yet) – hooray! Nonetheless, regardless of their shortcomings, the electronic gadgetry has almost completely taken over field surveying, not to mention the design office.

The reader should not imply from these observations that I believe all the effects of the new equipment and methods are negative. Just the electronic tools alone have resulted in tremendous increases in production, productivity and cost-effectiveness. However, the most basic influence in the success of any survey is still the surveyor, and hopefully it will remain that way.

Alaskan surveyors, like those anyplace else, seem to be trying to reach a time when dependence on, and trust in, the modern tools have largely replaced judgment. Soon, there will be no doubting the electronic wizard; such doubt will in fact be ridiculed. Even now, the surveyors of today will sometimes accept bizarre readouts and measurements that the 'ground-pounders' of yesteryear would instantly question. The old-timer's experience and intuition would alert them to indications that such numbers were highly unlikely, or even impossible. Alaskan survey crews are, in many cases, clearly becoming dangerously computer-dependent and lacking, losing or ignoring that traditional intuition.

As much as I'd like to think so, it wasn't the 'Managers', the oil boom, or even statehood that abetted the electronic dependence we are now afflicted with, it was, and is, the bewitching effect of technological 'progress' and the enticing button-activated gadgets that go with it. I think it started in earnest sometime in the early to mid 1970's and I fear that the subsequent decline of thought-driven survey practices in Alaska is not over yet. Back to the Goose Down.

It now became necessary to put aside most other matters and to propose at least two or three Taku River 'O' (office) lines for consideration as construction projects. As mentioned previously, these were the days when such considerations and deliberations were left to the expertise of the experienced engineers and construction specialists. However, I'm afraid that the MBA's, although at that time still in the minority among real working people, may have been lurking in the workplace shadows and licking their collective lips over the possibilities of moving in. To them, these supervisory decision-making situations would have appeared to be an obvious opportunity to stick some 'Management' on the process, regardless of their own glaringly deficient technical knowledge.

One major consideration on the Taku was that, if this was to be a federally financed interstate highway out of Alaska, we would obviously have to improve the first ten miles or so from Juneau to Thane so that it could accept the additional stresses imposed by increased traffic volumes and heavier wheel loads. Because of the closely encroaching side-hill cuts in the rock slope high above the beach, the age of the road, and the functionally substandard geometrics of that section, there would certainly be extraordinary construction problems, and the cost per mile would probably be much greater than for most of the rest of the project.

I don't know what cost figures the planners and administrators finally came up with for the Juneau-Thane section, but they were probably much too low, or maybe just erroneous out of simple ignorance of the actual conditions. Even then the managers, administrators and increasingly ubiquitous bureaucratic dragons usually just ignored things that they didn't want to hear or that they thought would not be well received by their political boss(es), so they may have just ignored or even scrambled the figures. They rarely had (or have) any saleable actual skills so their jobs depended (and depend) almost entirely on their ability to flummox both the politicians and the public.

These guys are the same today except more so, and they are getting worse. If the solutions or rationale they have refused to accept later proves correct, or if their own decisions/opinions prove bogus, today's 'Managers' can usually figure out some way to blame any misjudgments or faulty logic on someone else. Although despicable, the ability to shift blame is still a useful and frequently used skill in the 'Management' discipline.

At the time this was becoming an example of the sad erosion of the old Alaskan ability to get the work done with a minimum of bureaucratic bullshit. The managerial generators of meetings, memoranda and generic regulations were beginning to emerge even then and have now taken over almost entirely.

Changes in the workplace are not the only lifestyle

disruptions that have somehow robbed us of the atmosphere that helped make Alaska feel like home. The little restaurants and shops where the employees were almost like family members are gone now; or at least in most cases changed to the point that they are just like any such eating-places in the lower 48. This is truer in the Anchorage area than in other parts of the state, although it will surely spread throughout the state eventually. Anchorage has never been very Alaskan anyway. Unfortunately, The counter-Alaskan culture and attitude so pervasive in Anchorage is also becoming more and more prevalent in many of the urban and suburban locations within two hundred miles of the city.

Such unwelcome changes may be less evident in the more remote areas of the state, but the influences of the oil, the tourists, and the politicians will inevitably move in and pollute the lifestyles there too. It may happen tomorrow, next week, next year or maybe ten years from now, but it *will* happen, and I'm afraid it's too late now for us to do anything about it.

Downtown Anchorage today

These things were, in the early and mid-50's, barely beginning to enter my consciousness. My thoughts then were largely concentrated on love, friendships and survival with a little left over for job-related matters. This attitude, and the social aspects of inevitable change, along with the subsequent loss of the lifestyle many of us loved, was not then a major concern of mine and probably not of most of my contemporaries.

In the spring of 1954, we got word that Jack Rhodes (from the southbound Taku Lodge crew) and his father had disappeared during a flight into the Wrangell Mountains somewhere north of Skagway. Jack and his father were the only people on board the airplane. Jack's dad was a federal fish and wildlife officer who flew an agency Grumman Goose airplane all over the territory, frequently taking Jack with him just for pleasure. The area where they disappeared is huge and very, very mountainous so no wreckage of the plane was found until the early 1980's even though there was an extensive search mounted at the time. Given the nature of the country, it was actually surprising that they found it even then. I think that someone just more or less stumbled across it, perhaps a hunter. The wreckage would surely have been heavily entangled with vegetation by then and virtually invisible from the air. Perhaps with things having changed the way they have, someone built a hunting lodge or resort near there. The reports said that the remains of both Jack and his dad were found still in the deteriorated cockpit of the plane, implying that they were both killed during the crash. Hopefully, the end was quick and painless for both of them. God rest their souls.

Wrangell-St. Elias mountains from the Glenn Highway

During the winter of 1953/54, I still spent my share (and probably that of several others) of time in the places along Front and Franklin Streets such as the Imperial, the Triangle Bar, Sweeney's, the New York Tavern, and the Red Dog. Unfortunately, the other bars in town didn't altogether escape my attention, but those five held special fascination for me, and if it's not too late I should apologize to Irene for these selfish diversions.

Perhaps, except for the Imperial and Sweeney's, the

attraction was that they had large front windows making it possible to look directly out onto the street. As I described previously, one could watch the big, heavy snowflakes falling thickly in the fall or spring and hear the traffic crunching through the accumulated snow when it often became drier toward midwinter. The snow always sort of muffled the street sounds and made everything seem a little bit surreal. Even today, when the streets are wet and shiny, the reflections of the streetlights and neon signs usually awaken nostalgic feelings – at least for me. Often when the cold, cold Taku Winds ('Goose Down' winds) blew through town, as I'm sure they still do every winter, there was something very comforting about watching the street scene from a warm saloon behind a big front window. Alas, such experiences are long past, at least for me. Even if the saloons are still there (which Sweeney's and the New York Tavern are not) they have probably changed to the point of being unrecognizable.

Around the beginning or middle of March every year in Southeast Alaska, God begins to remind us that the annual rebirth is about to happen. The willows begin to bud out, the creeks begin to swell from the addition of upstream melt-water, and you can hear the mama and papa eagles chirping at each other; I guess in mutual congratulations for a new brood of three to five chicks in the old family nest.

The ever-elusive surveyor bird

This was also the time that the surveyors and engineers all over Alaska began to stir in the old days. They would start emerging in greater and greater numbers from the offices and bars, setting aside beers, calculations and drawings and stepping into the spring air, blinking at the sunshine. A friend of mine used to say that this was also the time you could hear the 'surveyor bird' coming out all over the woods with its distinctive cry "totheright-totheright-totheright; good-good-good-good" (say it quickly). Sadly, that old bird may be an endangered species judging from the crew behavior I've observed over the last ten or fifteen years.

For us, it was time to return to the Taku, and I daresay that that there wasn't a man among us who regretted it. When others asked us about the hardships of the job, our bravado was genuine: bears, brush, cliffs and canyons be damned, we are the men from the 'Goose Down'.

It was one thing to decide to move back to camp in the spring and something else altogether to actually do it. We always thought it wise to first conduct a thorough examination of the two project freight/crew boats. In the spring of 1954, we found that we hadn't done as detailed a job as we should have when we brought them in during the previous fall. This spring we took plenty of time to examine them and, in fact, we did find a couple of loose joints that would probably never have caused any serious problems while we were underway but could result in some leakage if not attended to. However, all wooden boats leak to some extent so we didn't consider it a symptomatic problem.

Small loaded riverboat – about half full size

Once the boats were repaired and ready to go, it was necessary to make up a complete list of supplies. Someone in the Juneau office had decided at some point that the camp should be prepared at all times for a one-month period of being completely cut off from Juneau by bad weather, equipment failure or whatever. We felt that this was a little extreme, especially when a few of the supply items were perishable over such long periods of time, and nobody could remember any month-long storms anyway. Foolish of us, even though *we* were on the job and even though these administrators were not the technically abysmally stupid 'Managers' of today, who were we to challenge their wisdom? Perhaps we should have sensed the early beginnings of a trend toward absentee management and loss of control for the supervisor (chief of parties or project engineer) in the field, but we didn't.

I want to contrast the conditions of those days and the way we made camp moves with the way such things are handled now. In the first place, today's crews probably wouldn't be housed in tents. Bunkhouse trailers or pre-fabricated portable housing would no doubt be required, as demanded by the unions. Moreover, transportation to the site would surely have to be provided in closed-cabin small boats with tie-up facilities on an engineered float constructed at the job site. The labor required for packing, loading and unloading of all the equipment and supplies could not be done by the crewmembers because such work would not be included in their job descriptions. Kitchen facilities and meals would surely also have to meet minimum standards as designed by professional kitchen managers[8] and dieticians. I think that most Alaskans at the time of, and immediately prior to, statehood were truly ignorant with respect to the influence the unions were capable of gaining over the workplace. I'm also pretty sure that none us even knew what a dietitian *was*.

The unions at that time were not influential in the surveying trades or the overall profession. In fact, I don't think that unionization within government agencies was even legal – it certainly never existed on any job where I ever worked. By the time we awakened to what was happening, they and the

---

[8] I'm sure there are such people these days.

'Managers' had agreed to almost total union control of such matters as job assignments, promotions, working conditions and a host of other things that had previously been under the purview of the field supervisor, project engineer, etc. Ah well, such is progress – no?

We worked out of the camp at Point Bishop, under the 'deplorable' conditions of that time, for about two months and then moved across the inlet and further east toward the Canadian border to a new campsite at Turner Creek that Robbie had chosen. This was about June 1, 1954.

Not surprisingly, the move from Point Bishop to Turner Creek went a lot smoother and faster than the move from Juneau to Point Bishop. We accomplished the whole move and had the entire crew back working before the end of the first week in June. Most of the crew only worked on the move until the heavy lifting was done. After that, just the cross-section crew (God bless 'em) stayed with the moving operation to put everything in place at the new camp before going back to work on the survey. Happily, the terrain moderated considerably on the south side of the inlet, probably because this was on the depositing side instead of the impinging side of the river. This made it somewhat easier for everyone on the crew, but I for one was particularly pleased for the sake of the cross-section crew. They deserved a break having borne the most odious and dangerous of the survey tasks over the extreme topography on the north side.

We conducted some pretty extensive bridge-site surveys at numerous creek crossings on both sides of the inlet – the Turner Creek crossing being the largest. Turner Creek was the last time I can remember using a plane table/alidade. I doubt if there is one engineer in twenty nowadays who knows how to use those tools, and probably not many more who even know what they are. Now they have what they call an electronic data collector – a soulless beast. In fact, I may have mentioned that a lot of today's engineers even get insulted if they are asked to do any physical survey or drafting work. Why would they know, or want to know, anything about survey or drafting instruments? Such things are of concern only to the 'great unwashed'. Graduate engineers must concentrate their trained brainpower on the more sophisticated problems of an engineering nature. So far, after fifty years experience, I still haven't been able to figure out exactly what these "more sophisticated problems" are – at least in the field of road design and construction.

Shortly after we crossed the inlet, Robbie was transferred back to the Juneau office. I later found out that he was reassigned as chief of parties for the surveys supporting construction of the proposed Denali Highway alignment between the MacClaren and Susitna Rivers; a job on which I was again fortunate enough to work for him.

The man who 'replaced' Robbie was called Richard – not Rich or Rick or Dick, but Richard. He was almost comic relief. As nearly as anyone could tell, he had no idea what was going on. It seems like all the replacement supervisors I've experienced have turned out to be duds. Maybe it's the comparison factor, i.e. these guys just didn't measure up to their predecessors, at least in my eyes. After statehood, there was an influx of people like Richard, and much worse. Perhaps they were somehow able to bamboozle their way into jobs that they were unqualified for because the federal folks felt they were sorely needed in what was, as far as they knew, a 'final frontier'.

Richard may have been a harbinger of what was to come, although most of us didn't recognize it then of course. He made absolutely no effort whatsoever to find out what the crews were doing or how the inter-crew arrangements could be periodically adjusted to expedite overall project performance. In fact, it appeared doubtful that he would even have known the meaning of such a concept. We were to see this lack of ability in an alarming percentage of the so-called professionals who followed statehood; probably in many cases escaping a situation where their incompetence had been unmasked and they were about to be fired anyway.

Perhaps I'm being a little unjust in my judgment of Richard in view of the quality of some of the other immigrants who came north after about 1959-1960, but the guidance (or rather lack of guidance) that he could provide was worse than useless because it was frequently misleading. However, he wasn't really the kind of guy you could dislike. He wasn't at all arrogant or officious; he was a really nice guy, just a little vacant. Occasionally (no one knew why), he would come out to work with us in the morning. His usual procedure would be to find a sturdy lath (1/2"x1½"x3' stake) and walk up and down the line swinging lustily at whatever piece of brush was fortunate enough to have escaped the machetes during the line clearing process. Once in a while the lath would break under this vigorous punishment whereupon Richard would exclaim forcefully that he intended to inform headquarters in no uncertain terms that we demanded a better quality lath. I have no comment about that; I guess he was just a lath person.

After all the ties and control data at the point of linkup between the eastbound and westbound crews were taken care of, Richard went to the Taku Lodge to meet with the chief of parties of the westbound folks. I would like to have been the proverbial 'fly on the wall' during that meeting. Here again was a phenomenon that I would become all too familiar with after the 'Managers' finally moved in and took over the workplace: THE MEETING – the management and bureaucratic dragons' ultimate forum.

I was pretty sure that Richard was totally in the dark about the goals and objectives of all this survey business. I really felt a little bit embarrassed for him because he was such a nice guy. If he'd been more arrogant like Gordon (Tonsina project 47-Mile camp) or some of the other overeducated fools I've known, I might have felt differently, but it just didn't seem right to let good old Richard walk unprotected into something of which he was totally ignorant. I suppose that if things went wrong, I wanted to be there to help him.

I don't want to put too fine a point on the subject, but Richard had to be regarded as something like a big St. Bernard who was softly generous and pantingly anxious to do right but totally unable to figure out how to go about it. I guess everything came out all right even without (or more surprisingly with) Richard's input; at least I never heard anything to the contrary. It's a shame that all the incompetent big shots to follow weren't as unassuming, modest and friendly as Richard. As Churchill said, "...a modest man with a great deal to be modest about."

There is a relatively unrelated story that must be told here. It is somewhat representative of the kind of incidents that used to happen occasionally before we were sucked into the federal fold. At the same time it illustrates the kind of specialists that were now being forced on us.

When we set out to move from Point Bishop to Turner Creek, John was still our cook. Although he was still desperately and constantly trying to get everyone to pick up some whiskey for him in town, he was still the best camp cook I had ever met, although I hadn't met them all at that point of course. As an example, on the evening of the day we finished the camp move to Turner Creek, John's stove wasn't fully assembled. All he had was a sort of cobbled-up assembly of loose cast-iron fireboxes, camp-stove units and whatever else we could pull together. Nonetheless, marshalling his consummate skills, John was able to prepare a full 'meat and potatoes' meal for our twelve-man crew. John was an expert of the old school, more anxious to do the right things than to ensure his own personal comfort or advancement.

It was even more astonishing, considering the equipment limitations on that moving day, when John produced a treat of delicious custard filled chocolate covered éclairs. There were enough of them for that evening's dessert, the late-night pinochle game and lunch the following day. Not only that, but by the time we were finished with dinner, John had all the dishes and pots washed and the kitchen completely cleared and shining with cleanliness. In the pursuit of his profession as a camp cook, John was a wizard. It's a shame that the booze got him, but that was an old story with camp cooks, especially the good ones. I suppose that today's more rigorous pre-hiring policies eliminate a lot of the truly great cooks like John.

About two weeks after that magic meal, John collapsed and had to be transported to the hospital in town. He never came back. Later on the following winter we heard that he'd died (God rest him).

Of course we couldn't hope to get a replacement for John who could match his culinary abilities, but we were not in any way prepared for what we actually *did* get; a product of the new hiring practices and the looming menace of generic management.

He was an Italian with a strong accent. There's certainly nothing wrong with that, but there was a lot wrong with Tony having nothing to do with his nationality, including his lousy cooking, his lack of cleanliness, his constant bitching, and his attitude in general. For one thing, he acted like he was paying for the groceries out of his own pocket. For example, if he prepared a sauce of some kind, and it wasn't all used up for dinner, he would store the remainder without refrigeration and keep using it until it actually stunk. Honest to God, it would sometimes really *stink* like something rotten. Whenever we complained, and we often did, he would call us food wasters and crybabies and such.

He also had all sorts of trouble with the dishes. It was at least an hour or two after every meal before he had them 'done', and when he folded his dirty dishtowel and apparently *thought* he was done, the dishes were still dirty, really dirty. To listen to him complaining while he supposedly washed them, one would think he was doing a really thorough job, not so. It seemed that all his griping and bitching about the so-called clean up tasks were, to paraphrase Shakespeare, much "sound and fury signifying nothing" as one could easily see by just looking at the pots and dishes he thought he had finished.

Sometimes it was possible to scrape enough old food scum off the supposedly washed dishes and pots to fill one's fingernails with grease and dried food, and still not have much of it scraped off. These conditions in themselves were intolerable, and when added to the fact that he just flat couldn't cook should have dictated that he be bounced out of the job immediately. We could easily have done a better job cooking for ourselves. Admittedly, today's union safeguards on behalf of the employees would have resulted in a quick one-way trip back to town for Tony. However, in their wisdom the administrators in the head office decided that we didn't need a different cook. I guess we should have invited some of them to dinner!

Even Richard called up Juneau and complained; he must have felt that the cook problem was even more critical than a faulty lath. Admittedly, Richard wasn't the sort of man for whom people snapped to attention in response to his demands, but at least he tried. I don't think he ever really made 'demands' as such – polite requests might be a more accurate characterization. However, one would think that his requests as 'commander on the spot' so to speak would carry some weight. These days, we all realize that we have entered the 'age of the manager' – the final triumph of ignorance. At that time, happily, our profession hadn't yet completely surrendered our decision-making prerogatives, and we were hopeful that Richard's complaints as the man in charge might carry enough weight to get Tony fired.

Alas, our hopes were dashed, perhaps due to Richard's benign approach to the Juneau administrators. Now it really began to look like we were all doomed to follow the project with extended hospital stays for treatment of ptomaine or salmonella poisoning, or worse. However, the fickle finger of providence stepped in and Tony himself provided us with such a monumental example of stupidity that he outclassed even the managers of today in his ignorance, and the administrators were forced to admit their mistaken judgment. Their mistakes were not – God forbid – theirs of course, but rather those of someone else whose counsel they had relied upon in good faith. Naturally it was not, then or now and *never*, *their* fault.

When you are in the woods, the smell of something cooking attracts all sorts of critters. The attraction is even stronger when the groceries are a little spoiled and the pots are dirty with accumulated food scum, as was usually the case in Tony's kitchen. As it happened, Tony was by himself one afternoon cooking up some kind of inedible slumgullion to serve us for dinner, and I was in the next-door office tent that day calculating survey notes. Tony always had a big pot of boiling water standing by on his stove for whatever purpose – maybe to wash his hands in if he ever did such a thing. I guess a big boar black bear must have been passing by on the Turner Lake trail. He was probably heading for some fishing spot where he thought he might grab up a fish or two without getting crossways with one of those confrontational brown bear bullies who always hung around this time of year. He probably then sniffed what smelled like either a freshly used outhouse or Tony's kitchen – a real spoiled food enticement for a poor hungry bear. I'm relishing the details of this story because what happened next really took the wind out of Tony's conceit, and because of the ultimate outcome.

Anyway, while Tony was puttering around in the cook-shack, probably looking for some spoiled leftovers to throw into whatever he was cooking up for us, our bear friend (my hero) stuck his head through the front opening of the cook-shack tent.

Tony now confirmed that he was the real jackass everyone thought he was. He didn't yell 'go away bear', or throw an empty dish at him like any sensible person would have done. Instead, he grabbed up the big pot of boiling water and threw it in the bear's face; exactly the wrong thing to do to a bear or to any other feeling critter, including a human. The bear was no doubt suddenly blinded, hopefully temporarily. and subjected to both exquisite pain and grinding fear. He reacted in much the same way that anyone, including a human being blinded and driven by pain or fear and with the only known path being forward in the direction he was already pointed, would probably react. He blasted straight ahead like I've been told a big boar hog goes through an electric fence after receiving a jolt of electricity. He knocked Tony over, without really hurting him, and barged straight ahead through the entire centerline length of the tent, striking at everything he could reach on both sides. He broke up most of the tables and benches, smashed almost all of the dishes, tipped over the stove and then crashed through the far end of the cook-shack. When he went out the back he took down the A-frame supporting that end, and when that went it pulled down the A-frame at the front, resulting in the complete collapse of the whole works, and from Tony the

Tony's dinner guest?

damndest wailing I'd ever heard.

Tony wanted us to find the bear immediately and kill it. However, we found plenty of reasons, including gratitude, not to do so, and we felt even more indebted to that bear when Tony quit two days later, somehow reasoning that the whole incident was our fault. Maybe he thought we had trained the bear to do what it did. If we could have, we might have done just that.

Within less than a week we had another cook. We managed to take turns cooking and washing dishes for ourselves during the interim between cooks. I really can't recall much about the new cook except that he wasn't bad, but he wasn't any great shakes as a camp cook either. He certainly wasn't of the same caliber as John, but he was one hell of a lot better than Tony, and we felt reasonably sure that he wouldn't poison us.

We experienced only one other incident regarding a bear around camp, and I'm going to relate the story because it was one of the motivating incidents that led to my final rejection of sports hunting as cruel, barbaric and totally unjustifiable behavior.

Bears, especially brown bears, aren't really that common in the woods. You're not likely to run into one unless you're poking around someplace that bears need to be. They might be around a creek full of fish in the fall, or in a productive berry patch in the late spring or summer. Contrary to what seems like popular belief, bears do not cruise the woods looking for humans to kill and, in very rare cases, to eat. Bears are not human. They don't kill things for recreational purposes or trophies as we do. I'm not a wildlife biologist, but my own observations indicate to me that except as noted above, bears, especially brown bears, will go out of their way to avoid human beings at least ninety-five percent of the time. One cannot really blame them in view of the fact that we have proven ourselves to be unquestionably the most dangerous and deadly species on the planet.

Bears, like all critters, including us, squirrels, cats, dogs, and even many bugs will almost always take measures (violent if necessary) in response to what is seen by them as a threat to either themselves or their young. However, sometimes what seems like a threat to a bear or other critter may not look that way to us. I've never spoken to the critters, but I think that they probably reason in a somewhat simplistic cause and effect or deductive manner. We must, therefore, try very hard to see things from their point of view and avoid actions that they might interpret as threatening.

I'm sorry to dwell so much on bears here, but it seems like every time I mention that I'm from Alaska, I get questioned about bears and the supposed dangers they represent. My sisters-in-law also spent some time in Alaska, and apparently at least two of them were told by someone that a can full of rocks is an effective bear repellent. I think the idea is to shake the can and thereby produce a loud weird sound that will supposedly frighten the bears and cause them to run away, leaving the can bearer unharmed. As an aside, I suggest tripod legs. (See a previous description of a personal experience north of Haines in 1951.)

I've personally observed that, like almost all wild animals, bears are intensely curious. I don't know, but it seems to me that the word would soon get around among the bears that the cans aren't really a threat. If so, wouldn't they be more likely to come out to see where the clattering noise was coming from than to run away or to hurt anyone? Anyway, the rocks-in-the-can approach seemed to work equally well against bears, elephants, zebras, crocodiles and numerous other wild animals. As far as I know, the girls never encountered any of these critters during their wilderness sojourns in Alaska while carrying the dreaded can-of-rocks weapon, bearing witness to the effectiveness of this approach. We must always remember that although they look, experience emotions, and express themselves unlike we do, animals are not stupid, just different. Is that such a threatening concept?

About a week after we moved to Turner Creek, we discovered that our larder had been the target of repeated raids by a young black bear. It's obviously easy to tell a bear raid from a squirrel or other small critter just from the extent of the litter left behind. Additionally, you can almost always tell what kind of bear it is because a black bear usually makes less of a mess than a brown bear, who will tear up everything he can get hold of. I don't think he does that because he's mean or angry, it just seems to be in his nature. Maybe he's looking for something extra, dessert perhaps. Anyway brown bears seem far less likely to raid larders, camp dumps, etc. than black bears. I think that brown bears just don't like people or anything that reminds them of us. The complete story of our clandestine raider is sad to tell, and it haunts me to this day, but nonetheless I think it's a story that should be told and that *I* should tell it.

We laid a sort of trap for this poor black bear. Actually it wasn't a very sophisticated trap; all we did was just sit up almost all night with our rifles and wait for the bear to show up. At about 4 a.m. when he did appear, we all opened up on him and chased the poor terrified critter up Turner Creek until he reached what he thought was sanctuary under his little pile of brush.

I think he was pretty young and inexperienced at den building. Had we allowed him to live longer he would probably have learned to make a bigger, more comfortable and more secure dwelling. But we couldn't let him do that, could we? We had to kill him, didn't we? Five or six of us followed him up the creek from our camp to his little brush pile, shooting at him constantly and repeatedly wounding him the whole way. After he was dead, we looked into his little den and found about twenty pounds of Darigold Butter in those little round cans that would keep un-refrigerated for months, and were therefore good for camp storage. They were a little less than half the size of a one-pound coffee can. We could have supplied him with that stuff for the rest of his life with no inconvenience to us, none.

After we got there, and I saw him lying so dead, so still and so full of bullet holes, I started throwing up and couldn't stop retching and gagging for least thirty minutes. It wasn't because of the blood or the guts or anything like that. It was because the pure horror of what we had done suddenly gripped me and wrenched my stomach inside out. I'm sure that his tiny cover of brush represented home and safety to him, and that the butter cans were his little treasures – he was still holding a couple of them to his body when he died.

The other guys wanted to skin him and keep his hide with all the hair attached, probably as some kind of macabre trophy. This was the hide and hair that had so recently been alive. It had shed the rain, kept the poor little guy warm, dry and cozy against the winter while he slept, and not so long ago had been licked, kept clean and cared for by his mother who loved and cuddled him just as human mothers do with their babies. He had spent the last hour or so of his life in absolute all-consuming terror, probably crying desperately for his mama, in his own way.

I wanted no further part of it. I walked away without saying anything more to the other guys. I was *terribly* ashamed of what we had done, and I still am. Even now it brings tears to my eyes when I think of that poor little animal guy and remember the years of his life that we took away from him. We have *never* been given any natural or moral right to do such things. It was a further step toward my now long-held aversion to the murder of wild animals. We say that this is the natural order of things, that the predators pursue the prey – bullshit! This is just a mechanism of self-justification no matter how undeserved. We're supposed to be rational and merciful creatures in the image of our Creator. Obviously we didn't turn out that way in many cases.

I've shot a few big critters since then and tried to justify my actions by telling myself that I needed the meat, or that it was for protective purposes. Despite my rationale, I always felt like I was lying to myself. The shame deepened with every killing. That little bear on the Taku kept invading my dreams for years, and I finally admitted to myself that the justifications were becoming increasingly transparent. About thirty-five or more years ago, I stopped hunting completely. I'm deeply ashamed of all the killings I did or helped with, and now I desperately wish that I could undo them. Unfortunately, like so many things in life, there are no second chances, and I can never give back the innocent lives of the wild critters that I've murdered. That sort of killing is not a matter of subsistence and there is no excuse or acceptable rationale for it, absolutely none!

Since statehood and the discovery of oil on the North Slope, more and more of the 'sportsmen' who enjoy murdering animals are infiltrating the state. Most of them are not used to being in close proximity to such large wild animals and killing these critters must be a twisted way of proving their masculinity to themselves. They often even hang pieces of the dead critters on their walls at home – sick, isn't it?

The guilt over killing the bear notwithstanding, it was time to set aside personal feelings and begin our move back to town. It would be the last time I saw the Turner Creek camp, and realizing that, I felt a certain amount of sadness. However, to paraphrase Bob Dylan, "the times they were a-changin", and we had our orders from the administrators and fledgling managers in Juneau. Being naively oblivious to the whispers of change, we followed those orders.

By this time, administrative interference in project technical matters was beginning to stir. It may have been a sign of things to come, but most of us were still probably too young and/or naïve to recognize it as such or to realize the deeper implications. Had we been more prescient in our outlook, we might have recognized the precursors of the 'Great Management Takeover', and had we been more mature, we might have taken steps to cut it off then and there. Perhaps not, we were dedicated to becoming surveyors and engineers and as such not really able to recognize the kind of insidious and subtle encroachment that is a characteristic of this type of management, and it was barely beginning to loom unnoticed over the horizon of our profession anyway.

It's a sure thing that if the Taku River survey were in progress today, the agency would be required to furnish safe and comfortable transportation back and forth to town for everyone on the job. In 1954, we weren't provided with amenities like that. If we wanted to go to town for anything other than official business, we had to provide our own transportation in our own boats or find someone else who had a boat and was willing to give us a ride. There were a few times when the sea was rough enough to cause some concern, but in general, the trips to town were uneventful.

The move back into Juneau this time was slightly more complicated than before because we were restricted from leaving anything at all behind – not anything, not a gum wrapper, not a stray peanut, not even a piece of dried-up eagle poop that we weren't responsible for. This was not yet the age of rabid environmental activism, although it would be coming sooner than we knew. However, even without constant haranguing from the rabbit trackers of today, we all knew enough not to leave the woods full of garbage. Unknown to most of us at the time, It wouldn't be long before there would be a whole discipline centered on this one simplistic concept and providing livelihoods for about a gazillion environmental zealots running around all over the woods and hiding in the bushes.

After we got all our stuff loaded and the clean up work was

done, we took one last look at our Turner Creek campsite and, reflecting on the individual memories we built there, we headed for Juneau.

There was something almost prophetic about the end of this job. It somehow seemed like the end of an era. We were departing the Taku project, but in some indefinable way that wasn't all we were leaving. Could there have been a subconscious sense that the mountains, the forests and the beaches of Southeast Alaska would, for me at least, soon be slipping into the past? It would be two years before Irene and I more or less permanently moved to the interior. Nonetheless, something sort of whispered to my inner self that leaving the Taku was like walking into a long dark tunnel with some sort of visible but indistinguishable images at the other end. I knew, kind of instinctively, that changes were coming, and I think that other Alaskans were beginning to sense it too. There were veiled, almost subliminal indications that the Alaska we loved was being eroded around the edges, but they were periodic and we couldn't know what the final outcome would be. However, the changes then barely beginning to emerge would make themselves felt soon enough.

Back to Juneau – Return from the Taku

Anchorage/Cook Inlet – Leaving on a Jet Plane

In the headquarters (Juneau) office, our efforts were now focused on the first section of the Denali Highway, running into the mountains west of Paxson. Ultimately, at the Susitna River, this section was to meet the road continuing on to Cantwell on the Alaska Railroad. Apparently, the political pressure was temporarily off of what we had thought was the *essential* connection from the territorial capital at Juneau to the outside world. Maybe it wasn't so essential after all, although I bet it became essential off and on every time some politician got hungry for a cause that would call attention to himself. There is still no such connection. The capital is still Juneau, and as far as I know, no final access route has yet even been decided upon, much less designed or built. Even then, we all knew that politics played a dominant role in choices like this, but it was before the 'reign' of King Wally I (Hickel), and Alaskan politics still seemed a lot more wholesome than was the case later on.

Although Bob Atwood is dead, his persistence while he lived has left a legacy of continual pressure about a capital move on the part of the pseudo-Alaskans in the Anchorage area. Unfortunately, statehood seems only to have intensified the arguments of the move advocates. This is probably because the majority of the post-statehood carpetbaggers who swarmed north settled in the Anchorage area. Most of them are barely aware that there is more to the state than just the south-central portion, and they have never even looked any further than Palmer, Seward or the Kenai Peninsula. They are thus easy targets for the resident capital-move proponents who for the most part, don't know any more about the rest of the state than they do about Siberia.

Before switching our major effort to familiarization with, and preparation for, the Denali job, we had a little work to complete on the Taku. We managed to find at least two alternative, buildable, and feasible alignments/gradients for the

Taku option, and get them on record by the end of January 1955 as ordered. We were a little later than originally anticipated, but no one made a big fuss about it. These days, written justifications for such a delay would require unending 'review' by a whole herd of different bureaucratic and management dragons, all but a very few of whom wouldn't know any more about surveying or road construction that they would about nuclear physics. Once the project was 'put to bed', we packaged up all the 'Goose Down' (Taku) stuff, labeled the boxes and stored them all away.

I was told much later that the data were all taken out and reevaluated several times, apparently in reaction to some political imperative of the moment. Regardless of all the time and money spent on these 're-evaluations', as far as I know nothing ever came of it. Knowing the way today's government agencies and their managers operate, I bet that if the project is ever seriously re-activated, the survey will be done all over again. Oh well, the taxpayers have lots of money, and besides, those old-time surveyors with their outdated methods and instruments probably didn't get it right anyway. That seems to be the attitude of this generation: "If it's old, it must be outdated, and if it's outdated, throw it out!"

It's the long-suffering taxpayer who finances such imperious attitudes, and who is increasingly kept uninformed about these things. The tragedy of the modern attitude is that most of the old data are *not* outdated. Technical ground-level data are technical ground-level data and remain so. Except in the case of major geologic upheaval, flood, or extreme environmental damage, they remain valid for many years – even decades.

Many, if not most, of today's modern 'Managers' don't understand such things. They often attempt to make project decisions such as discarding 'old' data without acknowledging, or even recognizing, their own ignorance. Discussions like this are interesting and they certainly go directly to the heart of what is largely responsible for today's obvious decline in engineering productivity not only in Alaska but throughout the profession. Unfortunately, knowledgeable suggestions for improvement are rarely heeded, and even more rarely result in any improvement, even if they are accepted.

In April of 1955 while I was in Juneau, I married Irene Albayalde in the Roman Catholic Church there. We managed to stay married for seventeen years and to produce eight fine children. I'm very proud of all of them now that they're well grown up, and I'm sure Irene feels the same.

In Juneau, we were able to organize and reconcile the available Denali project data for a quick start of the 1955 construction season by mid-May. We felt like we had everything prepared and were ready to go, so about four or five days before the end of May we packed up all our gear and left for the ARC Fairbanks district in general, and the Denali Highway project in particular.

The Denali Highway goes through the mountains of the Alaska Range from Paxson on the Richardson Highway west to Cantwell on the Alaska Railroad and intersects the Parks Highway, now running from Palmer to Fairbanks along the railroad corridor. At the time we were on this project, and even when the Denali Highway was first connected to Cantwell, the Parks Highway had not yet been built or even fully designed.

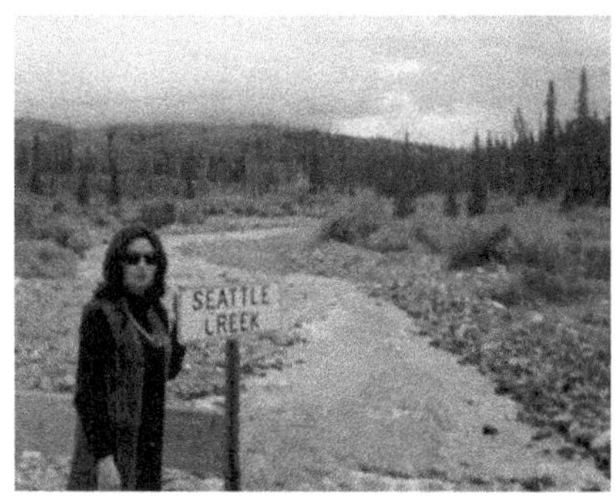

The Seattle connection Denali Highway – Cantwell-Susitna section

Cantwell is located about twenty miles south of McKinley Park, now called Denali Park, and about ten or twelve miles north of Broad Pass, where the railroad passes through its highest traveled point in the Alaska Range. It is, in fact, the highest point between Seward and Fairbanks on the entire railroad route. The road from Cantwell east to the Susitna River was already built by the time we began at the Paxson end of the highway. I don't know when the Cantwell-Susitna section was built, but it must have been some time ago since there was already a well-established maintenance camp five or six miles east of the railroad, and a couple of taverns along the way.

When we first got to Paxson, the old lodge was still operating on the east side of the Richardson Highway three quarters of a mile north of the Denali junction. This period is a little bit confused in my memory because a man named Stanley was there then functioning as the manager/owner of the new lodge located only about 300 feet north of the Denali Highway junction and on the west side of the Richardson. I think the new lodge was probably at least under construction during our first year, but all my memories of going to the lodge at that time seem to be set in the old log building.

There was an older couple named Wilma and Richard[9] Windust who ran the old lodge, and I think they had been there for at least twenty-five years. They had an old parrot that just sat in its cage calling, "Wilma-Wilma–Wilma," constantly. Parrots live a long time and I know personally that the parrot was still calling for Wilma as late as 1970. This was well after the old lodge had been abandoned and the parrot had been moved to the new one; I don't know if Wilma was even still alive by that time. Whether she was or not, the parrot didn't forget, and he probably wondered why Wilma didn't answer the call. They said that he could say lots of other words too, but I never heard any of them.

We came to know Stanley pretty well that year, and we frequently visited with him on a social basis. I clearly remember

---

[9] I think.

one particular party that we had just before we left Paxson for the Tangle Lakes, and it is worth talking about because I don't think such things go on anymore now that we've become more sophisticated like the folks 'outside'.

We invited Stanley to the party, I guess just because he really was a nice guy, and we were leaving for the Tangle Lakes soon. Anyway, about halfway through the party Stanley began to regale us with stories of what an athletic and happy fellow he had been in his younger days. We were sitting on the couch with a few chairs all gathered around a coffee table. Stanley pointed to the table, telling us that when he was younger he could have left the party by turning a full airborne somersault over that table, landing on his feet, tipping his hat and taking his leave by stepping out the door. We all agreed that such a feat would have truly been something to see and expressed regret that we never saw it.

The beer drinking and the conversation kept on going and at some point Stanley fell silent. I guess he kept thinking about his own description of his youthful leave taking because he suddenly stood, jumped straight up into the air and landed squarely on the coffee table with his legs sticking out straight in front of him. Of course, the table was flattened, the glasses went flying across the room in every direction, and Stanley just sat there on the top of the broken table. He had a really quizzical look on his face as if he was as surprised as everyone else at what had happened – those were good days and people like Stanley were good people.

We stayed at Paxson less than two more weeks, and we then managed to get another haul to the Tangle Lakes camp from an agency supply truck headed that way.

That party, or the hauling of a private trailer by an agency truck, would not have been tolerated by the bureaucratic and management dragons who moved in with statehood. Along with millions of other regulations, they would have had some strictly forbidding the private use of agency vehicles, as well as throwing parties on government property. Those kinds of people always have some logical-sounding rationale for acting like jerks. They would say, for example, that hauling private vehicles was prohibited by the insurers. Sounds logical, right? So why not buy some extra insurance to make such hauling possible for the convenience of the employees? I'm sure that if one asked that question, there would be a logical-sounding phony answer for that too. Anyway, I don't think such regulations existed then, and even if they did, everyone ignored them. No doubt about it, there were criminal elements among our group! As it turned out, my friend Mike also went to the Tangle Lakes, where he went to work as the lead equipment operator on the project.

Just as though we had been followed by the devil, some area entrepreneur set up a bar in a little glacial depression only about a half-mile east of our camp. Not surprisingly, Mike and I were almost his first customers. All he had then were about three empty oil barrels with two or three planks over them constituting the bar and some sawed off stumps with cushions for bar stools. It was pretty primitive, but at least he had a power plant for electrical power and was well stocked with beer and booze. I think he even had one of those old-fashioned jukeboxes that he probably got at a garage sale or a junkyard. We never thought much about it at the time, but that guy turned out to be just the first of a gazillion others who rushed into the country after the road connection was completed and statehood attracted the attention of all the outside opportunists. I haven't been back up in the Denali country for at least twenty-five years so I don't know how much the carpetbaggers have exploited it.

I remember the Tangle Lakes camp well; partly because it was the first time I ever heard such clear howling of wolves off in the distance. I had heard them before, but it's more impressive at a place like the Tangle Lakes. If one walks out to some location where the camp power plant can't be heard, the silence is deafening, and the cry of the wolves is unbelievably clear and crisp. I think it might be the cool mountain air that lends such beauty to their calls. There is no more beautiful sound in the whole world. It carries a sort of deeply mournful and nostalgic sorrow, and there's something about it that reaches deep inside you. It speaks of the unspoiled wilderness, the shelter of the forest, and to a part of us that is still there, only muffled by 'civilization'. Frankly, I doubt if the wolves think of it that way, but who knows? It wasn't the first or the last time I heard that cry, and its magic has never diminished – at least not for me. I fear that this sound is disappearing from large areas of Alaska. When it's completely gone and the wolves have left to seek the greater seclusion they prefer, perhaps one day we'll wake up and realize that our self-serving behaviors have driven away something very basic and profound. When it happens, maybe we can place the blame at the feet of the post-statehood 'immigrants'. They have never experienced the thrill and the unspoiled beauty of such things, so they can't have any appreciation or understanding of them, recognize the importance of protecting them, or miss them when they're gone.

In fact, I seem to recall that some of the politicians who arrived during the short 'smash-and-grab' period right after statehood formed part of the legislative so-called 'study group' who recommended, and pushed through the labyrinthine legislative process for which they themselves were responsible, the first bounty on Alaskan wolves. Through some idiotic rationale contrary to all common sense, this group felt, or said they felt, that by killing off a bunch of the wolves they could save more of the game animals such as moose and caribou, probably so that they would be available for the increasing population of stateside trophy hunters – a lower form of life. The temporary result, before these airheads became aware of what they had done, was that the number of grazing game animals really did increase. In fact, they increased so much that they were soon eating themselves out of natural fodder, and if memory serves me correctly, during the final winter of this insane 'experiment', the Fish and Game folks had to fly out tons and tons of baled hay to keep the herds from starving. All because a few dopey politicians thought they could outsmart nature.

Politicians, lawyers and 'Managers' should keep their mouths and ideas out of things they don't understand. Most of them wouldn't know a wild wolf from a Pekinese. Of course, as soon as it became obvious what a flop the bounty idea had turned out to be, it was almost comical to watch the politicians who had originally favored the idea tripping all over each other and desperately pointing fingers left and right trying to avoid any blame. Can it be any wonder why people look askance at so many of the crackpot ideas these guys come up with and have so little respect for them and their so-called professions?

The MacLaren River was where I first met Fred Pettijohn, at the time a prospector who owned a copper mine up near the headwaters of the MacLaren. I want to include Fred in this book because he was one of the types of long-time Alaskans who have largely disappeared. He was an original. At one point Robbie took a half-interest in one of Pettijohn's claims and dreamed of some pretty extravagant development to come as he exploited 'his' claim. Tragically, Robbie is no longer with us and his dreams were not to be, but that's another story that I may get to later. Robbie was really proud of his interest in the MacLaren River copper deposits and remembering his excitement about it and the events that were to come almost brings tears to my eyes. I really don't like to think about it.

During part of the first year we were camped on the

MacLaren, the crew lived in some tents with sideboards along the east side of the river right across from where the contractor latter set up his camp. I think that for a while the ARC had a cook-shack there too. However, when the contractor got established on the west side, an agreement was made for him to feed and house the agency crews too. Pettijohn also had his upstream copper mine on the east side of the river.

Fred wasn't a drunk in a derogatory sense, but he did like to drink whiskey, and he did so every Friday or Saturday night – a lot. After he got drunk up at his own cabin, he would climb into his tracked 'weasel' and come wobbling down the east bank of the MacLaren waving his bottle and singing lustily. Actually, he had a pretty good singing voice.

During our first season he ran through at least two tents, breaking down the sideboards, although not completely trashing all the canvas; most of it was salvageable. Fortunately, no one was hurt and no formal damage claims were ever filed. Apparently, there were no fee-hungry lawyers lurking in the nearby bushes or snorkeling along the river with periscopes as there would surely be today. All the tents that Fred ran over were unoccupied; perhaps he knew that ahead of time, although judging by his behavior, it was probably purely random; just pure dumb luck.

Fred's usual reason for coming down to see us was to get some of us to accompany him and give him a ride down to his favorite saloon near Paxson since he had no car. It was one of the best saloons in the Denali area; located on the east shore of Paxson Lake, about four or five miles south of the new lodge. Every time we arrived there, he would prevail upon the owner to play the piano and he would break into song with such timeless old classics as:

The Engineers, the Engineers
they don't care for trifles

they hang their b--ls upon the walls
and shoot at them with rifles

Or:

The Engineers, the Engineers
the dirty sons of b--ches
they line their a-- with broken glass
and laugh because it itches

And, of course:

Lady Godiva, through Coventry did ride
to show all the villagers her pretty little hide
now the men who took her off her horse and led her to a beer
were a bleary eyed surveyor and a drunken engineer
and so on and so on --------"

The last one went on for about twenty verses.

Naturally, he insisted that we learn them all and sing along with him. I was to run across Fred again about ten or twelve years later under very different circumstances. Fred was another casualty of statehood and the subsequent encroachment of the outside ways of doing things. It's another sad commentary on what happened to us.

The high country – Alaska Range massif

There's something about that high, treeless Denali country that seems to grow on a person. Bluegrass music often refers to such country as 'High, Lonesome'. At first sight it looks barren, bleak, ugly and inhospitable. After a few months, however, the emptiness itself takes on a sort of protecting and comforting aspect. Maybe that's because there is none of the 'spookiness' or threatening character of the deep woods after dark.

Even then, four years before statehood, there were signs as

far into the wilderness as the Clearwater, where there wasn't even road access, that we were stepping onto a sort of slow social conveyor belt leading to some very fundamental changes in our Alaskan lifestyle. Maybe some of the early signs were due to advanced knowledge of impending statehood that some politicians or influential (read 'rich') people possessed, but those of us in the trenches knew nothing of such things. Perhaps it was just the natural pressure resulting from the on-going increase in nationwide population; perhaps there was an expansion of the military presence for whatever reason, or perhaps some anticipated increased need in 'the states' for Alaska's resources.

Whatever it was, we were beginning to see unusual things like station wagon loads of hunters jumping out of their car and firing blindly into the huge caribou herds that used to pass through the Denali country. People dressed in suits and such were starting to show up for dinner at Paxson, and even some of the more isolated roadhouses. Overall, the indications were sprouting up everywhere, and although most of us couldn't yet define what it was, many Alaskans somehow knew that, in the words of Ray Bradbury, "Something wicked this way comes."

By sometime in late October of that year, the signs of the coming winter had begun blowing in from the high peaks. The chill of snow was in the crisp air, and it was time to go home for the season. We loaded up the old Plymouth station wagon and a U-Haul trailer, headed south to Haines and caught the ferry to Juneau. The trip was uneventful, and I think we were successful in finding a rental house on the beach on Douglas Island following a brief stay with Irene's mother and stepfather after getting home.

Our first daughter, Laura RoseAnn, came to us on November 7, 1955 at St. Joseph's Hospital in Juneau. I was dumfounded. I had known about chasing girls and the birds and the bees and all that stuff, but somehow I had never mentally connected those things with the production of little people. Not even Irene's obviously developing pregnancy seemed to prepare me for this astonishing outcome.

As soul-satisfying as this first birth was, we had to keep on working to provide for a family that we hoped would continue to grow; it did so to the full extent of our dreams. After she had recovered from the birth of Laura, Irene went back to work for what I think was the Department of Veteran's Affairs, and I continued working for the ARC in the Juneau headquarters office.

The winter of 1955/56 was almost as uneventful as the drive down from the Denali. All the pleasures of a winter in Juneau were there but the work at the office was depressingly boring.

We started out reducing and plotting all the Denali data available to us, although to this day I have never been able to figure out *why*. The ostensible reason was to determine, I guess just for the record, the quantities of materials involved in the construction of the Denali to date and the probable amount to be used in completing the job.

The exercise was pointless. We may as well have been doing all those calculations for some imaginary road to the moon because all the original ground data were taken from the alignment that we staked in the field prior to construction, and the agency construction crews built the road wherever *they* thought it should be. In several places, the two centerlines (staked vs. built) were as much as two hundred feet apart.

Interestingly, someone had assigned an administrative person to the design office during the previous field season. Perhaps, if he hadn't been a little ahead of his time authoritatively speaking, he might have been able to 'Administrate' or 'Manage' the problem of bogus data out of the way! In a very real sense, for better or worse, this business of the agency construction crews ignoring the surveyors was the old

Alaskan attitude showing up, i.e. you do it *your* way and I'll do it *my* way.

It was difficult to tell just what our new administrative guy was supposed to do and even more so to tell what he *did* do. He never used any drafting tools, and we never saw him do anything more advanced than add, subtract, multiply or divide on his calculator; one of those noisy old Monroes or Marchants. There was naturally a bit of talk over the bar about him and his duties. None of us realized, or would then have believed, that in a few years we'd be working for him or one of his administrative clones – tie, dark blue suit, briefcase and all. Anyway, Robbie didn't even seem to notice the guy, and as far I was concerned in those days if Robbie didn't notice him he wasn't worth noticing. Sometimes, blindness to events or even ignorance is a momentary blessing.

By the time we brought all the Denali office work up to date, it was late March or early April, 1956; a little too early to return to the Denali high country, and a little too late to take on any full crew assignment to a new project. We compromised by separating the crewmembers and accepting individual assignments to various other design jobs. We were able to do things like that then because it was before the management dragons took over and in many cases reserved the options of job assignments and scheduling for themselves.

It was sometime during the last week in April 1956 when we packed up and left for the Denali project once again. I was now assigned primarily to inspection duties and as a stand-by party chief whenever it became necessary to form an additional ad hoc crew. A man named Fred (obviously not Fred Pettijohn) was our new party chief for the permanent, all-purpose crew. Fred had spent most of the summer of 1955 in charge of a similar crew somewhere else, but I don't know how well he had performed in that capacity. He was now a college graduate and presumably capable of directing the activity of a transit crew in successfully completing the required tasks. He was a very sociable and apparently ordinary, albeit irritatingly meticulous fellow and *very* observing of all the events going on around him regardless of how trivial or meaningless. His conversation was the same way. He didn't seem able to tell a story or relay any information without going into every imaginable detail, whether it was germane to his point or not. His notes and daily reports reflected this personality trait.

As an example of Fred's conscientiousness, my dog, Tangle, occasionally flushed out small groups of Caribou. They bunch up like that before coalescing into the massive herd with which they will later migrate to their wintering ground. Tangle loved to chase these critters whenever he had the opportunity to do so, even though the grass and brush was well over his head. I don't know what he would have done if he ever caught one – an eventuality for which he was neither physically nor emotionally equipped.

South end of northbound caribou – Fun to chase?

Anyway, all of Tangle's escapades were duly recorded in Fred's field books and daily reports along with many other things, like miscellaneous game sightings, crew appearance and other such unrelated stuff. Of course, he also included the necessary information including angle 'wind-ups' and averages, curve data, control point and reference descriptions, etc. That was Fred's way and I bet it still is if he's still alive.

I may have mentioned previously that it was our practice to send out small long-range survey crews ahead of the main activity areas. During one of our inbound journeys from such a crew assignment we came upon a man on foot about ten miles west of the MacLaren River. He was all bloodied up with deep lacerations on his legs, arms, face and chest. It was obviously not the result of a bear attack because if a bear had scratched him up that badly, it would have finished the job and killed him – maybe even eaten him up. Such a possibility, although highly unlikely, was quite conceivable considering that he had no tripod legs to bang together.

He said he left his pickup at the MacLaren River and walked in. Of course, we had to pick him up and take him at least as far as the Clearwater where someone could clean up his injuries and then take him back to his pickup. During the ride he told us that he was out there collecting falcon chicks from the nests in the cliffs, putting them in a burlap bag and later taking them south to sell to pet shops and such. He said that this part of the Alaska Range was one of only three or four places in the U.S. where true hunting falcons could be found – or at least the kind that could be most readily trained. He went on to relate the gruesome statistic that by the time he got back to the states, about 60% of the chicks in the bag would still be alive, and he could get some really good prices for them; even from such prominent places as Walt Disney studios. He showed absolutely no concern whatever for the 40% of the chicks that would not survive. When I heard this I really (really – not just figuratively!) wished that we hadn't picked up the SOB and that a bear had killed and eaten him; no loss, he owed it to the environment. Considering what he was doing to those little falcon chicks, such an end would have been just punishment for his admitted despicable behavior.

His story was that with a bag about half full he had decided to raid one more nest that he saw on a ledge about fifty feet above him, so he climbed up there, found three or four chicks in this nest and began loading them into his obscene sack. While he was engaged in his disgusting and murderous activity, the hen falcon returned and really lit into him (hoorah-whoopee!).

According to him, she was responsible for all the damage to his tattered shirt as well as all the wounds on his chest, hands, neck and face; inflicting them with her raptor beak and her razor-sharp talons. Apparently he had been unable to defend himself because he had his vile sack in one hand and needed the other to hang on to the cliff. He must have lost the sack because he didn't have it when we picked him up.

We used what was left of his shirt for temporary bandages and small tourniquets to stop the bleeding (an effort to which I gave no assistance) and took him back to camp, where the cook, who was trained in emergency medical procedures, patched him up for a trip to Paxson. I saw the wounds after the cook got them cleaned up, and it was gratifying to see that they were mostly much deeper than we thought at first when they were all filled up with blood. When he left, everyone wished him good luck except me. I hope he developed fatal blood poisoning from his wounds, thus rewarding that heroic defense by the hen falcon. She should have been searched out and awarded some sort of falcon medal.

I know that this kind of commercialization at the expense of our wild critters became relatively common shortly after statehood, and I fear that it will get worse. Everybody from all those universities and museums down south wants to 'study' our animals for some reason, even when there really isn't any more to be learned. Why can't all these eggheads just leave our critters alone and let them live their natural lives? How do you think the studiers would like it if some moose or wolverine followed *them* all over the place poking instruments at them, putting collars around their necks while constantly taking flash camera photos of them and measurements of various body parts?

Occasionally we took trips into town that summer. We usually just went to Glennallen or Delta Junction, but I think we got into Fairbanks at least once or twice, giving Irene a chance for a little shopping in the 'big city'.

Some of the more disconcerting aspects of these trips were the tiny, almost invisible changes that showed up on every trip. It might be just a new, shiny hotel reception desk decorated with a commercial looking 'Alaskan' motif, or a few more parking meters downtown, or maybe some flashy formal wear in a men's store. Not much taken individually, but collectively forming an almost imperceptible trend toward a social change that would soon begin to permanently alter the Alaskan lifestyle. I was gradually beginning to notice such things.

The job closed for the winter sometime around the end of October. We got a ride to the MacLaren with all our baggage and headed back to Juneau around November 5. The fall of 1956 must have been pretty dry in the interior; it was cold, but most of the roads on the way home were bare. Although there was at least six inches of snow at Clearwater Creek when we left and maybe a foot and a half at the Three Guardsman summit on the Haines Cutoff, on average the trip was almost snow free. It was raining as usual in both Haines and Juneau when we arrived, but it felt good to get back anyway because we were home.

Upon arrival I reported for work at the design office as usual, and Irene went back to work. This winter in the office was looking a little more interesting, if only because we would be spending most of it working on the Denali project; something that we were more familiar with than anyone else in the office.

The Denali jobs between Paxson and the MacLaren River were due to be advertised during the late winter of 1961/62 for construction beginning in the spring/summer of 1962. This schedule allowed adequate time for collecting all the existing files and recorded field data, and for collecting, refining and extending the survey information in the field. At that time, planning for a project this far in advance of construction was almost unheard of, particularly since the Denali work would actually comprise two projects. Fortunately, this was before statehood and before the really intense proliferation of 'Management' with its attendant bureaucracy and procedures that almost seem aimed at delaying the projects.

Surprisingly, our 'in-house' administrator in the design office was starting to enter into conversations about the technical aspects of road design and construction. At first, a lot of what he said came out as just gibberish or, at best, meaningless nonsense, but he had apparently overheard enough of the professional words to at least pronounce them properly. Even in the face of these early, stumbling initial management incursions into our technical domain, we still didn't recognize the veiled threat inherent in such things, although we were starting to sense that changes must be coming.

All these usurpers needed then was some training in verbal dexterity in order to string the proper words together so that: 1) The overall impression would be one of familiarity with the subject. 2) The speaker could rely on obfuscation as a tactic to replace both intelligence and knowledge of the subject. 3) The speaker could tailor and twist his presentation to avoid sounding like a half-wit when any of the listeners are knowledgeable in the subject under discussion. These management folks might do well to speak with some lawyers to learn how such presentations are put together, i.e. in regard to what to wear and how to look self-assured when speaking. Even a well-trained and experienced engineer will grudgingly admit that lawyers are supremely proficient at such things. Fortunately, from the standpoint of actual practice, we hadn't yet surrendered to such lunacy by the spring of 1956. The idea then was to build roads, not to discuss them endlessly or to write reams of memoranda to each other about subjects of questionable relevance and then convene meetings.

The goal of the first two phases of the Denali jobs was to bring the road up to current standards from the Richardson

Highway to the MacLaren River. The road had originally been built by agency forces, and they recognized no constraints with regard to quality control or geometric standards.

In most cases, the field information extended only to the actual limits of construction, forcing the necessity of conducting more field surveys. We did what we could with what we had, and what we had was enough data to bring the road design up to BPR standards in several locations.

I was gone from the Denali during the next few years, but I knew that much of the time during the next four summers (1957-1960) was taken up gathering field data for both Denali projects. I was told that the project suffered numerous interruptions during this period, including the confusion accompanying statehood (1959), the change from ARC to BPR, and the onset of the 'Age of Acronyms'. All this brought on a concurrent scrambling for position by the politicians as well as all the 'Managers'. They were terrified of being rendered redundant by 'agency consolidations' – a term that strikes fear into the hearts of all bureaucrats. Much productive work was interrupted and delayed during this political upheaval, so it was probably good that so much advance time had been allowed for design and preparation of plans and specifications.

In January of 1957 our second child, Theresa Claire, came to us. I was just as flabbergasted as I had been when Laura was born. Regardless of all the sonograms[10], rational explanations of the mechanics of human reproduction, and my understanding of the 'birds and the bees' and all that, I was (and I remain) unable to bridge the intellectual gap between this and the sudden appearance of tiny little people. Theresa has since proven to be one of the most steadfast, honest and caring people I have ever known. As with all my children, I have a special love reserved just for her.

---

[10] We didn't have access to such advanced technology at the time.

Since we didn't intend to seek artificial intervention in order to limit our family size, and since we both knew that the profession I had embarked on required more education than my truncated high school effort, we both decided that I (we) should go to college.

Earlier that year, we had heard of a program initiated by Woodrow ('Woody') Johansen, the Fairbanks district engineer, that provided an opportunity for students to enroll at the University of Alaska (Fairbanks) and work nights at the Fairbanks District (ARC) Design Office. It sounded good so we decided to try nourishing my superior intelligence with some knowledge! It turned out to be very difficult, and it required a real mutual effort on the part of both of us. In the end, she deserved the degree and credit for all the work every bit as much as I did. However, in the fall of 1957, we were young, confident, in love, and on our way!

PART III
CHANGES

Chapter 1: A New 'Country'

I flew to Fairbanks with Pan American Airlines on one of the old Boeing Stratocruisers. I think there was a lower deck with three rows of passenger seats, and an upper lounge deck with a fully stocked bar, waiters and slightly larger windows for better viewing. For some reason that particular airplane model didn't stay in service very long, at least not in Alaska. The jet age was coming fast, so maybe Boeing saw the writing on the wall and turned their attention in that direction. Anyway, I heard there were problems with that airplane. There were rumors that parts such as engines kept falling off while they were in the air – no further comment.

They put Tangle in one of those airline cages with minimal food and water, and loaded him on the plane like a piece of baggage. I think he strongly resented that kind of treatment; I'm sure it was unpleasant and very unlike anything he'd ever before experienced. I guess he somehow escaped from his cage and began making a big fuss in the cargo compartment, finally poking his nose up through a ventilation hole in the cockpit floor and howling for attention. What happened next was purely Alaskan and could *never* be repeated these days.

The route from Juneau to Fairbanks at that time included a stop in Whitehorse slightly less than one hour out. There was barely time to reach 'cruising' altitude before beginning the descent. About fifteen minutes after we left Juneau, I got called on the cabin speaker and asked to please report to the cockpit, so I went up there. I don't know how the cockpit crew knew that Tangle and I were related; perhaps he had a tag around his neck. Anyway, after I got up to the cockpit the co-pilot opened a door in the floor and let Tangle climb up and join me in a fourth seat, which was unoccupied. People weren't as uptight about hijackings and such things then as they justifiably are now.

Tangle was delighted; he and I stayed there through the Whitehorse stop and all the rest of the way to Fairbanks without further incident. I think that the cockpit crew enjoyed it as much as I did, and I know Tangle loved being up there. He probably felt a lot more in control in the cockpit with us rather than locked in a cage down in the cold, dark cargo compartment – I know that I would have. He was probably scared and lonely down there too.

I only stayed in Fairbanks for two or three weeks, working on several survey projects within one or two driving hours of town as an instrument man and living in a BOQ (Bachelor Officers' Quarters); a Quonset hut that had reportedly been bought as surplus from the army. The room was comfortable but small and certainly not luxurious.

It was around the middle of May that I left Fairbanks for Dot Lake on the Alaska Highway, twenty miles or so north of Tok Junction. Dot Lake is actually a little village, and as a result of previous work in the area the agency already had some trailers there. With a little persuasion and a few phone calls I was able to rent a thirty-eight-foot trailer about 500 feet south of the Dot Lake Lodge.

The project that I had been assigned to was essentially a paving overlay job, although there was some reconstruction and widening of shoulders on the inside of most of the curves. The reconstruction methods for the shoulder widening were in accordance with some specification that was apparently written by an office-bound and probably overeducated idiot with no construction experience at all – certainly no Alaskan experience. The drawings and specifications called for widening merely by end-dumping some gravel over the edge of the road without benching the existing slope or incorporating any other precautions to keep the new fill from sliding against the old slope. We seemed to be getting more and more people like this showing up in Alaska for reasons that weren't yet apparent.

This project was unusual in that the staff had to be willing and able to perform a variety of tasks; in most cases a certain amount of working knowledge in several different construction engineering techniques was necessary. I don't recall hearing about any labor unions whining over this interdisciplinary practice or any staff complaints either. Times have changed.

After I was sure we had been guaranteed the use of the trailer at Dot Lake, and I had contacted Irene, I drove to Fairbanks to pick her up at the airport. Irene was traveling with the two children by herself, and it was quite a load. Laura, our oldest, was about one and a half, but our second daughter Terry (Theresa) was still a babe in arms, unable to walk very well and requiring a lot of attention.

After Irene's flight landed and taxied up to its parking place, the ground crew wheeled the steps into place, and she walked down onto the pavement as about the third passenger out of the plane.

After all the appropriate affectionate greetings, I took the baby from her arms, and I was appalled at Irene's appearance. She was down to just a little over ninety pounds, and her face and eyes looked as though she hadn't slept or eaten for a week. Ninety pounds! My God! One of my legs from thigh to heel weighs more than that. It was still fairly early in the day, so we had something to eat and then left for Dot Lake.

We met a lot of interesting people while we lived at Dot Lake Village. They were all real Alaskans of the type that has by now almost disappeared. One of them was an old Athabaskan guy who made and sold a lot of really exquisite and intricate carvings. I can't remember his name, but he was a remarkable man.

Whenever Irene and/or I talked to him informally or during the several times he came to visit us, he spoke flawless English and had a surprisingly accurate grasp of history, mathematics and literature, as well as what was currently going on in the world. He was obviously well read, and occasionally when he came to visit he was dressed in slacks, sports shirt or jacket and regular shoes. However, the Dot Lake gift shop was one of his market outlets, and if there were enough tourists present when he went into the lobby, he would abandon this urbane image and assume the role of poor, uneducated Indian in appropriate 'costume', i.e. moccasins, old jeans, old fringed leather shirt and so on. When some of the potential customers discovered that he was the artist who created many of the carvings, they were eager to ask him questions, and he delighted in telling them some of the most bizarre stories I've ever heard. Maybe some (or even most) of them were actual legends and such, but they sure sounded weird to me. To impress some of these tourists he would come into the lodge asking for a particular candy bar or coke or whatever, and when told what the price was he would lay a whole pocket full of change and bills on the counter, implying that he didn't understand the money and telling them to take what they needed. This from a man who I was told served markets all over the country (not just Alaska) and probably even in a few foreign countries.

I know that he had a number of accountants and marketers who reported to him periodically about sales, expenses, profit, taxes etc., and I think he mostly controlled them by telephone since there was no Internet or e-mail then. Does this sound likely coming from a poor old, uneducated Indian guy? I don't think so, although maintaining the image was probably a good PR strategy, and I admired him for it. He was pretty old even then, so I doubt if he's still alive, although I hope so – if not, God rest his soul.

After about two or three months at Dot Lake, we moved our residence about ten miles south to Cathedral Bluffs and rented a new apartment in a recently built three-unit building owned by a man named Marvin Warbelow. We became pretty good friends with him, his wife Lou, and his boys, who were quite young at the time, and we had dinner with the family numerous times. I have to use his first and last name here because I refer to his legacy in a later paragraph and because he founded a sizable flying service out of Tok, and the company still bears his name.

Marvin was a man completely absorbed by flying small bush planes all over Alaska. I think he chartered out to individuals or companies who wanted to get to some of the more remote villages that had no scheduled air service.

Bush plane parked on a sandbar

When his airplane wasn't around, it meant he was out flying, and when it was, it was always parked in his front yard. He had no nearby private airstrip, so the obvious implication was that he was landing on the highway whenever the traffic was light enough. He freely admitted that he was doing so, even though it was actually illegal even then. However, he never got caught doing it, and even if he had, I think the territorial police would have looked the other way unless he caused an accident, which as far I know he never did. Since statehood of course, Alaska has turned into just another state, and I doubt if he could get away with it now.

In those days Marvin's kind of aviation services were essential to Alaska's isolated rural residents and many of the tiny settlements. Accordingly, most of the involved agencies did what they could to encourage them by limiting non-safety-related restrictions. Such services are still vital to much of Alaska's trackless interior.

Marvin, like most of the long-time residents in that part of Alaska, was an interesting guy. He was very cost conscious, some might say cheap, although he never demanded anything regarding cost or price unless it was absolutely justified, or unless I asked. For example, if I needed a bolt, a screw, or whatever to repair something I was working on, I could always count on Marvin to have one somewhere in his shop/garage and to give it to me without mentioning anything about a price. However, if I said something like, "How much do I owe you?" Marvin would, without fail, reply, "Well it ought to be worth a dollar," or fifty cents, or whatever. He was definitely not greedy, but he *was* frugal, and I think it paid off for him in the long run. I believe Marvin is dead now (God rest him), but Warbelow Air Service, operating out of Tok, is one of the largest 'fixed-base' operators in interior Alaska. His wife, Lou, still lives in Tok or did during 2007, and although we try to contact her every time we go through there, we have so far been unsuccessful. His boys apparently run the air service now, and I feel this is a proud and fitting legacy for Marvin.

The interior of Alaska up and down the Alaska Highway, the Richardson Highway, the Glenn Highway and now probably the Parks Highway, formerly served by the Alaska Railroad, was an unusual if not unique part of the territory. The people who lived along these highways seemed to look upon them as neighborhoods. The neighbors got together and formed such groups as neighborhood improvement committees, neighborhood crime watches, and all such activities as can be found anywhere else in the country. The residents are essentially the same kind of people as those in neighborhoods everywhere. The only real difference is that the people who live there have decided that they don't want to be all jammed up within a hundred feet or so of each other. They preferred to be thirty, fifty, or even a hundred miles apart despite the inconvenience in getting together. They were no less friendly or any more anti-social than anyone anywhere else.

Neighborhood street – interior Alaska

We were privileged to experience some of this highway camaraderie, and we found it delightful. I suppose the increased traffic, regulations, imported distrust, and so on have acted to dampen the character of this pleasant aspect of living in the Alaskan interior. I guess that's progress, isn't it?

The summer of 1957 gradually changed to fall, and by September 15, after a major party thrown by the contractor at the Tok Lodge, it was time to close down and head back to town. The contractor also left a bottle of whiskey in each of the inspectors' pickups, an act that might even result in some jail time today. At that time, we all knew the whiskey was just a gesture of goodwill, given with no thought of return favors or anything like that. It may be my imagination, but I seem to recall that relations between the agencies and the contractors were less adversarial in those days than they are now. Distrust is an insidious thing and it's getting worse.

For Irene and I, heading back to town meant moving up to

Fairbanks so we could enroll at the University of Alaska. Sadly, we would not be going home to Juneau for many years, not even to visit. In fact, we were destined to never go back there *together* again.

Of course, we had to make arrangements for housing and other such domestic necessities before moving, but it was surprising how easy it was to line up a thirty-eight-foot trailer all hooked up and winterized in the Graehl section of NE Fairbanks, where the ARC trailer park was located. Even though we had been on the telephone for two or three weeks lining it up, there were no real problems.

The university is actually located in a small community called College, which is about ten or twelve miles west of Fairbanks on what was then called College Road. It has since become the last few miles at the Fairbanks end of the Parks Highway, running between Palmer and Fairbanks.

There were a number of small to medium-sized trailer courts surrounding the college campus, mostly populated by married college students because the rents were relatively low and the campus was easily accessible. In those days, sanitary regulations or restrictions in small communities like College, and in most rural areas, were pretty minimal, although that by no means implies that people were living in any kind of unsanitary squalor.

It happened that I had a friend named Tyrone who lived in a trailer near the edge of his trailer court immediately adjacent to an apartment complex, maybe four or five units, on a separate piece of property. There was no central sewerage in College then and that may still be the case. Individual developments and residences were responsible for the installation of septic systems that theoretically were inspected and approved by the 'Alaska Department of Something About Sewage Disposal'. In fact, although the process today is about a thousand percent more effective, at that time I think there were many 'bootleg' systems that were built without the approval or even the knowledge of the territory/state. I don't want to imply that Tyrone's water supply was polluted, but I was told when the apartments next door decided to pump out their sewage disposal system, his well went dry. That's probably a true story – only the names have been changed to protect the innocent.

Chapter 2: The Dragon Rises

It was a day or two past mid-September, 1957 when I reported for my first shift on the night crew. This was the second year that the crew had been in existence, and there were three men who had been there since it started in the fall of 1956. The man of really significant intelligence on the crew was named George, and he was subsequently to become a close and respected friend of mine. The other two members were Gordon and Lee. They were, as Lieutenant Clark said of Charbonneau (Sacagawea's 'husband'), men of "little substance", although they were very nice guys and typical of long-time government civil servants.

George, of course, was the de facto boss by virtue of the fact that he was both senior and by far the most knowledgeable and dynamic member of the crew. He remained the boss until he left about four or five years later. I think that he was one of about three or four men that I ever met who were truly natural leaders. Besides, he was smarter than me and that's something I hate to say about anyone.

The first project assigned to us as a crew was called Badger Loop Road; or alternatively, the 'Survey from Hell'.

The south end of Badger Loop departs the Richardson Highway about fifteen miles south of Fairbanks, heads north and east then north and west for a total of maybe twelve miles before re-entering the Richardson approximately eight miles south of

Fairbanks. The northern part of the road follows along the southwest bank of a slough called Badger Slough that over the years had been eating away its south bank because it wanted to move southwest, probably due largely to the Coriolis effect, a consequence of the earth's rotation. The people who lived along the road had noted all this for years and had kept dumping old busted up concrete slabs, refrigerators, car bodies and such all along the banks of the slough in an attempt to keep the water from taking out the road at flood stage.

At some point about a year or two before we moved to Fairbanks, some overzealous local bureaucrat began haranguing on the residents along the road, telling them that all these 'amateur attempts' (his term) at bank stabilization, albeit effective, which he either didn't understand or wouldn't admit, were causing a nuisance in the form of an unsightly condition. As I understood it he had moved to Fairbanks two or three years previous to these incidents and to most Fairbanksans of that time, that was about the same as having just stepped off the plane. I guess he was from someplace in the states and no one had even asked him to go look at the condition. It was easy to tell that he was new to the country because anyone who has lived around Fairbanks for a number of years knows (or knew then) that the surest way to get a Fairbanksan to refuse to do *anything* is to *order* him or her to do it. Reportedly, this guy took it upon himself to strut around giving orders about various matters and just generally acting like an officious, arrogant horse's ass. He didn't live anywhere near Badger Loop and knew nothing about the conditions there, or about bank stabilization in general. Nonetheless, he recognized an opportunity to exercise some invented authority that his ego needed and maybe position himself for a lucrative position in the future political regime. I suspect he was one of those so-called 'visionaries' who saw the coming of statehood and wanted desperately to place himself in a perceived position of authority so that he could jump in quickly when the time was right.

Unfortunately, he wasn't a solitary dragon. His clones began popping up everywhere as statehood approached. It's uncanny how administrative dragons who have no real knowledge of anything of substance are able to sniff out these veiled opportunities even before they become a reality. Maybe it's because, having little else to do besides making up new, useless and irrelevant regulations, they have plenty of time to get together and hatch plots aimed at expanding and complicating the bureaucracy and their own role in it.

In those days we didn't have all the electronic gadgets that remove much of the necessity for a surveyor or designer to really have a 'feel' for the ground over which a project is to be constructed. The procedures that we used then required that we choose, in the field, the data points and terrain details that would best provide a data set specifically suited for the design of the construction contemplated. Of course, this meant that the project survey crew party chief had to be knowledgeable about the project and its particular data requirements; just being a good surveyor in general, no matter how technically competent, was not enough.

Today, the 'surveyors', with their 'data collector' can simply blanket the entire area with an infinite number of data points, some of which are bound to be irrelevant, and a few even misleading, for the purpose of showing a 'picture' of the terrain. This collector machine then delivers a digital product which is subsequently surrendered to a 'fixed-base' computer. Presumably, the office computer then sorts out all the collected data and prepares a mathematically precise but 'cold' map of the terrain. A human being is often hardly required at all in the process up to that point except to transfer stuff from one machine to another, and if some electronic wizard has hooked everything together properly, maybe not even then.

Our old-fashioned methods involved numerous iterative procedures offering many self-checking opportunities. Inconsistencies, errors, and irrelevancies would thus be largely caught and eliminated before the data were reduced and plotted. It was much slower than today's methods, which is a point favoring the electronic systems. However, who wants a method that's fast at the expense of producing a result of questionable suitability (not accuracy but suitability) as a result of attempting to incorporate misleading extraneous data? If a racehorse ran around a racetrack in record time but was going in the wrong direction, the speed, although remarkable, would be irrelevant, wouldn't it? I use the word 'irrelevant' frequently because irrelevancies introduced into a chain of data analyses (or administrative procedures) will render all the subsequent results useless. Such useless results will, more often than not, go undetected until the damage has been done, and because of the nature of the contamination, its source will be almost impossible to trace.

The Badger Loop Road design project broke down almost from the very beginning. The project 'P' (preliminary) line started at the north intersection with the Richardson Highway, ran south along the highway to the south intersection, then around the loop and back to the starting point. The problem was that after calculating all the bearings and distances, the line didn't come back (mathematically) to the starting point; it missed by about a hundred feet in a southwest direction.

Before the night crew came into existence, the daytime designers tried to find the problem for about two years and then just got disgusted, gave up and set it back on the shelf. I guess they thought that if left alone to 'simmer', the calculations might straighten themselves out. They didn't, obviously, and after listening to George's complaints during the 1956/57 season about getting a complete project for the night crew, the big shots downstairs assigned us Badger Loop Road – thank you very much!

We started out by re-turning angles and re-measuring distances as long as the weather stayed mild enough to work outdoors. In Fairbanks, 'mild enough' is any temperature above fifteen degrees below zero Fahrenheit…just kidding, but it isn't far off!. Since we had to miss a few days when it got *really* cold, or in the case of class scheduling conflicts, it took us a little over a month and a half to do the work, and we finished up about the end of October.

I think that much of the error we set out to correct was actually in the original calculations, although one would think that the apparently exhaustive repetition would eventually catch such errors. We fixed it up and were ready to begin the design work when the day crew took our figures and began the final line location and design work themselves. This was an outcome that George was not prepared for, and he got very upset about it. He complained bitterly to 'Woody', the Fairbanks district engineer, and about two weeks later we got the job back. This is an important incident because since the day crew supervisor was an old-timer, it shows that we did have a few homegrown jerks even before statehood.

Alaska was always a little laid back when it came to rushing into projects. I can't remember ever feeling a sense of urgency in those days, and Badger Loop was no exception.

The whole question was mooted by mid-January because the job was then set aside in favor of some preliminary work on the Denali Highway west from Paxson. I had originally worked on the Denali as a kid in about 1953, and, of course, also in support of agency construction in 1955 and 1956. Much to George's disgust and apparently in spite of his lamentations to Woody, the night crew was again temporarily relegated to piecework sent to us from the day crew projects, and at the discretion of their supervisory staff.

The other two guys on the night crew that year, Lee and Gordon, were both, as mentioned previously, typical long-time civil servants. It's hard to describe people like that or how they seem to think. You have to conclude that such folks have worked at these government jobs for so long that their minds can only grasp concepts that are strictly codified and require little more than the ability to read and to translate government language/acronyms.

Lee didn't last more than a semester or two in college and on the night crew, and for some reason I can't remember very many details about him, perhaps because there simply isn't much to remember. I *can* remember that he and George both bought one of the early edition manufactured homes during the first or second semester that I was there. George seemed able to handle the stress of putting the house together, working nights and carrying a full scholastic load at the same time, but it was apparently just too much for Lee, and he soon dropped out of school.

Gordon, on the other hand, lasted for at least three or four semesters, and I had a little bit of time to watch him and his extraordinary approach to education. He seemed to believe that, regardless of the subject he was studying, if he bought enough books about it, he would somehow automatically come to know all that he needed to know. He must have felt it unnecessary to actually *read* most of the books because no one taking more than two or three subjects could possibly read the entire collection that Gordon accumulated. He always made it a point to show me his new books whenever he bought one and there were a *lot* of them. Maybe he was right, but I couldn't afford all those books anyway. It was hard enough for me to come up with the money just to buy the specified texts for a given curriculum of courses, particularly in the cases of technical or professional subjects.

During one of our brief breaks on the night crew I caught a glimpse of Gordon's method for 'learning' mathematics. We were doing a little break time homework when Gordon called my attention to one of the math problems on his assignment. He pointed out proudly that he had found an *exact* duplicate in one of his numerous extra mathematics books. I suddenly realized that he actually thought he could memorize every conceivable math problem and then pull it out of his memory bank whenever confronted with that problem or its twin. He seemed to feel that he had overcome a major intellectual hurdle, but surely it must have dawned on him at some point that similar problems sometimes could use different symbols (a, b, c, x, y, z, etc.) for variables and still be governed by the same principles of logic. I once asked him politely if he might have noticed any thread of continuity in the *processes* of how these problems were solved during his extensive searches from text to text. He seemed to be studying math *problems* rather than math *principles* and *procedures*. I can remember that he looked at me with the most quizzical expression I ever saw him display and said nothing. I don't think he had a clue what I was talking about.

Actually, Gordon *did* have a phenomenal memory; it seemed, however, that in spite of all his beguiling character traits, he just didn't have the mental wherewithal to combine all those memories into some sort of whole cloth so to speak.

I don't want to speak ill of Gordon, and if it seems like I am, please don't think of it that way. People like him and Lee make up the backbone and framework of our government's civil service structure. Without them, and folks just like them, the whole system would collapse. Unfortunately, the wannabe bureaucrats who flocked north immediately after statehood possessed the same sort of mindset as Gordon and Lee. Many of them apparently meant to perpetuate their methods through new little administrative empires of their own making. Folks like that don't think that they have any psychological problems, and they probably don't. In any case, I'm certainly not a psychologist.

In April of 1958, I was detailed as instrument man/party chief on a survey crew working toward Nenana, a railroad and riverboat marshalling town about fifty-two miles west of Fairbanks. At that time of year at that latitude daylight lasts well into the evening hours, making it possible for me and a couple of other night crew members to work very late.

When I went to work on this springtime survey crew, there was a road from Fairbanks to the Tanana River at Nenana, but there was no highway bridge over the river. There *was* a private ferry running from the end of the road to Nenana, but like most Alaskans, the ol' boy who ran it only operated sporadically at best, and then only if he felt like it. God, how I miss those kinds of attitudes, they really embody the old Alaskan spirit of independence. The result of this transportation disconnect was that we couldn't stay in Nenana with any assurance of being able to get back and forth to work, so the ARC set up a survey camp about forty miles out of Fairbanks and put us up there.

It was a pretty fancy camp, and although constantly running back and forth to town to keep up with my scholastic efforts, I could appreciate the extraordinary comforts. There were tents with sideboards, regular electric light hookups, and the traditionally great camp cooking. Irene stayed at the Graehl thirty-eight-foot house trailer in Fairbanks with Laura and Terry. She was pregnant again with our third child, and her delivery date wasn't far off. I stayed in the camp for about two or three days every week and went back to Fairbanks to spend the other three with her, even though it was a long Friday commute.

There's a bridge at Nenana now. The ferry operator has disappeared and I've heard that many of the traveler-oriented businesses in Nenana have closed, probably because almost everyone passing through on the 'new' Parks Highway just wants to hurry up and get to Fairbanks or Anchorage.

Because there was no highway bridge at Nenana or even any reliable ferry service at the time of our survey, we tied off our part of the Fairbanks-Nenana survey at the river and most of the crew went to other jobs. In Irene's and my case, we moved south, across the river, and I went to work on the survey from Nenana south along the railroad corridor.

There were nominally four three-man crews assigned to the Nenana-Healy survey – a total of twelve crewmembers, two of which were young women. Additionally, there was the project 'engineer', a full-time office engineering technician, and me, the newly appointed chief of parties.

Irene left what was apparently a fairly fulfilling job at the Fairbanks office of the Alaska Public Health Service (PHS). I don't remember the name of the guy she worked for but he looked a little like Leslie Nielsen, the actor.

Irene's boss at PHS was obsessed with wall-hung plaques proclaiming his accomplishments. His office wall was covered with impressive-looking framed, signed and sealed documents testifying for completing everything from a three-day piano-playing course to some testifying to his attendance at, and completion of, various short courses and conferences about all manner of subjects. He was a nice enough guy, and I never heard Irene complain about his being hard to work for, but I doubt if he was truly competent at anything productive. Maybe he was a 'Manager', the only high-level position in our society that doesn't require the practitioner to know anything specific about anything in general. If he was, he must have been one of the few Alaskans of the day who openly admitted it. He would have been, that is, one of the few who had 'come out of the closet', so to speak.

Unfortunately, Irene was in some discomfort during the first two months or so on that job because she was already about six or seven months pregnant when we moved down to Nenana. About the second week in July, she started having labor pains or some such indication of the imminent arrival of the baby. She was reasonably well experienced with this sort of thing, so I figured she must know what was probably about to happen. We contacted a local bush pilot named Paul, who was well certified and recognized as the best bush pilot in the area. Luckily, he had enough time to take Irene into Fairbanks that very day – I think it must have been a Saturday or Sunday.

There is a deep, and relatively broad, canyon along the Tanana River between Nenana and Fairbanks, and there is often a sizable air pressure difference between one end and the other, frequently causing rather violent winds along that stretch of the river. The canyon was part of the normal bush plane route between Nenana and Fairbanks. Nonetheless, we had to get Irene to town by plane because there just wasn't time to drive there considering the ferry delay. Later she told me that the plane was tossed around like a cork going through the canyon, and I suppose she must have been as scared as hell – I know I would have been. However, either she wasn't frightened or she wouldn't admit it. Behind that facade of loving tenderness, there existed a very tough lady, and she proved that to me many times during our marriage.

Anyway, when they got to Fairbanks it turned out that she wasn't ready to deliver after all, and I seem to recall her telling me that her doctor said she was about a month away from bringing home baby number three. He was a bad estimator. On July 28, she started having serious labor pains again, and this time she knew it was the real thing. Paul was out flying around somewhere, and we didn't know of any other way to get to Fairbanks. I was in something of a panic, although Irene wasn't. She was always the epitome of the 'unflappable Molly Brown' in situations like this. I say again – a tough lady.

I drove her to the airport hoping to find a pilot hanging around who, for a price, would take her to Fairbanks. By the grace of God, and I really believe it was, we got there at the same time as a BLM (Bureau of Land Management) DC-4 that was refueling at Nenana while returning to Fairbanks after dropping off a bunch of firefighters up in the deep interior.

When we described our crisis, the plane crew welcomed Irene on board, provided her with some sort of relaxing refreshment and left for town with her being the only passenger. I guess there was even a stewardess on board, and Irene told me later that she had never received more solicitous and attentive service. That was an example of the true Alaskan way as it used to be.

This sort of thing simply wouldn't happen today because of all the codes, regulations, insurance and so on. It's almost certain that there's been some sort of dragon-ridden agency or department created for the purpose of regulating civilian use of government airplanes, regardless of the nature of the need. In general, the traditional Alaskan concern for others has been badly eroded by the influx of all the neo-Alaskans.

When they got to Fairbanks they rushed her to a cab and on to St. Joseph's Hospital, where Irene brought our third daughter, Denise Jay, into the world. I can't remember whether I got into Fairbanks before Irene left the hospital, or if I didn't see Denise until they got back to Nenana. In either case, I was just as nonplussed and incredulous as I had been at the arrival of Laura and Terry. I know that it's

Fairbanks: Chena River with St. Joseph's Hospital on the left. Birthplace of our third child, Denise.

all just biology, and I've read and I understand all the details about the physiological mechanics involved. Just the same, I can't seem to come to terms with the obvious fact of the juxtaposition of all these human biological conditions that must come together properly in order to interact and produce tiny human beings. It seems like, in the normal world, the chances of all these things happening at the right time and in the right place to cause such a thing would be almost nonexistent. I guess the same sorts of mysteries happen with most all critters, and I bet that the male of the species is just as bamboozled at what happens as I always was.

Irene brought Denise home to Nenana, and she joined our growing family as a full-fledged member.

We lived in the teachers' quarters until about the end of September when it was time for the teachers to come back and for us to leave and go sign up for our second year at the university. There were at least two other notable events that happened while we were stationed at Nenana. I'd like to relate them because, as the Alaska of my memory fades out of sight, such things are not likely to happen again.

The responsibility of a chief of parties on any job involving primarily surveying includes a requirement to maintain constant contact with all the separate crews and to shift crewmembers and assignments as necessary to most efficiently accomplish each of their tasks, while keeping in mind the primary overall project goal. If they fail to do so because of confusion in objectives or of inappropriate crew make-up, it's the fault of the chief of parties. Individual party chiefs are not to blame for inefficiencies or failures in communication arising out of any lack of survey party communication/coordination. Obviously, on a project the length of the Nenana-Healy job, discharging this responsibility requires a lot of time just traveling between crews over trails that double as access roads, however primitive. It's therefore always a good idea to seek out shortcuts to save time whenever possible. Pursuant to this idea of timesaving, I was always looking for possibilities, and on one occasion I spotted a large meadow, on the other side of which there was another point on our access road. Going around this meadow was almost two or three thousand feet longer than just cutting across. I was soon to find out why the road had gone around rather than across the meadow.

All the survey crews and I drove Dodge Power Wagons fitted with big airplane tires to turn them into swamp buggies. However, if one counts on that vehicle to go through everything, they will sooner or later get irretrievably bogged down in some bottomless swamp hole. Accordingly, whenever coming to a spot where passage might be at all questionable, it was always a good idea to stop the rig, get out, and walk ahead to make sure that there wasn't some deep hole or swamp waiting to suck you in. When those big swamp buggies get stuck they are *really* stuck. So, I stopped my truck, got out and began walking across the meadow to check out the ground in the direction I hoped to go.

As I walked out into the clear area, I noticed a bunch of big mounds made up of sticks, grass and other such detritus along the edge of the meadow. I don't remember thinking that there was anything special about this, or even if such things were unusual until I got about three quarters of the way across and a bunch of the mounds began first moving and suddenly sort of exploding. It turned out these were nesting mounds for those big sandhill crane hens, and they very obviously took my presence there to be extremely threatening to their eggs and/or young, if not to themselves.

These birds are the ones that used to fly over in the fall in big flocks making a sort of resonant gargling sound as they passed. I haven't seen any of them for years. Why did they make such a weird sound? I guess because their throats are set up for it, and because like all birds, most of whom are pretty stupid, they feel it necessary to make some sort of noise for no particular reason.

Apparently in reaction to their anxiety over my presence, what seemed like about a thousand of these big hens jumped out of their nest mounds and came after me. Fortunately, they didn't have enough sense to plan any sort of strategy like cutting me off or surrounding me, and I managed to get back to the truck with only minor scratches and a few bruises from running through the brush. Interestingly, most of their attack seemed to involve using those big bones at the top of their wings rather than their long beaks, which seem to be mostly for squawking, I suppose to impress the other crane ladies, their mates, or their babies. Those birds are big. Standing up with their necks fully extended, they seemed to be at least a foot or two taller than I am. That's just an estimate because I didn't stop to get any precise measurements.

I decided not to use that meadow as a shortcut, and I advised the party chiefs not to do so either; not only because of the threat of injury from the birds, which was probably less than I imagined, but because we could easily damage, if not destroy, some of the nesting mounds. At the very least, our close presence might well cause the birds to abandon the nests. We actually figured that out by ourselves without being harangued on by some extremist environmental group. In a previous chapter, I said that I had never been threatened by any species of Alaskan wildlife except bees, mosquitoes and such. I don't count these old hens because the incident was actually occasioned by an attack on my part against them.

I haven't been back to that part of the country for years, but if I had to guess I'd say that by now, private or government expansion has probably caused those old hens to pack up and leave. They are pretty stupid but not so stupid that that they don't recognize our human species as vicious and dangerous. We seem to enjoy killing other critters for no really good reason, and if we can't find enough of them, we start killing each other. As noted, I haven't heard one of those huge gargling flocks of sandhill cranes flying over for a very long time – not down here or up north either. It would be tragic if they were another casualty of our increasingly wasteful and destructive behavior. I wonder where they all went.

There was one other incident on the Nenana-Healy job that has since shaped much of my thinking about wildlife.

During almost the whole time of our survey, except for the few areas near groups of human habitation, we were shadowed by a pack of wolves. We never saw the whole pack or even parts of it, but after the snow showed up in late September we found their tracks almost every morning all over the dozer we used for clearing. There were always indications that they had investigated all our stuff and had even sat or lain down on the warm hood of the dozer or in the seat. In those days we usually left the survey instruments outside too, covered and mounted on tripods and looking I suppose to the wolf folks like some sort of critters standing there without moving. We could always find tracks going around and around the instruments, apparently made while cautiously investigating and then front paw prints on the instruments themselves at the top of the tripod; maybe that was when the investigator finally drummed up the courage to overcome his/her trepidation and have a closer look.

One morning I experienced the most memorable thing that ever happened to me concerning Alaskan wildlife. It was only a fleeting few seconds, but I've never forgotten it and I never will.

After Denise was born, I often picked up lunch for the day at the Tortella (not Tortilla) Lodge where most of the rest of the crews were furnished room and board. Irene was so busy with the new baby and getting so little sleep that I hesitated to ask her to pack my lunch. The lunches from the lodge weren't very good, but it saved Irene (or me) the trouble of preparing the next day's lunch every evening.

I had been traveling between crews, and I stopped alone to have something to eat. I took out the first sandwich, ate about three quarters of it and threw the rest away because it tasted pretty ugly. I then heard a soft rustling in the brush, and to my astonishment a male black wolf stuck his head out and grabbed the bit of sandwich. He must have been watching me, and he must have been *really* hungry to go after one of those sandwiches. I still had another one and a few other tidbits like cheese, cookies, etc., so I kept throwing pieces out for him, trying to entice him closer and closer, until finally I was dropping the enticements only about three or four feet in front of me, at least it seemed that close. At that point I took the rest of another sandwich and a piece of cookie and held them out, hoping to get him to take them from my hand. After several very cautious and hesitant approaches he did just that but then ducked back into the brush like a flash, and I never saw him again.

I threw down the rest of what I had and left, hoping he got it. I hope he survived, although I fear that he may have been an outcast from the pack with, I've been told by wolf people, less than a fifty-fifty chance of making it on his own. I want to think that he found some new friends with whom to make a home, and that he lived out the rest of a long and happy life. I've also been told that such things sometimes *do* happen to wolves that get kicked out of their pack; the idea of them being alone, deprived of their familiar surroundings and so very lonely makes me extremely sad.

I liked that old wolf, although our encounter was too brief for him and me to 'bond'. I must say he had a lot of guts if he was able to eat those Tortella Lodge sandwiches and keep them down.

Since that experience, I've always had a soft spot in my heart for wolves[11] and have met many of their domesticated brethren (and/or hybrids) on closer terms at the homes of friends who have raised them. Despite all the propaganda about inherent viciousness, etc., I've always found them to be deeply affectionate and fun loving.

The Nenana pack continued to follow us, as evidenced by the tracks around the stuff we left out at night and the footprints in the woods, but we still never saw them except for rare, fleeting, almost imaginary glimpses of a shadow or a shaking bush. Occasionally, we also thought we could hear muffled footfalls or the quiet swish of disturbed underbrush. I think there must have been other packs somewhere far off because we could often hear them howling back and forth at night. That far-off lonesome sound is still one of the most beautiful in the world and today, even in Alaska, one is very fortunate to hear it.

It was about the end of September when we left Nenana and moved back to Fairbanks. Irene and I found a basement apartment just southwest of downtown, so we moved in and settled down for another gloomy winter, made more so by the claustrophobic atmosphere of our new apartment.

When I registered for school that fall, I was accompanied by a graduate geologist friend of mine named Bob. I guess he was a good geologist, but neither his vocabulary nor his math skills were what he wished them to be. His intent this time was to take a few courses in both creative writing and mathematics.

When we got to the first sign-up table, the lady handling the books asked Bob, "Have you ever matriculated at the University of Alaska in the past?"

Bob looked at her for a moment or two and then replied, "Not to my knowledge."

She seemed a little nonplussed by that reply, but then she

[11] I love dogs anyway – and always have.

went on to the other questions. I've often thought about that incident and wondered what Bob thought 'matriculated' meant. Anyway, back to the night crew.

At the beginning of the 1959 spring semester in January, our constant unrelieved pressure to keep up both the scholastic effort and the wage earning was becoming prohibitively burdensome, so I went to work for Gray, Rogers and Osborne, a Fairbanks consulting firm. However, I didn't slam all my doors behind me. Woody said that trying the private sector was a good idea, and that I would be welcome when I wanted to come back – he was that sort of person.

The company consisted of three principal members: Bob Gray was the engineer, Les Rogers was a surveyor, and Osborne was an architect.

In the early spring, I had the opportunity to do some surveying for them and my memory tells me that the only project on which I did any significant amount of fieldwork was in establishing the airport boundaries in preparation for an extension of the runway at the Fairbanks International Airport. There was at least one humorous incident that happened while we were on the airport job, and we were lucky enough to get to watch it.

The inaugural flight of Pan American's new Boeing 707 into Fairbanks took place that spring, and the city officials saw that as a very significant event. Fairbanks was like that about almost any occurrence that was even slightly out of the ordinary. Sometimes the city would sponsor parades just to celebrate a third-hand rumor that the executives of some off-the-wall industry had just *mentioned* Fairbanks during a meeting about opening a new plant. That's a bit of an exaggeration, but not much. The city promoters were eternal optimists; they either didn't realize or were unable to admit that for a lot of people, Fairbanks is almost uninhabitable during much of the winter, although it must be added that there are long-established families who remain throughout the year and have done so for many generations, perhaps due to some sort of mental imbalance!

I'm only kidding, Fairbanks is actually a very friendly town and a pleasant place to live except during the relatively brief and intermittent wintertime periods when the temperature drops to thirty or forty degrees below zero, and the thick ice fog covers everything. I wonder if, in view of the unpleasant and sometimes destructive effect that the post-statehood northward migration inflicted, Fairbanks still has those parades that seem to celebrate the possibility of attracting outside industry. Maybe what's happened in recent years has opened some eyes to the negative aspects of attracting new industry and residents. I digress – here's the story.

The arrival and departure of the first new 707 was considered a very significant event and, in keeping with the customary local practice, a rather elaborate send-off was planned for the first departure of the big airplane. To make sure everything was handled with appropriate dignity, several airport officials dressed up in white coverall uniforms, and with their official badges of rank affixed, took their newly polished white sedans to the end of the runway. They positioned themselves so that they would be behind the 707 as it prepared for take off, and then they were to salute or something as it left.

I don't know if the pilot knew they were there or not. If he did, he gave no sign of it as he pointed his airplane down the runway in the direction away from the little delegation and cranked up his jet engines. In those days, the aviation industry was apparently not yet required to use smokeless, non-polluting aviation jet fuel, and as he revved up and departed, the engines emitted huge clouds of coal-black smoke and soot that were pushed back by the jet blast and settled right over the 'official' departure delegation.

We were at the same end of the runway where these guys were but further away and shielded by some trees. As they turned to go back to wherever they came from, which I hope was the shop and not the terminal, we could clearly see that their uniforms and their shiny white cars were now 'crow' black. Our whole crew really yucked it up over that, but I suppose the guys who got all blackened didn't find it so amusing. I guess what made it seem so funny was how the solemnity that started the ceremony turned so suddenly to slapstick humor. I still wonder how they were able to maintain their dignity when they passed in front of the unavoidable public areas on the way back to their shop.

I stayed with Gray, Rogers and Osborne all the rest of the following summer season until fall registration time at the university came around.

Sometime during the early spring of 1959, Alaska became the 49th State of the American Union. By now, virtually all of us knew it was coming, but this was sort of the 'Official Notice of the Beginning of the End' (ONBE perhaps?) for the real Alaskan lifestyle. Sadly, it must also have been the beginning of the end for most of the unique personalities that characterized the Alaska I had come to love. It seems like they have just sort of retreated into the fog of memory like those wisps of morning mist in the dark forests of Southeast Alaska that slowly break up into raggedy fragments and disappear into the trees as the sun comes up. In this case the disappearance seems to have been largely caused by the assault of conformity and pseudo-sophistication brought by the dragons who quietly (at first) snuck in behind statehood.

The ARC was soon to no longer be the road-building agency, with the responsibility temporarily accrued to the Bureau of Roads (BPR) during the interim prior to the formation of Alaska's own road-building agency. Now some of the subtle signs that we had mildly noticed in the recent past but had failed to recognize as significant or permanent began to form a more coherent picture of what was happening to us.

The aim and purpose of the gradually increasing managerial interference in technical matters began to reveal the tactics that would ultimately destroy our emphasis on *production* and force our focus onto *process,* i.e. the proliferating codification of irrelevant and time-wasting regulations, the increased frequency of meaningless meetings, the incredible volume of pointless memoranda, and the creation of new and counterproductive managerial and bureaucratic positions. All these things began to coalesce into a massive body of smothering changes that couldn't possibly accomplish anything except to increase the prominence and prestige of the administrators, slow normal project progress to a crawl and 'justify' a bunch of new and useless administrative jobs. Now we began to recognize it; the dragon was among us and attempting to reduce our productivity and creative inventiveness to the bureaucratic governmental mediocrity that characterizes most of the lower 48 agencies. We were suddenly required to endure a workplace where the local bureaucrats continually strived to complicate their supplications to the great God 'FEDERAL AID'. The more complicated they could make it, the more secure their own positions because most of the time the arcane wording used comes out as just pure gibberish to any normal person. From this point forward, it became less and less important what or *how much* we accomplished, and more and more important *how* we went about it; it was the early but no less brazen arrival of the dragon-sponsored policy of *process* over *product.*

Regardless of whatever agency the ARC was to become, Woody was still the district engineer, and he saw that the night crew continued to exist. Not only that, but he hired me again so that I could go back on the crew and continue my education.

After leaving Gray, Rogers and Osborne, I registered for the 1959 fall semester at the university and re-joined the (then) BPR night crew where George was still working. The departure from Gray, Rogers and Osborne was quite friendly. In fact, I seem to recall that Bob Gray, who doubled as a math instructor at the university, said he was glad to see me going back to school. Maybe he was also glad to get rid of me but just too polite to actually say so.

The night crew had accomplished quite a bit on the designs of both the Steese Highway from the Chena Hot Springs intersection to the Elliot Highway intersection, and on both of the Denali Highway projects from Paxson to the Tangle Lakes, and from the Tangle Lakes to the MacLaren River (all without *me*, imagine that!). There was, however, still a considerable amount of work that could be done on both jobs before the need for additional field data would force delays.

We began with the Steese Highway job because that was the one we had the most data for, and also because it was scheduled for construction earlier than the first Denali job.

Most of the Steese Highway design work was finished around the end of February or the first week in March, except preparing the final ink on linen contract drawings. Incidentally, nobody uses 'ink on linen' anymore, largely because nobody knows how. Like most things these days, it's hard to tell which came first, the 'not knowing how' or the abandonment of the procedure. We also had a little fieldwork to finish up before we could put together the final drawings.

Fairbanks usually has enough 'reasonable' (a relative term) weather off and on during late March and April to allow a limited amount of outdoor work. The longer daylight hours start coming back by that time, so we went out on the Steese whenever possible to make a few field ties to control monuments and property corners in the vicinity of Mark Acres.

This was where I first met Joe Vogler, a real, vigorously self-proclaimed Alaskan, albeit a bit extreme. Joe belonged to some wacky political group called the Alaska Liberation Party, or something similar. He was strongly and sometimes almost violently opposed to Alaskan statehood and a lot of other things, many of which had already become law or had already happened. For a while, he was also a backer or a member of some politically obscure but quite vocal group advocating Alaska's secession from the American Union.

Joe was a very unusual person, some would say he was just plain nuts, but he was an Alaskan nut so we respected his right to his own opinions. I was told that he had left a lucrative law practice back east to move to Alaska. I have nothing but hearsay to verify such a rumor, although it might well have been true. He sounded like a lawyer in that he was always mouthing off about technical matters without knowing what he was talking about. Conversely, an argument could be made that the stories about his mysterious past were pure hogwash.

Before statehood, and for a while afterward, Alaskans loved to make up off-the-wall stories about anyone who acted a little weird, espoused some goofy political/philosophical viewpoint, or seemed reticent about discussing their past. We used to have plenty of fodder for stories like that, but, alas, our new and enlightened lifestyle has somehow caused such people to fade away. Folks used to say that Alaska attracted such budding lunatics because unless they physically hurt someone, we really didn't care or pay much attention if they ran up and down, waved their arms about, or carried radical signs. In fact, we sort of enjoyed those people. I wonder where they all went.

As an example, some such fringe group once scheduled a midwinter demonstration in Fairbanks while I was city engineer there. The night before the planned event, the temperature dropped to between fifty and sixty below zero, which is unusual even for Fairbanks, and it didn't get much warmer when the late winter sun briefly came up. The demonstrators showed up all right, but nobody came to see them so they took all their signs and attention-getting devices and ducked inside the downtown post office entryway on Cushman Street. They stayed there for over three hours, probably hoping that someone would at least ask about their cause. I don't think anyone showed the slightest interest in what they had to say, but nobody told them they should go away either. They didn't even make the newspaper.

During the brief times that I spent on the Steese construction project that year, I spoke with Vogler several times. None of our conversations made it any more evident to me exactly what he was trying to say. He was, for some abstract reasons I couldn't translate, very much opposed to our imminent construction project. He seemed to think that just about everyone working on the job was empowered to shut the whole thing down if he could convince us to do so. Of course, such an idea was nonsense, but when we told him that, he just ignored us. It was a good thing none of us wore those bright orange jackets in use today; it would have been very much like the imaginary effect of waving a red flag at a bull.[12]

There used to be a little coffee shop beside the highway at Mark Acres about ten or so miles north of Fairbanks. I don't think it's there anymore, but when it was, most of the guys on the survey and inspection crews often stopped by for some morning coffee and maybe a roll or something. Vogler frequented the place too and was well known by the owners who, judging by their comments and reactions, were always sorry to see him come and glad to see him go. Sometimes, if he was preoccupied when he came in, it was possible to avoid him, which I was able to do once or twice just by keeping my mouth

---

[12] Can a bull really tell that a flag is red? Does he really care what color it is? I'm not a bull person, but I'd like to know.

shut and sort of staying in the corner.

It was a real lesson in aberrant human behavior to just sit there and listen to him while watching what he did. He would come in, sit down at the counter and engage himself in a spirited and gesturing argument over some matter that sounded controversial. Pretty soon he would argue himself into a near fury and then stomp out of the shop muttering about some obscure cause that was apparently important to him at that moment.

Joe was always a subject of a lot of controversy, and finally his perception of himself as a fiercely independent frontiersman apparently got him involved in a gunfight with someone he didn't agree with. He lost the fight, and his opponent buried him on the Vogler property, finally confessing to the shooting and leading the authorities to Joe's grave. There's even a blurb about Joe on the Internet, although I think they got the date of his death wrong. Check it out![13] Joe was so opposed to Alaskan statehood he even requested that he not be buried under U.S. soil when he died. He was buried somewhere near Whitehorse, Y.T. I guess they must have dug him up from his property and shipped him over there.

Is there a moral to Joe's story? I doubt it, unless maybe it carries a warning not to go around arguing and getting into gunfights with other people. This is especially true if the other people are better with a gun than you are. Go home and shoot at beer cans instead. So, Joe Vogler is dead, but time marches on.

Despite the digressions, to finish up the work on the Steese, the Denali design remained our primary objective during the winter of 1959/60. It was actually a pleasure to take on the first section of the highway leading out of Paxson. This was a piece of road that held a lot of memories for me personally, and since I was still married to Irene, I felt almost like I was reliving a

[13] http://en.wikipedia.org/wiki/Joe_Vogler

cherished part of our lives – memories reincarnated.

Of course, it was no mystery why the alignment and dimensions of the Denali Highway did not meet the standards of the BPR, which was the funding agency for the outside states at the time. They could enforce their standards down there by making the federal funding contingent upon compliance. However, we were a territory when the first construction on the Denali was accomplished, and we got little or no federal money for our roads, so the loss of any minor BPR funding wouldn't be a big deal. In the event, apparently not impressed by the BPR standards, the ARC construction crews had built the road according to the way *they* thought it should be. It *was* true that many of the BPR requirements were not compatible with Alaskan conditions, and our construction crews knew this; their attitudes and practices reflected that knowledge: "Standards? What standards? We know how to build roads. Who is this trying to tell us what to do? Get out of the way and let us get this thing done." This was the guiding principle of the first crews that pushed the Denali Highway through, and it was hard to get them to realize that, although the pioneering work they had done was admirable, maybe even heroic, the time had come to recognize that if we didn't meet certain standards, we wouldn't get any money to help us reconstruct our existing roads or to build the new ones.

We were aware of these standards even before statehood. There were also those among us who knew the BPR was coming, and that if we wanted to qualify for any of the federal funding after statehood, it would be necessary to begin complying with those BPR standards *right away*. The big boss dragon was just over the hill, and he was on his way to straighten us out.

The first Denali Highway from Paxson to the MacLaren River was built by the foremen, operators and laborers working on the ARC payroll with the ideas that they had always believed in. Those folks assumed they were doing the right things in attempting to get their projects done and functioning as quickly as possible and, given the needs and circumstances of the time, *they were*. It shouldn't be forgotten that pushing the first road or the first survey through from Paxson to the MacLaren River was no small accomplishment. There were, and still are, a lot of Alaskan roads like that. They may not be northern transplants of interstate highways, but they *do* provide access to a lot of places that weren't accessible before they were built, and they might not even be there today if it hadn't been for those 'maverick' road builders.

George now told me that I would have to dig out what field data I could and set up some kind of design strategy so that the night crew could affect a quick start with the Denali design project when we came back the following fall.

My first move was to call up the Valdez office of the old Alaska Road Commission because at the time the Denali Highway was first started Valdez was the headquarters of the district or sub-district that covered the Denali country. My intention was to find some record of the work that we did in the early 1950's. I could hardly believe it when I was referred to the office 'Manager'. He must have been an early arrival from some of the flocks of 'Migrating Managers' who headed north in their gazillions after statehood provided so many slots for managing all that extra federally mandated administrative crap that never even existed prior to statehood. There would obviously also be positions for people who would set up meetings for obscure purposes and make up (and codify) a lot of inapplicable regulations that no real working person could, or yet does, see a need for.

The manager didn't even seem to know what I meant by 'survey records', although it took him a long time to say so. In fact, I got a strong impression that he didn't know where the Denali Highway was either.

Finally, I reached someone in the Valdez office who *did* understand what I wanted, and he rounded up and sent us all the Denali-related field notes they could find, along with a few old field books (survey notes) from 1952/53. I couldn't find my name in any of those old field books; that's how important *I* was in the early fifties. Fortunately, but not surprisingly, the notes were in good order and well kept in a manner that could be easily understood and retraced by any competent surveyor. This may not be true today since most of the thinking and note keeping is now done electronically.

On October 10, 1959 God sent Irene and me Kathleen Louise (Katy). She's still with us, but she's a lot bigger now and has babies of her own. Even her babies (my grandchildren) have pretty well grown up except for Halena (not H*e*lena), the teenager, who still lives at home. Katy was a sweet baby, and now she's a sweet lady. She was sort of accident prone as a little girl, and sometimes she would become hyperactive for reasons I never really understood, although I think Irene probably did. I can remember waking up very early one morning and finding her climbing all over the furniture in her room; up to the top of the bunk beds and the dresser, then down and up again repeatedly. I can only remember two incidents that were really frightening.

She once fell out of a tree belonging to a lawyer who lived about two blocks from us when we were living on McCullam Street. I think he was one of two brothers named Cole (last name) who went wrong at an early age – they were both lawyers. He was probably terrified that we'd sue him since that would no doubt have been the kind of action *he'd* have taken, even before looking to the welfare of the child. There didn't seem to be any ill effects from that fall, but there was one other accident that *truly* frightened both Irene and me.

I think Katy was four or five years old, and we were driving either from Fairbanks to Anchorage to visit my mother or to Kenai/Soldotna to visit some old friends. I don't really remember what our destination was, but it isn't important. We stopped at Paxson Lodge for something to eat, and while we were inside just before leaving, the kids went out in front of the lodge building to play. There was a three-foot-high retaining wall about twenty feet from the front of the building, running the full length across the front except for two ten-foot gaps where concrete walkways and steps from sidewalk level entered the lodge. There was a street-level concrete landing at the locations of the gaps in the wall.

Katy was walking along the foot-wide top of the wall, and she apparently didn't see one of the gaps. When she got there, she fell off the wall and landed on the lower level concrete, right on her head. When she hit, the sound was more like a muffled crunch than the real bang as one might expect from a hard skull. It was extremely scary.

We debated whether to return to Big Delta or Fairbanks to find a doctor, or to continue on to our destination and find a doctor when we got there. There wasn't a whole lot of difference in distance either way. Katy was crying pretty hard all this time but aside from some scratches and limited bleeding, she didn't seem to be seriously injured. We couldn't find any soft spots in her skull or anything like that, so we elected to continue our trip while closely monitoring her condition and behavior.

Amazingly, once she stopped crying she went right to sleep. She didn't seem to be in undue discomfort, and her breathing, etc. was normal. I think we did take her to a doctor at some point during or immediately after our drive and were told that she was actually suffering from nothing more serious than a bad and painful bump on the head. Maybe God does indeed keep a special watch over little ones like Katy.

It seems almost unbelievable that Katy will be fifty years old in just a little less than three years. I've always seen her as a sort of brunette Goldie Hawn (Hawn's comedy persona that is). It doesn't matter how old or sophisticated she gets; she'll always be my beloved little sweet, scatter-brained Katy. She was the first of our babies to be born in the new state of Alaska. Just recently, Eloise and I met her and Deirdre (her daughter – my granddaughter) in Olympia for a brief visit. It was an emotional, if not unnerving experience to hear this beautiful young twenty-five-year-old woman addressing my dear little Katy as 'Mom' and me as 'Grandpa'. Deirdre was married in June 2008 – God, how cruel time is. It takes away our babies and makes us old, ugly, fat, or sometimes goofy and/or crippled up.

I have a Fairbanks story that I must relate because it illustrates how Alaskans used to be. It's a story that just couldn't happen today. The time was just before Christmas, 1959, and I'll probably remember it as long as I live. It involved Stanley the Barber and a remarkably realistic toy model of a thirty-caliber machinegun and tripod that we had placed on the back-bar at Tommy's Elbow Room. We had hung a nicely lettered sign over the muzzle reading 'Peace on Earth'.

For some reason, Stanley took a real interest in that toy gun and often asked to hold it and point it around, making gun noises with his mouth, etc. Early on the night before Christmas Eve, we were sitting around at the Elbow Room (Stanley included) talking about not much of anything of consequence when suddenly Stanley walked over to the back-bar, picked up the toy gun and went out the front door onto Second Avenue. For a few minutes nobody noticed that he was gone, but when we became aware that he was, we noticed that the gun was gone too.

Stanley was an Eskimo guy originally from some very remote village – King Island sticks in my mind, but I can't remember for sure. Anyway, nobody lives on King Island anymore so I guess that if anyone asks Stanley where he's from, he just has to say, "No place." At some point he moved to Fairbanks, went to barber school and set up a little shop where he did quite well. Anyone who knew Stanley knew that he was one of the most gentle, considerate and caring people you would ever expect to meet, not to mention his outstanding skill as a barber. His sensitivity was demonstrated when his wife fell ill with some kind of cancer. He was devastated, and that Christmas (1957 or 1958) he bought her a coffin and a cemetery plot as gifts.

Given the proper circumstances Stanley was capable of very good humor; upon request he would deliberately take on the fierce facial expression and the mock mannerisms of the Genghis Khan warriors, who were in fact representative of his long-ago ancestors. If one didn't know him, and if he was armed with what appeared to be a real machinegun, a confrontation could be a genuinely alarming experience.

Stanley knew how he looked, and if it was to be done in good humor, he was more than willing to go along with almost any practical jokes as long as it was really funny, not just silly, and no one got hurt. I guess his adventure on that night was to be such a practical joke, launched on his own initiative with the help of more than a few drinks – about as much as we'd all had – and armed with a plastic machinegun.

We wandered up and down the three or four main east-west streets that make up downtown Fairbanks, each about five or six blocks long, looking for Stanley. We were about to give up, thinking that he may have frozen to death or met some other such grisly end when we heard a loud commotion in about the 600 block of Second Avenue, approximately two blocks west of the Elbow Room. By the time we got there, the Fairbanks police had turned off the 'popcorn machine' lights on the roof of the squad car and were talking to Stanley very cordially and laughing uproariously over his immediately previous antics and the stories he was telling them.

Unlike most of the big city cops we hear so much of today, the Fairbanks police, at that time, were local people with an in-depth understanding of the uncommon folks who lived there. They were laughing *with* Stanley, definitely not *at* him.

Stanley was, of course, enjoying all this immensely and all the more so because these particular officers happened to be personal friends of his, having helped with the handling of several unruly customers at his barber shop in the past.

Stanley, armed with his toy but realistic looking thirty-caliber machinegun, had (we were told) burst into several of the downtown 'high-end' cocktail lounges, pointed his 'weapon' around and cried out something that was later described as unintelligible. I wonder if it might have been something in Eskimo; knowing Stanley's flair for the dramatic after a few drinks, I wouldn't doubt it. Reportedly, he scared the hell out of more than a few people, but the police in the squad car that we encountered on Second Avenue didn't seem to be upset. In fact, they were getting a really good laugh out of the whole incident, and they asked us if we could look after Stanley. Of course we agreed to do so and we sort of took charge of him. He too thought the whole thing was incredibly funny, even offering the cops his services with his machinegun to help with any Christmastime troublemakers.

Today, Stanley would be locked up for disturbing the peace and surely fined some exorbitant amount. Even the Alaskan cops take themselves so seriously these days that the humor of the incident would be completely lost on them. A sign of the times? What a shame!

One of our group was a reporter for the *Fairbanks Daily News-Miner* who had only moved into town about six months prior to Stanley's Christmastime shenanigans. His name was Jim, and he wasn't yet fully familiar with our kind of behavior, although once he understood that we were harmless and interested only in 'intellectual' pursuits, he became a very good friend and a long-time Fairbanks resident.

After we took control of Stanley on Second Avenue, we decided that it might be good idea to take him someplace where he could wind down and have a few cups of coffee. Jim suggested that his own apartment might be a suitable place since it was reasonably close by, and we wouldn't be disturbing anyone except him and his wife, Bonnie. I think that he may also have felt that meeting Stanley would help to give Bonnie some sense of the Fairbanks ambiance, if there was such a thing. Jim had moved to Fairbanks from Washington D.C. where, as I was given to understand, his family was at least third-generation Navy, and I guess his wife came from the same sort of D.C. culture, although perhaps not military. In any case, this occasion with Stanley was to be the first time I met her, and it provided a clue to the sort of truly gracious, genuine and cultured person she really was.

When we got to Jim and Bonnie's apartment, Jim proposed that we let Stanley greet Bonnie at the door with his Genghis Kahn expression and plastic weapon so we could laugh at her reaction and put a satisfactory ending to our early Christmas celebration. We did exactly as he suggested, and when she opened the door and was confronted by Stanley at his intimidating best she simply said, "I think you must have the wrong apartment," whereupon I was immediately stricken by a crush on her that has lasted until this very day.[14]

This was only one story from memories of the many things

[14] I should explain that I am still usually stricken by crushes on women who impress me, even at my age. It has nothing to do with sex, only with admiration.

that we discussed or celebrated when partying at Tommy's Elbow Room. My behavior during that period was probably one of the many causes gradually building up and eventually leading to Irene and me getting a divorce. She didn't like the Elbow Room or its effect on my behavior, and now I think I can understand why.

Finally the daylight hours increased and the air temperature warmed up enough to allow occasional outside work. We often worked under conditions that today's crews would just look at through the window, call their union representative and refuse to go out into. We used what few breaks in the weather we got to pick up 'spot' field data or to make property ties on the Steese Highway project, scheduled for award sometime in the mid to late summer of 1960. In the meantime, we continued with what we could do on the design of Phase I (Paxson to the Tangle Lakes) of the Denali Highway.

During the early spring of 1960, two or three other agency employees and I had been doing a fair amount of private property surveys, as well as some boundary work and a couple of construction layout jobs. We were doing this private work while still on the agency payroll, which generated a lot of complaints from many (or maybe most) of the local surveying/engineering firms. There were increasing claims that we were working on agency time, using agency equipment, and other such nonsense – none of which was even partly true. Nonetheless, there was the *appearance* of impropriety and Woody (the district engineer) had no choice but to advise us in writing that in view of this appearance and the possible formal complaints alleging conflicts of interest, he must direct that we cease our 'moonlighting' (private) work while in the employ of the agency.

Accordingly, I and another employee left the agency for the summer, although it must have been with some kind of understanding that I could return in the fall because that's what happened, with no problem that I can remember.

It's doubtful that that such an arrangement would even be considered today. In those days, however, the refugee bureaucrats, now in the employ of the new state, had not yet completely wormed their codifying and complicating tentacles into the administrative guts of our workplace. Consequently, they could not yet strangle our efforts at production, nor had they yet written enough unnecessary regulations to completely control every facet of employee behavior. At that time, such actions as allowing us to work away from the agency just for the summer were apparently left to the discretion of the local supervisor; in our case the district engineer Woody Johansen.

I personally found the complaints on the part of the local firms about our extracurricular private work to be hypocritical in the extreme. Virtually all of the principal owners of these firms in Fairbanks had begun their private work with 'moonlighting' while working for some agency or other. Evidently, their rules of ethical conduct were pretty flexible and were to be applied only to others, not themselves. I can't remember if it was my friend Tom who left the agency with me at that time, but I do remember that we were on at least one fairly large private sector job together before the season ended. I'll describe that job later.

I wasn't yet registered as a Professional Engineer (P.E.) at the time. For this reason we worked under the aegis of Donald MacDonald III ('Mac'), a Fairbanks P.E. of long standing and impeccable professional reputation. Mac was the scion of a real pioneering Alaskan family with deep roots in northern transportation development. Donald MacDonald II had been highly influential in the location of most of the major transportation routes throughout south-central and interior Alaska, including several railroad proposals that subsequent events rendered unnecessary. As I recall from reading, he was also involved in a proposed railroad route from Alaska to 'the States'.

The railroad idea, of course, never became a reality but had technological development taken a few different directions, it probably would have. Rail was and still is the most economical *point-to-point* means of shipping bulky items or large quantities.

At first almost all our work was in land surveying; mostly city lots. However, it soon expanded into construction layout, which is more lucrative and early payment is more assured.

Urban property (lot) surveying in a relatively small town with a long mining history like Fairbanks often presents opportunities to meet some unique characters. Unique characters were not uncommon all over Alaska at that time anyway. When some activity requiring individual enterprise and hard physical outdoor work, as with private small claims gold mining, accelerates an economy, a lot of such characters often move in, planning and expecting to make their fortune. These folks were nothing like the opportunists and politicians who have polluted our state since statehood and the oil discoveries. They were hardworking, independent, stubborn and productive folks who came up north to work and produce, not to leech off the efforts and productivity of others.

As we now know, and as history tells us, very few significant gold-rush fortunes were made, but many of the 'unique characters' stayed anyway. I think just the inherent challenge of the country attracted and held them.

Steese Highway – Small mining claim north of Fairbanks. My son-in-law with my granddaughters.

In those days, Alaska was a country well suited to an independent lifestyle and generous to those willing to work with their hands to accomplish real goals. I wonder where most of them have gone;

it's a question that has haunted me since statehood. They can't just morph into similes of everyone else and simply vanish into the crowd, can they?

Before the stateside lifestyle began to permeate Alaskan life, there was a certain sense of individual freedom that appealed to people like the old miners. Sadly, that sense of freedom has, by now, largely been rendered almost completely impractical over much of rural Alaska and certainly in all the urban and suburban areas. There are a lot of reasons why this happened, and is still happening. The outside observer may attribute these conditions simply to statehood and the oil boom. However, most real Alaskans know that the general loss of the Alaskan lifestyle was much more subtle than just the direct and obvious result of two events that, although very significant, were not in themselves capable of acting as the sole engines of such profound change. It may be a little complicated but as the book progresses I will *try* to identify some of the causes for, and the early indications of, the most significant and in several instances the more subtle changes.

I think Mac is dead by now, God rest him, but he grew up in Fairbanks while much of the gold mining activity was still a significant factor driving the local economy. When we were doing property surveys all over town, it turned out that, in many cases, Mac had known the property owners for years. Whenever there was controversy involved, as there sometimes is over property line locations, he was usually able to defuse any volatile situations.

There was one case involving setting out the corners for two lots directly east of the city center, bordering on the old graveyard established during the gold rush and abandoned shortly after WWII. There were two property owners involved, fronting on adjacent parallel streets. Between them, the two lots extended north-south across the full width of the block. They thus had a common back lot line, the location of which was the source of a long-standing dispute because apparently they had lost the back lot corners. Both guys were real old-timers which, just in itself, almost ensured disagreement about something or other; they knew Mac well, and he knew them. Apparently, after all the years of arguing they both agreed to call in a surveyor to reset their lot corners and fix the location of the disputed back lot line. They called Mac because he too was an old-timer, and they trusted him.

At that time, most long-time Fairbanks residents were outwardly very friendly and accommodating, but in their heart-of-hearts they were not truly trusting of newcomers; defined to be anyone who had not lived there at least ten or fifteen years. Maybe they believed that most people from outside were just grifters coming north to take advantage of them. As it turned out, such a belief soon proved remarkably accurate in many cases.

Unlike Anchorage, Fairbanks is an old town with deep roots and more than a few well-established families of several generations' residence. One lady, who is reasonably well advanced in years, is even named 'Alaska' (first name). It's not apparent on the surface, but Fairbanks is also a clannish town, suspicious of outsiders and slow to accept new ideas. That's the way it used to be when I lived there, but I suppose that Fairbanks, tragically, has also felt the encroachment of the new and unfamiliar lifestyle from outside.

Anyway, Mac went with us for the first couple of visits to see the property owners of the two lots described above. He suggested to them that since they were the only two residents involved in the argument, they should just settle on a mutually agreeable location for the back lot line, tell us where they wanted it, and we would stake it that way, making sure that there was no encroachment either way between them and the property bordering them on the west or the graveyard on the east. We would then go to the courthouse, record the new dimensions (file a new drawing), and that could be the end of the matter.

They wouldn't hear of any such agreement, insisting that since they had both purchased their property from the original Fairbanks town-site layout, they wanted the dividing lot line to also be in accordance with that same document. It seemed to me that there was a certain logic to that point of view, and maybe Mac thought so too because that's what we set out to do.

After we finished the boundary survey work, dimension adjustments, etc. we set all six corners for our two clients, and, as should have been expected, the final location of the common lot line didn't satisfy either one of them. In fact, for two or three nights in a row, one or the other of the owners went out, pulled up our corners and moved them to where he thought they should be. This seemed like an affirmation of Mac's wisdom in the original suggestion that the two property owners decide between themselves where (north-south) they wanted the common lot line, let us know and have us stake it accordingly.

Mac came with us when we went back after the third or fourth corner-pulling occasion and told them that we weren't going to set any more corners unless they agreed to stop pulling them up every night and repeated his suggestion about deciding for themselves where they wanted the line. I don't remember what the final outcome was, but I hope they were satisfied, or at least equally disgruntled.

The final bill was horrendous; both because of the necessary initial research and the dimension adjustments/re-recording of the portion of the town-site plat enclosing the four-block area. Of course, there were also extra costs in replacing the corners every time the clients pulled them up. I think they complained to Mac about the high bill, and I suspect that he paid part of it for them just because they were old friends. In any case, it made no difference to me; we got our money and walked away grinning, so to speak. I probably used up too much space describing that job, but I think it was space well used because the job was so typical of the several that we did in the old part of town. I want to go into detail about just one (I promise) more of the many property surveys that we did that summer.

This one was on the west side of town in a newer section. The area had only been completely covered by residential development for fifteen or twenty years, and many of the old-timers around town considered most of the people who lived there to be carpetbaggers or worse – newcomers. Although, as a surveyor I was only there to establish the lot boundaries in a professional (representing Mac) and dispassionate manner, I have to admit that the final outcome here was very satisfying for me personally.

As usual, there were two property owners involved, one of whom had been settled on his lot for about thirteen years while the lot immediately north of his had been vacant most of that time. The fellow of longer residence was very pleasant; mild-mannered, polite and not at all critical of his new neighbor to the north despite all the mean-spirited, loud and sometimes obscene squawking about encroachments, his rights as a property owner, and so on and on. I believe the mild-mannered fellow worked as some kind of civil servant for the City of Fairbanks, and that the squawker was an Air Force or Army officer stationed at Fort Wainwright.

Apparently the new neighbor on the north (hereinafter referred to as 'the Officer') had gone out with a twelve-foot carpenter's tape, measured 100 or 150 feet south from the next intersection north, then twenty feet (or whatever) east to clear the street right-of-way, stuck a piece of wood in the ground and proclaimed the point that he arrived at to be the southwest corner of his property. I was told that he then pulled his little twelve-foot tape eastward, bending through the trees, for whatever the plat said was the east-west dimension of his south lot line and stuck in another piece of wood that he labeled his south*east* corner. Judging from the reported comments of his other neighbors, the Officer was, all in all, a very self-confident, overbearing and obnoxious jerk. I guess the easygoing neighbor to the south just watched all these antics without saying anything.

I'm unfortunately familiar with people like the Officer, and I'm absolutely certain that he noted the non-aggressive attitude of his neighbor to the south and took it for weakness. It's been my experience that people like the Officer see folks in only two classes: strong or weak. They consider themselves strong and thus empowered, if not obligated, to take advantage of those they see as weak. There is no doubt in my mind that the Officer immediately began bullying his easygoing neighbor to the south, saying that his 'ACTUAL MEASUREMENTS', which were ludicrous at best, proved that the easygoing fellow was encroaching on his (the Officer's) property. He then tied (through the woods, from tree to tree) a yellow cord between the two bogus so-called 'corners' that he had set, cleared off most of the trees, hauled in many loads of gravel, leveled the lot and moved in a doublewide trailer[15] just ten feet north of his meandering yellow cord. All the time that he was doing this he was constantly (I was told) badgering his polite neighbor to the south, telling him to move his stuff off of what he said was his (the Officer's) property because he was going to put up a fence. The sad part for the Officer was that he believed all this crap he was unloading on his easygoing neighbor. He finally said he was going to call in a surveyor for a legal determination of the location of the line after which (I was told) he said he was then going to sue his neighbor to *make* him move his stuff. For some reason, perhaps through word-of-mouth or some kind of cross-

[15] They were pretty unusual and impressive in those days.

reference, he called Mac, so we went out to do the job.

Our completed survey showed that the southern neighbor was *not* encroaching. In fact, the Officer had located his 'carpenter tape' lot line almost seven and a half feet (average) too far south. This meant that the true lot line was only two and a half feet from the south exterior wall of his newly installed doublewide trailer. He had already built and attached a six-foot exterior porch for the entrance on the south side about halfway along the length of the trailer. In order to avoid *his encroachment* on his southern neighbor, he would have to cut off four and a half feet of that new porch and, in fact, unless he moved the trailer north, he wouldn't even be able to open his side door.

The Officer was furious. He seemed to think that since he had hired and was paying us, we were supposed to find in his favor.

The man disgusted me, and I declined to even talk to him. However, Mac told him that things didn't work like that and gave him a copy of the survey drawing and the bill, whereupon he (the Officer) declared that he was going to hire a 'real' surveyor who would 'get it right'. I'm not sure, but I think Mac suggested that he go ahead and hire anyone he wanted to, but in the meantime please pay the bill.

As far I was concerned personally, the outcome of the job couldn't have been more satisfying. Despite his honest and straightforward approach to almost everything, Mac was a lot more diplomatic than I am. I cannot abide phony people like that Officer, then or now, and I'm inclined to let them know it, either directly and insultingly, or (if they're too big physically) indirectly through sarcasm or innuendo.

I guess whatever 'real' surveyor the guy hired after we left came up with about the same results that we did. Just out curiosity, I drove by the place about three or four months after we finished and saw that one of the two neighbors had built a fence, and the Officer had moved his trailer further north ten or fifteen feet. Maybe he apologized about the trailer out of embarrassment for being such a jackass about the property line and then being proven wrong, but I doubt it. For some reason, guys like that never get embarrassed about the consequences of their own childish behavior. You may attribute it to optimism or confidence; I attribute it to blockheaded stupidity and unabashed arrogance. Alaskans would meet more and more of them as we 'matured' into political and social sophistication.

Mac didn't cover for this guy's payment like I think he may have done for the old-timers on the east side, and we waited for our money until the Officer paid – almost six months later.

Mac was pretty closely involved with the property survey parts of this intentionally short-lived business because it was his stamp and signature that sealed all the survey drawings we recorded. However, he took less interest in the construction layout jobs that we did for various contractors on various jobs in the Fairbanks area.

Glenn Highway: approximately 120 miles east of Anchorage. Tahneta Pass – note small hill.

When the end of July approached, we were forced to face the fact that it would be less than two months until time to return to school. As luck would have it, we were fortunate enough to pick up a pretty sizable job for a contractor who had won a contract to build a repeater station. It was to be located atop a high knob in the middle of Tahneta Pass – about 120 miles east of Anchorage, through the Chugach Mountains. I suppose the name Tahneta comes from some Indian word, but I don't know what it means in English. We resolved that this would be the final job of the season so my old friend Tom, a man named Bill, and I got all our gear together and moved down to the site.

Bill worked for the University's Civil Engineering Department. I don't think he was an instructor at that time, although he may have become one (or a professor) later. Before we left town, he announced that he had just struck a very good bargain and obtained a spacious four-man tent with room for a large layout table in the center. It had built-in provision for a stovepipe with a prepared fire retardant material and a metal reinforced roof vent. He also said that the tent material would be especially good for us because it was darker than canvas, therefore affording better shade I suppose, and it weighed a lot less. It was called 'balloon cloth'.

Neither Tom nor I knew enough about the material to say anything at the time, but we would find out a lot about it over the next two or three weeks. I guess we figured that a man with Bill's advanced scholastic standing must surely know what he was talking about. So away we went.

The centerline of the access road from the highway to the repeater station site had been previously flagged out by the Corps of Engineers. In addition to building the road itself, it was the contractor's responsibility to set out the centerline, reference the control points, turn all the P.I. deflection angles, compute and stake all the curves as shown on the plans and set whatever stakes they (the contractor) felt were necessary to control the construction. Setting out all these stakes, including those required for grade control at the site itself, was what we were hired to do.

We had located our campsite in what seemed to be an old gravel pit, perhaps used during construction or reconstruction of the main Glenn Highway. The location was at about milepost 118 (from Anchorage) on the Glenn Highway; we were approximately two miles east of Sheep Mountain Lodge and 300 feet or so south of the highway. We spent a fair amount of time at the lodge partly because it only cost two or three dollars to take a shower there, including towels and soap. Bill wasn't much of a beer drinker so he never spent much time at the bar, but Tom and I did, mostly me I guess. I stopped at the lodge about ten years after we finished that job. The sign over the door off the lobby doesn't say 'Bar' anymore, it says 'Lounge' – I guess that's OK, times change after all. I think that by now, the lodge ownership has changed too. I didn't ask when the previous owners had left or where they had gone when I stopped there. I think that, like most of the old Alaskans, they disappeared too, but I still have some pretty good memories of them.

The man's name was Duke,[16] and his wife, or whatever she was, was called Ellen. Duke was my idea of what an Alaskan businessman should be like; he had his priorities in order. Occasionally, he would be with us at the bar enjoying good company and good beer when a customer off the highway pulled up at the gas pumps. If Duke preferred to stay in the bar with us, he would go to the door and shout to the potential customer(s) that he was out of gas or that he was closed, or something similar. Sometimes the customer didn't take Duke's attitude in good spirits and would say something intended to insult Duke because he did in fact have a sign out on the highway saying 'Gas' in neon. However, any such insults would roll right over Duke's back just because he was Duke. He never said a word in reply to such remarks; he just closed the door and came back to the bar.

I think he acted pretty much the same way with people who came in to eat. If he felt like serving them, he would; if he didn't feel like it, for reasons known only to him, he wouldn't.

Ellen was much more of a businessperson. We could often

[16] Maybe this was a nickname or maybe not; I once knew a man with the given first name 'King'.

hear her arguing with Duke over his behavior, particularly the stuff about turning away customers. She seemed especially upset whenever the customers were tourists from someplace other than Alaska. At such times she would often refer to him as an 'irascible old curmudgeon'. Personally, I loved it.

If those tourists came to Alaska to see typical Alaskans, they wouldn't find anyone more typical than Duke. They should have been grateful for the opportunity to experience such authenticity, even though they might suffer some minor inconvenience. Duke just couldn't see himself as anyone's servant, regardless of the business or the tips or whatever. It begs the question of why he got into the lodge/service station business in the first place. I wonder where all the Dukes have gone.

The balloon cloth that our tent was made of was indeed lightweight and easy to handle, just as Bill had said it would be when he bought it to bring with us to the job. When we got to the campsite and set everything up, the weather was good – it was warm and the sky was clear. It stayed that way for about two weeks so we set up our tent and even an outdoor table protected by a sort of patio cover (a shelter-half also made of balloon cloth) that Bill, in his wisdom, had foreseen would be needed when he bought the tent.

Everything went really well with regard to our tent and patio until one night about ten p.m. when it started to rain. All three of us were asleep, but we slowly awakened as we realized that the balloon cloth was making no pretense of even *attempting* to shed the rainwater. The only difference between the rain that was falling outside and what was falling inside was that the drops inside were smaller. Everything, and I mean *everything*, exposed in the tent or under the 'patio' got completely soaked. Our boots wound up with about a half-inch of standing water inside them, the few field notes and sketches that had been left on the table were ruined, and water had splashed into the oil drum stove and put it out – it was smoking profusely.

Fortunately, the notes and drawings that mattered most had all been put under the table for some reason and the outer covers of the sleeping bags were water repellent. We lost some food that was exposed, and our clothes that were hung up also got soaked, and we had to take them up to the lodge and pay to use the dryer for a few hours.

Of course, Duke had never heard of such a thing as a balloon-cloth tent, and he thought that the whole business was uproariously funny. Fortunately, he had a bunch of large vinyl ground cloths. He was agreeable to renting us enough of them to cover both our tent roof and the patio. Thanks to Duke, we had no further leaking problem when it rained, which it did almost continuously for the rest of the job. Naturally, we didn't let Bill forget about the marvelous balloon-cloth tent, even after we had returned to the university for the 1960 fall semester. He didn't seem able to appreciate the humor in the incident.

Although he had a deep and thorough understanding of what we were working toward on the project, as well as the details of what we were doing and why we were doing it, Bill was still a little bit scholastic in his approach to the work. One night he sat up really late preparing a listing of all the stakes we had set out. The document that came out of all his work was very impressive, very comprehensive, and no doubt very accurate. Bill was never known to produce second-rate stuff.

When we went out on the job the following morning, he presented his pieces of paper to the superintendent, who kept right on talking without even a brief pause to look at them. He took Bill's documents, thanked him very much, then unceremoniously folded them up kind of sloppily and stuffed them into his shirt pocket, still talking about other matters the whole time. I'm not sure Bill fully understood that most dirt superintendents are primarily concerned with keeping the equipment operating at peak efficiency, maintaining continuous load counts and ensuring accurate quantity measurements. It's been my experience that they more or less just expect the staking to be accurately done and never pay much attention to it unless they run into a gross error. Anyway, it's often true that dirt projects are heavily over-staked, particularly when the agencies do the construction surveying. Most good dirt contractors, or experienced equipment operators, don't need much more than just a few grade stakes here and there and some idea where the centerline of the road is supposed to be.

Once, when I was a young and eager inspector, a grizzled old dirt superintendent asked me why we didn't just tell them what towns we wanted to go through, step back and leave them alone. He assured me that given that kind of latitude, they could indeed build us a fine road, one that would meet all our specifications/standards and, if we wished and were willing to pay for it, guaranteed to last for a thousand years.[17]

Although it actually has no relevance to the subject of the book, I must include the following incident out of respect and remembrance. I do so whenever I have a reasonable opportunity.

From a personal standpoint, this may have been one of the saddest early springs of my life. My dog Tangle, who had been with us since 1955, was shot and killed by the Fairbanks dogcatcher. It was my fault because I just wasn't watching him closely enough. At the time, we were living in the Queen's Court Apartments before we moved into a new house on McCullam Street. One evening I left to drive to the local Foodland grocery store, neglecting to take Tangle with me. He saw me leave and ran behind the car all the way to the store, where he watched me go into one of the doors and then he ran over to sit there and wait for me to come out.

The Fairbanks Foodland had two or three entrances/exits,

[17] Perhaps a slight exaggeration.

and I came out of a different one than the one I had gone into. I didn't know that Tangle had followed me, and he didn't know that I had come out by a different door. That night he didn't come home to bed, and I was terribly worried about him.

As soon as I could, I called the animal control people. I don't want to describe the event in detail because it still brings tears to my eyes and makes me sick to my stomach with sorrow. The upshot of the whole business was that my sweet and loving Tangle was shot to death by the dogcatcher. I never saw him after leaving him at home that day; I never even got to look at his ashes.

At first I couldn't really accept it and for at least a year or two I kept calling to every yellow Husky that I saw, hoping against reason that maybe Tangle just wandered off, got lost and was now running around lonely and homeless. Of course, these were forlorn hopes. Tangle was gone and it took a long time before his presence, albeit ethereal, stopped being part of my daily life and became just part of my past. I miss him still; maybe I'll see him again on the other side.

Fairbanks: 2106 McCullam. Purchased: in the fall of 1960 for $25,000.

Before we enrolled for the 1960 fall semester, Irene and I moved into our new house on McCullam Street, located south and west of the city of Fairbanks about a block and a half off Airport Road. I don't know how she felt about it, but I was very pleased and proud. It was the first (and last) house that we ever owned together. I think that we paid something like $25,000 for it, which these days isn't even enough to buy a full-sized car.

It was now time to go up to the university, explain why we

were about two weeks late, set up our curriculum and start classes. I was back on the BPR night crew in the attic of the district headquarters building as was agreed to by Woody Johansen the previous spring. Now began what might have been my final year in college if I hadn't had to work and adjust my class loading accordingly – poor me! Actually, it *was* beginning to get very, very burdensome for both Irene and me, but I figured that, as long as she was hanging in there, I could too. Although we're no longer together, I must give her full credit, respect, admiration and gratitude for sharing the load with me during those college years. It was no small thing, and if she hadn't stuck with me, I'd still be cutting brush and driving stakes.

At least my studies were becoming more interesting, and it seemed to me, more practical and applicable to the real-world practice of engineering. I was now beginning to move away from the lower division classes at the university and getting into the subjects that I thought were my reason for being there. The winter thus promised to be a great deal more rewarding as far as the academic aspects were concerned, but nonetheless, as a practical matter, I still had to address the more mundane design and design support work to be done on the night crew.

When we left in the spring of 1960 to pursue our private survey work, there were still a lot of field data needed before the design of the Phase I Denali project could proceed from Paxson to the Tangle Lakes. During the summer, field crews working out of Fairbanks had picked up almost all these data, so we moved on with the design work. This was before the proliferation of computers and computer-generated design in the workplace, but the transformation was a lot closer than any of us realized if we even thought about it at all, which we probably didn't. At the risk of again sounding like a hopeless anachronism, I still believe that dependence on all these modern devices separates the designer too far from the actual field conditions and makes it harder to see the drawings as representative of actual dirt surfaces. Besides, the computers of that time filled whole rooms, and it really didn't seem likely they would ever fit into our little attic drafting room, much less accompany a survey crew out into the field.

In my opinion, the designer or even the draftsmen should not, if possible and practical, be allowed to work on any project without at least having actually walked over the ground and preferably even worked with the field crew in some capacity for a few days. When we designed the first phase of the Denali Highway reconstruction, we relied on both the actual 'on-the-ground' knowledge of each designer as well as their technical experience and ability. Fortunately, in this case they had all visited the site at least once, which assured a much greater 'team' feeling within the office crew as well as a collective appreciation of what was actually on the ground. This design crew knowledge avoided numerous errors that might otherwise have arisen out of misunderstanding or unfamiliarity with actual ground conditions.

The construction that we were designing for that winter was scheduled to begin in 1962 and to be built under contract in accordance with the BPR standards then in effect. In order to avoid creating another Badger Loop Road situation we decided to run a brand-new continuous line all the way from Paxson to the Tangle Lakes, later extended to the MacLaren and then on to Susitna River. There were ample and accurate government control points, both horizontal and vertical, all along our route. So we climbed eagerly on our stools, bent over our drafting tables because none of us yet had any of those white-collar executive desks and went to work – after daytime classes, of course.

The field survey data with which we were furnished were quite complete and well documented. However, if I were to receive the same information today, I would note the fact that we had virtually no soils information and could not proceed until we were furnished with the parameters governing the behavior of the material. Fortunately in this case, myself and at least one other member of the design crew had lots of experience in the Denali country and were familiar enough with what was there to allow us to begin the design.

We finished the design decisions and the detailed calculations for the first two 'pieces' of the Denali Phase I project before the beginning of April 1961. It would be nice to be able to say that we overcame some great technical challenges in our design of this project, but unfortunately such a claim wouldn't be true. Virtually all of what we did was ordinary stuff, except maybe for the decision to throw all the old stuff away and start our new alignment as though it was the first one in there. There was just such a mass of overlapping information that we recognized the similarities to Badger Loop, which was a classic example of what *not* to do. Our frequently expressed view of Badger Loop might have offended the day crew a bit, and if so, I'm sorry, but don't take it personally. We just didn't want the Denali to wind up in that kind of mess. We had done about all that we could do with the first two pieces of the Phase I Denali project, so now we had to scare up some interim jobs to last us until school was out for the summer. Ironically, we were thus assigned to review the finally completed drawings for the Badger Loop construction project.

The finished project design that we were given for review proposed two main things that were not really sensible. First of all, the title sheet presented a lot of gibberish about seasonal records, flood frequencies, rainfall statistics and so on. Out of all that, the designers came up with a finished flood level elevation that the residents knew to be at least a foot lower than the average floods they had historically experienced. I was told that when these residents came in to the design office to point out their concerns, they were treated with infuriatingly patronizing tolerance and told that everything would be just fine – "Just trust us," they were told. This is, of course, just hearsay on my part, but I don't doubt it, and I wouldn't have been surprised if it was the chief of the daytime design crew that these folks talked to. This was an attitude toward the public that was increasingly coming north with the new concepts of management. What these stateside imports in Fairbanks didn't seem to understand was that in many cases, they were talking to Alaskans who weren't then, and never had been, satisfied with the imperious 'just trust us' answer.

The newly completed plans also called for the removal of all the debris, car bodies, old appliances, etc. that the residents had been placing in the dikes for a lot of years. I for one felt that its removal was another ill-advised action.

All that debris was, by that time, well integrated into the dike structure. In fact, it *was* the dike structure, not to mention a probable home for a lot of resident fishes and whatever other little critters live in water like that. Digging all that stuff out would have caused a mini disaster both from an environmental and a construction standpoint. If there were any fish, etc. in that slough, they were by now habituated[18] to the dike and all the elements that made it up like the car bodies, old appliances, etc. Sudden removal of all that stuff would have been very traumatic for those aquatic critters.

As I recall, we made some field reviews, determined that all the debris in the existing dike had either filled up tightly with stream deposited silt/sand or had been completely crushed. We recommended that it all be left in place. Of course, even by that time a few of the management dragons had already begun to insinuate themselves into the decision-making processes.

[18] I love that word.

Lacking any knowledge whatsoever about the technical aspects of such a project, they would not hesitate to overrule an engineering decision for political or administrative reasons. Their time was imminent, and they knew it.

Badger Loop was to fit nicely into the convoluted administrative structure and apparatus that statehood brought with it. There were plenty of different opinions about what to do; each accompanied by an extensive enough body of social, economic and environmental arguments, to furnish material for an almost endless series of meetings and a truckload of memoranda. With any luck, the newly installed bureaucratic dragons might also have found enough simplistic and irrelevant things for which they could codify a few arcane regulations just to help plant their 'claw' more firmly in the door.

Sometime during the last week in April, I was assigned to be project engineer on a project for supply and placement of riprap bank protection and stream current 'diversion groins' on both the Delta and the Big Gerstle Rivers. The Delta River job was located along the Richardson Highway about thirty miles south of Delta Junction near Donnelly Inn. The majority of the rock was planned for placement at this location.

I remember that we surveyed and laid out a proposed bank protection dike on the Big Gerstle River too, maybe twenty to twenty-five miles south of Delta Junction, but on the Alaska Highway instead of the Richardson. Incidentally, that road is sometimes called the 'Alcan' Highway, but actually there is no such road as the 'Alcan'. I don't know how it got that name; I suppose someone made it up during the wartime construction because the route goes through both Alaska and Canada.

Even after doing all the control surveying and layout work for the Big Gerstle, we never built the job. I don't remember why not. Maybe it had something to do with finding out that the Gerstle flood plain, which was limited to about a quarter-mile-wide corridor stripped of overburden by the seasonal meanders of the river, served as a testing ground for the Army Chemical Corps from time to time. In those days people weren't as spooked by such things as they are now, but the Army told us they sometimes used the area without warning for testing the effectiveness of potentially hazardous chemicals. Maybe that's why we never did anything more than just notify the Army and then simply locate and stake the proposed dike and groin alignments for the construction that never happened. Although we *were* more liberal in those days, none of us were really enthusiastic about the possibility of getting gassed.

The contractor on the Delta River job was an outfit called Yutan or Yutana or something similar. I remember that the name either was the same as or sounded a lot like the Yutana Barge Lines, which served the Yukon River and its tributary system throughout Alaska's huge interior. Their project superintendent was a man named Harvey who must have been at least sixty-five years old. I think he told me he had more or less come out of retirement to do the job, both because he knew and liked the principals of this company, and because he enjoyed heavy construction, particularly rock work. He thoroughly demonstrated his skill during the progress of the work and surprisingly he did so without any application of the new concepts of 'Management'. Considering all the claims and procedures of today's managers, it seems impossible that he could have accomplished such a feat!

The company used a little two-seater airplane for bringing small parts and supplies back and forth between Fairbanks and the project, allowing almost immediate response to Harvey's requests. He once told me that he could call up his expediter at ten a.m., order five gold toothpicks, and they would be on the job by three p.m. the same day. He said that with this company, no one would even *think* to ask why he needed the toothpicks.

He added that such unquestioning responses from a project expediter were absolutely essential for the efficient completion of any construction project. The expediter was, said Harvey, a truly critical member of the project team. That's still true, by the way. Of course, any action by an agency expediter today would almost certainly require a flurry of memoranda, several meetings, numerous copies of approved purchase orders and an approval by the 'Manager' prior to taking any action.

I think that Harvey may have been the first dirt superintendent to thoroughly explain (and demonstrate) to me the principles, practice and importance of setting up dual haul routes on projects involving hauling units. He emphasized that this was especially true with trucks because trucks were more susceptible to frequent breakdowns than other hauling units. He pointed out to me that by doing so, it is possible to vary the haul distances and still maintain the load count if mechanical problems took out one or more of the trucks. He also drove me to the blasting site several times to demonstrate the efficiency of his blasting crew. At the time, I felt that such knowledge was extremely important for my career because in those days it was more or less assumed that engineers were 'nuts and bolts' people; capable of supervising, or maybe even performing, actual work. Engineers who restricted themselves to 'Management', 'Leadership', or theoretical calculations were in the minority and were not well tolerated.

In the event, every blast that I ever saw on Harvey's job didn't seem like anything more than a thump, followed by a sudden swelling of the rock surface, a lot of dust and then a settlement of the newly fractured rock – a typical sign of a well-placed charge. Harvey was extremely demanding in his hiring of powder men. He often used that hackneyed expression, "There are old powder men and there are bold powder men, but there are no old, bold powder men." If he even suspected that any of his blasting crew harbored only a slightly casual attitude about powder work, he would fire them and send them back to town without a moment's hesitation. His blasting crew knew that, respected him for it, and probably felt safer on the job because of it. I doubt if Harvey would put up with the workplace control that the unions enjoy today. He would also make his objections known in less than diplomatic language. I wonder where all the Harveys have gone.

Our Delta River job was located within the range of a large herd of Buffalo (American Bison) that had originally been introduced by some government agency or other in about 1933 as a part of an experiment; they were probably testing 'species adaptability' or something like that. The buffalo didn't know they were being tested, and since then the herd has at least tripled in size. In a few cases, the interface with the human population has caused some problems, albeit pretty minor ones. The herd shows up all the way from the Delta/Tanana Rivers junction to the foothills of the Alaska Range, at least seventy-five miles south of our project. It's relatively well developed in the Delta Junction (Richardson and Alaska Highways) area, and occasionally a big old buffalo will fall into the basement excavation of an unfinished house or get his or her head stuck in a garbage can while looking for something to eat. In either case, I'm sure that such an incident is more traumatizing for the poor buffalo than for any nearby humans.

Buffalo: (American bison) Note newborn calf on the left.

Although it's not fair to be critical of other living critters, it seems like the American Bison is not very bright. They don't look very bright either. They just seem to wander around in whatever direction they happen to be pointed unless some food distracts them, and then they wander off in a new direction.

Although there were many rumors of an occasional old bull challenging cars, tipping over Volkswagens and so on, we did not experience a single incident involving the slightest sign of aggression from any of these beasts, even when we encountered them on open ground when we were carrying no weapons. I think that by the time they were able to figure out what we were, we were gone and they just forgot about it. I can clearly remember one incident when I was wandering around in one of the clearings near the project looking for something or other when I came upon an old bull peeing on a flat rock that happened to be directly under him. He was making a lot of noise, which seemed to really puzzle him. He kept looking from side to side and behind him trying to locate the source of all that racket. It finally occurred to me that he didn't know he was peeing. He had no idea where all that noise was coming from.

Nonetheless, they are a handsome animal in their own way; strong, beautifully muscled and well suited for their environment. They *do* look a little hunchbacked and their head is positioned so that it appears it would be impossible for them to look behind them or up into the sky. Perhaps they never feel like doing that anyway.

When the bison (buffalo) were first introduced in the Delta area back in 1933, there was some doubt that the animals could survive the extreme winter conditions of interior Alaska. Obviously, they have not only survived, they have prospered. I believe they are now one of the largest free-ranging buffalo herds in the U.S., if not *the* largest. I have encountered these animals many times in the Delta area while alone and on foot and have always found them to be mild-mannered, polite and certainly non-threatening. In the one instance wherein I had a really close experience with a buffalo, I was the aggressor (although unintentionally so), and the buffalo certainly did nothing to justify my aggression.

I was driving a BPR pickup south toward our project when I ran into a cow buffalo with her calf just south of Delta Junction, right next to the Fort Greely airstrip. There was another driver coming north who hit and killed the calf. The accident broke the cow's back, and she was struggling to get to her feet after her mortal injury; she was bawling and obviously trying to get to her calf. It was tragic: I grieved about it for weeks, and it haunted my dreams off and on for several years. Since I quit hunting, I seem to have developed an almost obsessive empathy for innocent animals who get hurt through no fault of their own. The pickup was 'totaled' and the car was badly damaged, but these things were trivial compared to the buffalo fatalities.

These are gentle beasts with no murderous intent toward us, yet the Alaska Department of Fish and Game takes several 'hunters' out each year, points to an animal for each of them and tells them to kill that creature. Many of them are from outside seeking what they want to describe to their friends as their 'Alaskan' adventure, the phony bastards. Do they think that they are really hunting? How can they sleep at night? More than that, how can these fish and game people, who are sworn to protect animals, rationalize such behavior? Both this subject in general and the outcome of my collision depress me.

The survey crew that was sent to us out of Fairbanks seemed to be a sort of 'scratch' crew consisting of four young men who were either cashiered or surplused out from other projects, and I must say that they were not the best I'd ever worked with. I need to describe them and to relate some of their behavior because, admittedly, there were a few such kids and crews running around during the statehood transition before our pre-electronic surveyors became as skilled and efficient as the transitional BPR crewmembers were.

Fortunately, we were able to cut the crew back to two men after about two or three weeks. All we needed was a large enough crew to set out and maintain the reference stakes. We then requested and received an experienced instrument man to monitor and assist with grade control during construction. He was, thank God, unlike one of our surveyors, who seemed to be a little bit off center. He (the 'surveyor') kept insisting that he expected a Playboy 'Bunny' to show up in his sleeping quarters[19] sometime within the next two or three days. When we were out in the woods working, he frequently told us that he'd been in contact with a beautiful "wood nymph" that had offered to share his life. I was forced to function as party chief for these two boys from time to time because they had not brought anyone with them who could do that job. When I told him to get back to work and forget about things like wood nymphs and Bunnies and such, he turned and looked at me with a very odd, almost scary, expression. Maybe he thought that *I* was nuts for taking him seriously about all that stuff.

The day before the two kids left, they cornered a poor little porcupine against a tree and were teasing it unmercifully; maybe that was the 'wood nymph' that the one kid had been fantasizing about. The helpless little critter was completely frustrated; its tormentors were too far away for it to strike with the tail, but the sad little creature tried to do just that. These little punk sadists laughed at its futile efforts and just teased it more intensely.

I heard the laughing, and when I got there I told them to stop their behavior immediately. I probably should have fired them; mistreatment of animals is a very sensitive subject with me. Fortunately, after composing itself and regaining its dignity, the harmless little critter waddled off with no damage except maybe to its pride. I know from experience that if these small animals

[19] We each had separate rooms on this job – a real luxury.

get too stressed from teasing or from some other form of human inhumanity, their little hearts will just burst. Most real Alaskans are as considerate of the animals' feeling as I am, but there are exceptions. It's mostly the 'big, brave woodsmen' and hunters from outside who can't wait to shoulder their rifles and go out to murder everything in sight.

Donnelly Inn was operated by a lady named Billie[20], who must have owned or leased the inn. She had previously been married to the Doug with whom I had briefly worked on the job north of Haines. He was the guy who scared the bear out of the brush and then ran like hell when the bear came up on the road. The bear actually ran too, in the opposite direction. Billie married Doug in Juneau and during the brief time that they were together, Irene and I visited them several times. Every time we saw them, they were slobbering all over each other and proclaiming their undying love. Apparently, the slobbering had stopped and the undying love had collapsed after three or four years of marriage, and they went their separate ways. I can understand that sort of end to the marriage because Billie was a pretty intelligent woman, and Doug was, in my opinion, sort of stupid, arrogant and a monumental bore. I don't know how he captured Billie in the first place, or how she put up with him as long as she did. I wonder where all the Billies and the Dougs have gone.

During the time we were at Donnelly Inn, I put in numerous weekends (and frequent weeknights) bartending for Billie. I was a little awkward at first, but when I got used to it, I found the work to be interesting and educational. Educational because of the opportunity to meet a lot of different kinds of people on an informal basis. It was a little surprising that so many of the patrons coming into the bar were from the lower 48. Most of them were tourists and this stretch of the Richardson was not on

---

[20] Probably a nickname.

the route that they would normally take when traveling between the states and either Anchorage or Fairbanks. At the time, however, it *was* part of the shortest route between Fairbanks and Anchorage.

It was always a pleasure to have traveling Alaskans come by the inn for a drink or two; no self-respecting long time Alaskan would stop for just *one* drink. Almost all real Alaskans have a large repertoire of stories (yarns) to tell, and they are usually delighted to do so. Many of the stories are embellished a bit, and they get better with each telling (and why not?), but they are almost always based on true events, and most of the tourists who happened to be listening seemed genuinely enthralled. I hope that some of them who passed through also stopped at Sheep Mountain Lodge on the way to or from Anchorage and got a chance to talk with Duke if he chose to serve them.

Of course, Billie didn't pay me for the time I spent bartending. I had suggested that I work for nothing except drinks, so no payment was expected. I considered that gaining the experience and encountering the people that I met to be payment enough. Fortunately, there were no aggressive drunks or stick-ups while I was there. That sort of thing was far less common in those days than it has become today. Besides, Billie was a pretty tough lady and if there had been trouble, I think she would have protected me! Actually, I think I might still have been pretty tough at the time myself, although I hadn't been tested since my South Franklin days.

Anyway, most of the Alaskans ordered straight shots of whiskey or beer, but many of the tourists wanted some sort of cocktail concoction that I hadn't ever heard of, much less mixed for customer consumption. However, when I started bartending, Billie had given me a little book with recipes for just about every kind of mixed drink ever conceived.

The construction of the new Parks Highway would

drastically affect the traffic along the Richardson within the next ten years or so. That new stretch of road along the railroad corridor virtually destroyed many of the roadhouse businesses on the Richardson between the northernmost junction of the Richardson/Glenn Highways and Delta Junction. While it's true that the Parks Highway significantly reduced the time and mileage between Anchorage and Fairbanks, such a reduction does not justify the economic impact on those old roadhouses. Many of them were originally built during the gold rush, and any single one of them has more historical significance than the whole city of Anchorage.

On September 2, just before I returned to school, God sent David Jeffrey to us. He was our first boy and a dear, good-natured little baby. As he grew up, I tried to impress on him how important it was to be polite to people, to not be mean and aggressive, and to try to get along with everyone. I may have tried a bit too hard because 'Jeff'[21] turned out to be super polite to the point of submission. In fact, this characteristic was instrumental in his briefly falling in with bad company at one point. However, he joined the Navy in about 1981 and the change in his outlook and attitude by the time he was discharged was astonishing.

When he was very little, Jeff was somewhat slow in learning to talk. Because he was a boy he was a curiosity to the girls, who could already walk and talk, and they did all his talking for him. "Jeff needs this," and "Jeff needs that," so he could usually get what he wanted without saying anything. Jeff has fulfilled all the dreams I had for him, becoming a graduate civil engineer and supporting himself comfortably. I love him a lot, and I'm very proud of him. Of course, I'm very proud of all my children, but these are Jeff's paragraphs because my chronology has reached the time when he was born.

[21] We called him Jeff to avoid confusion around the house with two Davids.

By mid-September 1961, we had completed all the construction work on the Delta River erosion control project, and it was time to go back to Fairbanks and climb up into our night crew attic. My first task would be to take care of all the calculations, reports, etc. necessary to close out the season's project and make the final payment to the contractor. Any happy anticipation that there may have been when preparing for my first two years in college had pretty much disappeared into a less than enthusiastic outlook for another winter of classes. For Tom and me the office work facing us that winter consisted first of closing out the Delta/Big Gerstle project and after that returning to the design work for Phase I on the Denali.

There were a lot of field notes, scale tickets, daily reports and so on to pull together in order to justify the final payment and to review all the previous payments made during the progress of the Delta project. As long as the total of the progress payments didn't exceed the total due for the actual work done, I could never see the reason for exhaustively close review of each progress payment, and in this case the contractor's representative agreed with me. Nonetheless, I always did it anyway because it just wasn't worth arguing about with all the bureaucrats who were, by that time, becoming more and more ubiquitous, and in some cases even aggressive. The dragon vanguard had arrived and they were beginning to test their limits.

I think that recalculating all the previous progress payments, preparing the final estimate, checking and putting in order all the daily reports and other project-related stuff took Tom and me until about the middle or end of October. We then turned our attention to the final design, plans and contract documents for the Phase I Denali Highway project (Paxson to the Tangle Lakes), which was scheduled for advertisement and award in late winter 1962.

This section of road as-built had several curves that required major changes in order to meet BPR standards. At the time, the survey crew that re-measured and re-staked those curves wasn't working for us, so we never knew if they had any problems with our requests, although we would probably not have heard about any such problems anyway. The field data that we got from the crew that fall were good, complete, apparently accurate, and unambiguous. I can't remember who the party chief was, but he was obviously very good at what he did even though he had no electronic gadgets to do his thinking and decision-making for him. The few contacts I had with him demonstrated to me that, unlike too many of today's 'surveyors', he had a firm grasp not only on how to do what he was doing, but also why he was doing it.

We had to ask the day crew for some drafting assistance that winter or spring. Our request, of course, somehow gave their supervisor (a real pain in the ass) the impression that he and his crew were in charge of the project. However, when he started sending us memoranda telling us what to do, it didn't take George very long to straighten him out and explain that all we wanted was a little drafting help (technician work) without any advice, direction or supervision.

With a little help from the day crew draftsmen, and the fact that George had finished putting the specific technical specifications and the legally required general provisions together, we were able to rush the project and advertise for bids during the last week in March. At that point we were, as a crew, pretty proud of the fact that this was a completed project with which we had demonstrated that we could begin and end the whole job, and take care of everything in between, with no input from any of the daytime designers, the meddling managers or the budding bureaucrats.

Times were changing; putting projects like this together were unnecessarily involving more people and consequently becoming more and more complex. It's well known among competent engineers that the complexity of an originally simple task increases exponentially with the number of people involved. This is a very fundamental and logical fact that managers, bureaucrats, and most lawyers seem unable to grasp. Of course, these are the people who benefit from increased complexity, and by this winter it was becoming sickeningly evident that we were getting caught in their dragon-like claws.

It was sometime in April that the bids were opened and the contract was awarded to S.S. Mullen Construction. I'm not sure where Mullen's headquarters were, although they *did* have an office in Fairbanks, and I think that was where they had put the bid together. At the time they didn't have much equipment in town, but I assumed they must have had some stationed at another location close to Fairbanks. The fallacy of this assumption was to become evident during the first season of the Denali construction.

Having completed the design and preparation of the plans and specifications for the Phase I construction and watching the contract go to Mullen, we needed some interim work to take us up to the time we were to go to Paxson to set up our project office. There was about a month and a half during which we could work around the Fairbanks area. The delay until mid to late April or early May had nothing to do with the contractor's schedule. It was the weather on the Denali that delayed things. Nothing fully thaws out before the end of April up there, and the probability of vicious late winter storms would still be high.

I think this was the year that George graduated and put in his last shift on the night crew. He was the first to start and to stick with the program all the way through college. We all congratulated him, but there was absolutely nothing sentimental about it as there often is with retirements and such. We all knew what a difficult burden working full-time and going to college was, and still is, and we were pleased for him that *his* burden in this respect had been lifted.

During the interim period from March to May while waiting to move to Paxson, I went to work as an afternoon and early evening party chief/inspector on the Steese Highway construction project, which had been awarded to Morrison-Knudsen the previous fall. After the award, the Steese project was almost immediately officially shutdown for the winter (October to early April). This allowed M-K plenty of time to prepare detailed project schedules, line up necessary equipment, prepare an on-site project office, set up a project shop, prepare an equipment yard and the myriad of other pre-construction tasks that can be taken care of during an official shutdown period without charging time against the contract.

The Morrison-Knudsen project people, from laborers to superintendents, were real professionals. They all knew how to do what they were hired to do, and they didn't waste any time doing it. I suspect that there was little or no tolerance of incompetence, and that if it became otherwise apparent, or even suspected, it didn't take long for the offender to be sent down the road.

In about mid-April, I met with 'Roxy', who was to be my project office engineer for the next two years. We went to the district supply depot and loaded up with just about everything we could conceivably need, and what we'd just like to have, in the project office. We picked up stuff such as two drafting tables, pencils, pens, paper of many varieties, file cabinets, file folders, field books and about a gazillion other things. Additionally, we had to requisition all the instruments, steel tapes ('chains'), transits, levels, cutting tools, plumb-bobs, and everything else necessary to equip and supply at least two survey crews. Naturally, we forgot a few things, but nothing that was vital. We got whatever we had forgotten during two or three subsequent trips to town.

This was to be the first *major* project (1.7 million in 1962) for which I would serve as project engineer. I was only twenty-seven years old, and naturally I was pretty excited and proud at the prospect of having a large job of my own. To make it even better, Paxson was just far enough out of town that the district officials and management bureaucrats couldn't conveniently make the roundtrip in one day. Consequently, we welcomed very few supervisory visits from the Fairbanks district office. It was a good, clean, straightforward job while it lasted; there are undoubtedly no more like it now that the 'Managers' have more or less taken over.

The fact that the contract hadn't been awarded until *very* early spring, and that the Notice to Proceed was issued less than two months after the award, more or less forced the contractor to begin work before they were completely ready. They did not have the opportunity to prepare for the project over the winter as M-K had on the Steese project. We felt at the time that this was really unfair to our contractor. It would have been far more beneficial both to S.S. Mullen *and* to the state to delay the Notice to Proceed long enough to allow the contractor to bring in a more efficient combination of equipment types, and to put together a better project game plan, so to speak.

Since it seemed logical to postpone our Notice to Proceed until warmer weather, I attempted to reason with the head office dragons about it. I tried pointing out the benefits for everyone concerned, but sadly, the age of project control by project people had passed without warning or whimper. My requests were naturally turned down by these administrative lightweights whose only equipment experience involved a coffee cup and a pencil.

Sometime later the district construction engineer at the time told me that he had never received my request. Maybe one of the

'Managers' sat on it, thinking, in their dangerous ignorance, that their management 'skills' better equipped them to judge the merits of such a shutdown request – the end of the age of reason was upon us. Knowing most of the 'Managers' at the time, I can say with assurance that being 'sat on' by at least one of them would have been a decidedly unpleasant, if not fatal, experience.

I told Mullens' superintendent (a man named Don) what I thought and what I had tried to do, and he thanked me, saying that he hoped to save as much of the mobilization work as possible until after the winter shutdown. I knew the Denali country, and I was pretty familiar with how quickly the weather could deny the possibility of any outdoor work anytime after September 30. However, Don seemed confident that he could schedule his operations around the weather, so I said nothing further about the matter. Suggestions to a contractor by an agency representative can easily backfire.

There were one or two matters of procedure when we felt it necessary to demonstrate early on to the contractor, and I guess to ourselves, that we were the authorized representatives of the owner (i.e., the public) and that as such, we intended to enforce the plans and specifications as *we* interpreted them. We were in charge from an administrative and technical engineering standpoint, and we needed to make that clear. I'm sure today there are now strict and codified regulations directing the field representatives in exactly how such things must be done. The ludicrous aspect of this is that such regulations are almost all written by today's bureaucratic dragons, who wouldn't know a scraper from a road grader. There was one incident that still stands out clearly in my memory.

Although there are exceptions, most contractors have a number of preconceived stratagems that they will try to use for one or two reasons: 1) For the contractor looking for a slight edge in saving money, or making extra money, it is desirable to keep the agency representatives as confused and hurried as possible. If that can be done, it is a wedge that can be continuously pushed further and further until the agency project personnel no longer feel capable of making independent decisions and must defer to higher authority. There are built-in delays here, and delays are traditional grounds for contractor claims. 2) Many contractors will try to elicit decisions from inspectors when they (the contractors) think they can convince the inspector that such decisions are not within his or her authority. This, it is assumed, will result in even more delays and another addition to the list of claims that with some contractors will inevitably follow project completion. Shortly after the job got organized we were confronted with a situation much as described in number 2 above.

When Mullen had finally received a sufficient complement of operators and equipment, they opened up a couple of well-organized scraper cut and fill spreads. We had a very competent grade inspector on the job, but the contractor began demanding directions in writing from me every time the inspector told him to do something at a particular location and/or in a certain way. It was obvious what Mullen was doing; it was part of the time-honored game, and although there were no real hard feelings, it had to be nipped in the bud. They hoped that the delay of getting things in writing might help in establishing grounds for a later accumulated delay claim. When it became apparent what was going on after three or four instances, we printed up about a hundred and fifty pre-authorization letters, leaving the description of the work and the location blank. I signed them all and the inspectors carried a bunch with them.

Thereafter, when asked for something in writing to back up a request or direction, the inspector had only to return to his truck, get one of the blanks, fill it in with the description and location and hand it to the foreman or whoever was asking for something in writing.

At first, the contractor's supervisory people acted furious about these "pieces of paper", but when it became obvious that this practice was henceforth to be part of our project policy, they seemed to mellow a bit. I think that Don realized we had just 'checked his move', so to speak. In any case, the requests for stuff in writing stopped, and although Don said that he was going to complain to the district office, we never heard any more about the matter. Personally, I doubt that he contacted anyone in Fairbanks because if he had, the now burgeoning bureaucrats/managers would have leaped at the chance to demonstrate some project authority – the old 'claw in the door' method of gradually gaining authority.

I described this incident in some detail because it demonstrates an occurrence that today would no doubt be a perfect opportunity for some bureaucratic dragon to write a policy memorandum, follow it with others, and who knows, maybe even grasp the chance to write an official regulatory code provision after, of course, a gazillion meetings.

About halfway through the project we set up a little soils lab under the very capable direction of our lead soils engineer named Dave (not me). Dave had a graduate degree in soils engineering and for about two years he had been mentored by the old Russian running the Fairbanks District Materials Lab. We were lucky to get him, so I sort of left the setting up of the lab to him, remembering how I had hated being interfered with without my request earlier in my own career. He was particularly valuable in that, at the time, he was largely unfamiliar with many of the useless and burgeoning bureaucratic regulations, or at least pretended to be. Predictably, the managerial dragons in Fairbanks never even realized that they were not receiving all that nonsensical paperwork crap they had recently invented. I fully supported his 'negligence' in this respect.

It soon became evident that I had also been fortunate in acquiring an office engineer. As mentioned before, the man assigned to the job was nicknamed 'Roxy' and beside being very good at what he did, he had a terrific sense of humor. A sense of humor is not specifically authorized during working hours these days. Believe it or not, there's more truth than sarcasm in that remark.

A lot of the younger folks who came down to work on the project were completely inexperienced. Of course, they had all been issued plumb-bobs with holsters and strings, which they were wearing conspicuously like some sort of badge of office. A few of them even had hand-levels on their belts, although it was doubtful that most (or any) of them had the slightest idea how to use them or even what they were used *for*.

When they started coming in, Roxy usually asked to inspect their plumb-bobs. He would then make an elaborate show of driving a hub-tack in the office door about five feet off the floor and, using a t-square, placing a mark at a point about three or four feet lower, saying that the point was exactly vertical below the tack, which it obviously wasn't. He next explained to them that, when hung from the tack and allowed to swing freely, the point of the plumb-bob must fall exactly on the mark he had made on the door below the tack. He said that if it didn't, it would be necessary to adjust the plumb-bob by adding little pieces of solder on the point until it fell 'correctly'. It was all nonsense, of course. First, the mark was probably not exactly below the tack and second, the plumb-bob would roll against the door while swinging so it wouldn't even stop at the same spot twice. Nonetheless, the great majority of the surveyor wannabes dutifully hung their plumb-bobs from the tack and tried over and over to get the point to fall where they wanted it to. We happened to have a small soldering gun and some solder (although not for this purpose) in the office, and the kids kept attaching lumps of solder until Roxy told them that it was OK, and that they'd just have to make allowances for the supposed maladjustment of the plumb-bob. Perhaps some of them actually had the plumb-bob point stop where the mark was, but if they did, it was strictly coincidental and had nothing to do with the solder. I'm sure that there were some of the young 'surveyors' who realized that the whole thing was a joke, but apparently they didn't tell the others. Some of them kept coming back for days to get their plumb-bobs adjusted. Roxy is dead now, God rest him.

By the middle or end of September, the weather in the Denali country turns unmistakably toward winter. There is no more rain; any precipitation is in the form of snow. The ever-present howling wind from the mountains can create blizzard conditions; sometimes within an hour the weather might go from clear and calm to impenetrable blowing snow squalls. Drifts can, and often do, build up from ground level to roof eaves overnight during deep winter. Folks who live up there just go into the cabin and wait out the storms. A contractor can't do that because the frequency of the storms causes prohibitive delays, and temperatures during the storms frequently drop to ten or twenty degrees below zero Fahrenheit. Equipment won't start, and when it finally does, it doesn't run properly and is more prone to breakdowns. It's tough on the equipment, but it's just as tough on the crew. Morale drops and most of them, even the most dedicated, want nothing more than just to park all the rigs, stow all the tools and supplies and go home.

During the second half of September 1962, there were signs of a rough winter to come and Don, the superintendent, wisely decided to request a winter shutdown order about four or five days before the end of the month. We gladly complied with his request, and he called all his equipment back to their own yard, closed and locked their office and left the jobsite. I think that they made a deal with someone who worked at the lodge to watch all their stuff over the winter. We, as agency people, were able to leave our survey equipment in the space that the maintenance superintendent had provided for us. We packed up the records that we would need to bring the project up to date when we got back to the office and left for Fairbanks.

I was already late in registering for the fall semester at the university, so I left most of the packing of the office stuff to Roxy and hurried back to town to sign up for the next-to-last semester in my college career. There were two more pickups and two Suburbans to drive into town and park in the lot next to the Fairbanks district office. I have no idea how Roxy got the vehicles back to town, but he did, so I never looked into it. In those days we didn't question success very closely, and if we were confident of a subordinate's competence, we certainly didn't interfere. I think that today such interference and meddling must be written into the job descriptions of most of the 'Managers' et al.

Anyway, I was sort of looking forward to the coming school year because, unless something drastic happened, it would culminate in my graduation.

Almost all of the engineering courses that I signed up for that semester were 'professional' courses like structures, a couple of graduate courses in soil mechanics, mathematics of physics and engineering, and a couple of other things. The 'couple of other things' were probably liberal arts, history or business courses that I took just to make my semester hours add up to fifteen, which as I recall was the minimum required to remain a 'regular' student. Signing up for anything less would require payment to the university by the semester hour. I don't remember the cost per semester hour, but I do remember that it added up to significantly more than just padding your class schedule with a few 'Mickey Mouse' courses requiring little or no real mental effort. Courses like that also had the salutary effect of raising one's grade point average (GPA).

After I got all signed up for this next-to-last semester, I realized that, after completing it, only about ten hours of engineering courses that I hadn't already taken would be available to me. I thus anticipated that during my final semester, except for the demands of the night crew, both Irene and I would probably be under a little less stress than during previous years. It was a happy thought, and I felt good about it for both of us.

Ever since I had started working on the night crew, George had been there. He had become the de facto boss, and everybody accepted his role as such. He had protected us from the incursions by the day crew and built us an identity as a separate unit. George graduated in the spring of 1962, and we all realized that if the day crew started sending us piecework, we would have to show that we were busy with something of our own. I don't remember how we worked it out, but I was able to bring Roxy onto the night crew even though he wasn't going to school, and getting him thus assigned served as evidence that we were heavily engaged with the Denali projects. He was allowed to split his hours between us and the day crew. That's another thing that probably couldn't be done today because it would almost certainly conflict with some stupid and unnecessary policy made up by some of a multitude of managers, bureaucrats and administrators no doubt at one of their meetings. There was enough office work just on the Denali project to keep both Roxy and me busy for most of the coming winter. As I recall Roxy signed up for some university classes during the 1963 spring semester and thus became a 'legitimate' member of the crew for the second half of the 62/63 winter.

Since George had left, I may have become the heir apparent as supervisor of the entire night crew, and maybe that's what the other crewmembers thought. However, I had no desire to become the supervisor for the entire crew and I said so. Roxy and I would be fully involved with closing out the 1962 season for our project, and after that, we would begin design on the Denali Phase II project – Tangle Lakes to the MacLaren River. This was all in accordance with our plan for the winter already submitted to, and approved by, Woody Johansen. We had all this in writing in case the day crew supervisor persisted in his confusion about how the night crew was supposed to function.

We suggested to the other three or four night crew members, if they chose not to help with the Denali, that they seek advice from the day crew man who was next in command to Woody. I seem to recall that his name was Andy, and he that was a really nice fellow, although, like many government employees who just stay with the agencies waiting for automatic pay grade advances, he was pretty much a technical lightweight. He would have been a perfect candidate for one of the glut of upper-level 'Management' positions that were beginning to proliferate. However, I doubt if he applied for any of them, even though there must have been a long list of such positions, each for 'managing' a totally different discipline and each with identical background requirements devoid of anything specific. To some small extent this was still the 'age of innocence' when many of us still thought that managers had to know something about what they were managing. We were gradually learning the truth.

I think that Andy would probably have made a good party chief or even chief of parties, but when confronted with the necessity for decisions beyond that level, he seemed to become more and more puzzled. He always had an expression of intense concentration on his face, although the problems he had to deal with were usually administrative in nature, something that could usually be taken care of by a secretary, an administrative assistant or a 'para-something'. I don't want to say derogatory things about Andy because he was such a nice fellow. He was very honest too – if he didn't know the answer to a technical question, he would just say, "I don't know." He said that a lot.

It took us a long time to finish plotting up all the Denali cross-section notes we had and to check the slope stake numbers because it turned out that the survey crew had gotten a lot further than we thought they had. Here goes another diatribe about the differences in surveyors between then and now.

These days, all it would take would be an instrument man and a 'rodman'. The instrument man would not really be a surveyor anymore – more like an electronics technician. He would, as I understand it, take a bunch of rod shots by pointing the so-called instrument at the rodman in various locations. I'm told that the instrument takes all the information into a sort of storage place populated by some kind of electronic intelligence. All this information is, according to my friends who know all about this stuff, easily retrievable in the form of a topographic map just by 'downloading' it to another machine and touching the right buttons. Isn't that amazing? Isn't that disgusting? Surveyors, except for the unfortunate man carrying the rod, don't even have to get their feet wet anymore in order to pick up a lot of detailed topographic data. However, our story here refers back to 1962, when such devices were not available to us.

If you think it's boring to read about all this office engineering stuff, you should try doing it the old-fashioned way. It seems like it's never going to end. Finish one page of cross-section notes, turn the page and there's another one, and another, and another and another and so on ad infinitum. If you had to do just that for a living, you'd surely go nuts at some point. As much as I resist admitting it, the elimination of the old methods for cross-section data gathering, reduction, and plotting is a good thing. The only negative aspect is that it has become so simple and routine from the technician's standpoint that small errors can easily slip by and project disasters can arise from unnoticed accumulations of small errors. Fortunately, the cross-section stuff was not all we had to do. We also prepared a myriad of other project-related drawings and finished calculating quantity volumes, reducing survey notes.

We then started with the basic design work for Phase II of the Denali Highway. Here again, I had been on the survey crew that first went into this area during the early 1950's, although I had been transferred to some other project before the season was over. I was there when we reached the MacLaren River with our 'P' line, but that was around the time I left.

From early February 1963 until my college graduation date sometime during the first half of May, we worked almost exclusively on calculations for quantities of construction materials on the Denali Phase II project. We made no changes to anything done previously by the first Phase II designers because there was no reason to do so. It was well done, and all we had to do was just slog through the already prepared drawings, plotting up design templates and calculating end areas; very, very boring and highly susceptible to the kind of mistakes that arise from inattention.

On February 2, 1963, Irene and I were blessed with another boy – our sixth child. This was Richard (Ricky) Austin, who has grown up to be the true renaissance man of the family. Even when he was a baby, it wasn't hard to see that Ricky was to be a man of strong convictions – a man unwilling to accept other's opinions or directions without rational reasons. In many ways, he demonstrated early that his personality was to be almost the exact opposite of Jeffrey's. This turned out to be a very good result because as Jeff grew older, he mellowed out more and more until it almost seemed that he would do whatever anyone told him to do. He needed a little counterbalancing, and I think that Ricky provided some of that, at least within the family. Ricky cried a lot as a baby and I have to think that it was more out of anger than discomfort or real need. He may have been angry about being a baby, and he wanted to get it over with. Nonetheless, even though he was our sixth child, the whole business of creating little midget human beings was still unfathomable for me. How can you not love such a little creature that is somehow given to you from an unknown benefactor? It is definitely not all biology. I (we) loved Ricky the same as all the others, and he has since proven that love to be well placed.

There were at least a couple of other interesting incidents that took place that winter, and perhaps I should relate them before my narrative leaves the night crew period. I hope that relating these stories does not unduly distract from the theme of the book, i.e. *The Americanization of Alaska.*

I mentioned a few pages back that being sat upon (meaning 'delayed' in that previous context) by some of the administrative or managerial people at the district office would be a decidedly unpleasant experience. In particular there was one lady of extraordinarily prodigious dimensions. We on the night crew had all dealt with her personally once or twice because she had something to do with personnel.

One night during one of our infrequent break periods, we decided to go downstairs and put one of those extra-long tacks like an upholstery brad or a carpet tack on her chair. We placed it a little bit off center to be sure of hitting some flesh and added a small dab of glue to keep it in place and pointing upward. The tack was very nearly the same color as the cushion of her chair so it wasn't likely to be seen unless one was looking specifically for such a thing.

I didn't have an early class the next day, so I agreed to show up in her day crew area using some excuse that would put me in her office when she came to work. I did so, and in fact, I got there about ten or fifteen minutes before she did. I used some personnel-related reason for coming.

When she got there, I told her what my trumped-up reason

was for being there and while answering my question she plopped down into her chair with one of those mammoth cheeks falling directly onto our tack. She didn't say a word – nothing. Not only that, but when she grunted up to her feet for some reason, the tack was gone.

That evening, I related the whole incident to the night crew as I had agreed to do, and we all had a pretty good laugh about it. George would definitely not have approved, but he wasn't there. Actually, she was a pretty nice lady personality-wise, and I suppose that what we did was a little bit cruel. In the end, however, she didn't seem to even feel the tack, although if it fell out of her clothing later, I suppose she must have wondered where it came from.

One of the day crew people had a desk upstairs right next to our workspace, and he too was also unfortunate enough to be a victim of one of our practical jokes. As I recall, he was the only day crew member who worked up there. His name was T. Hugh. I don't know what the T stood for and, in keeping with my general practice here, I'm not going to use his last name. He had been a surveyor for the agency for many years, but at the time we knew him he was getting older and had become the district right-of-way agent.

Since T. Hugh was upstairs right next to our attic quarters, he was sort of out of touch with the other offices and probably because there was no one up there to talk to during the day he frequently fell asleep, and he was a prolific snorer. He also had a fancy intercom on his desk with which he could call any individual office in the building as well as any combination of offices, including all of them at once.

It was irresistible so we set T. Hugh's intercom to broadcast to every office in the building at maximum volume. Every noise he made, including the snoring, was heard by very nearly everyone in the building. I guess someone must have finally discovered the prank because after two months or so T. Hugh began locking the intercom keys, which was another feature of that particular device. Although someone must have guessed that it was us doing this while it was going on, we never heard anything about it.

We missed George a lot during that winter, even though we knew he wouldn't have allowed any of these pranks and practical jokes that we kept trying to pull off. None of those actions ever got us into any trouble, although they were admittedly childish – everyone has to do something childish now and then. Even if we had been revealed as the perpetrators, we probably wouldn't have suffered any punishment. However, things have changed a lot since then; in those days, we never took ourselves as seriously as people in the profession do today.

During the middle to late part of May, I had to make several overnight trips to Paxson, where Roxy was busy setting up the project office and familiarizing our new assistant project engineer with the project. His name was Henry, he was a registered engineer in Texas, and a graduate of the University of Texas.

All this running back and forth between Fairbanks and Paxson kept me from taking part in most of the non-academic events connected with the 1963 graduation ceremonies, although I made sure to attend the commencement ceremony in particular because that was where they handed out the diplomas. However, I was unable to attend much of anything else except a few off-campus parties, at least one of which Irene and I co-hosted at 2106 McCullam. It would have been nice to take a few days off after graduation and the accumulated stress of the six years leading up to it, but the Denali country was calling and my professional responsibilities forced me to respond and return to Paxson.

Chapter 3: Escaping the Dragon

This season Roxy, Henry, a guy named Dan (with his old Elkhound), and I shared a four-bedroom trailer that must have been at least forty feet long. Actually, it was pretty comfortable, but it might have been more so if it had been doublewide. At first Roxy had some concerns about having a dog in the trailer, but since Dan had brought his Elkhound, with which he was very close, and since the dog was well behaved and housetrained, and since neither Henry nor I had any objections, Roxy was sort of outvoted.

The contractor's project engineer, Roger, seemed to have really come out loaded for bear, so to speak, to greet the new construction season. We hadn't been on the job more than two or three days before he came over and told us that he wanted to have a meeting with us to discuss project procedures, whatever that meant. When we did sit down for his meeting, he told us, among other things regarding project management, that he intended to check our construction staking methods, calculations and information on the stakes at frequent, but irregular, intervals. I think he must have been taking some 'Management' classes during the off-season because although he was very sure of himself, everything he said somehow sounded like he was reading it out of a prepared text. Interestingly, I have since encountered a number of young engineers who sound like that, particularly if they have recently entered into a job with a modicum of responsibility.

We advised Roger that although his ideas might be part of the wave of the future and were probably valuable, we simply couldn't tolerate him going directly to the survey crew(s) to complain about any errors that he thought he might have found. He was to bring any such complaints to us in the office, and Henry or I would go out and look. When he said that coming back to the office might take too long and might delay the construction, we suggested that he keep his stake checking efforts far enough ahead of the construction to avoid problems like that.

At the time, we had no idea that he was germinating a strategy for creating uncertainty in our administration of the project. This issue would lead to a few problems before we recognized Roger's real motives. I also realized later that Roger was using his new awareness of the increasingly prevalent management philosophies in the hope of making us feel inadequate and anxious to learn these new procedures from him; thereby allowing him to maneuver us into a vulnerable position. I think he was probably tailoring these increasingly popular management principles to put us at an initial disadvantage. In any case, it didn't work and his efforts to explain his ideas actually made the whole thing sound ridiculously overcomplicated, and even a little childish. Hopefully, he has matured significantly since then. Incidentally, none of our surveyors, inspectors or anyone else on the agency payroll *ever once* saw him checking out stakes on the job.

Up until then, all this new administrative bullshit had, I thought, been confined to office procedures and was being promoted by the well-dressed management types who wouldn't know a front-end loader from a dump truck, and was thus relatively harmless in the real world. Having Roger bring it all up in a specific construction project context was scary. Things were beginning to get serious; the management dragons were now apparently trying to introduce their arcane and unnecessary nonsense into the actual construction process where production *must* be of primary importance. If this trend continued, as it ultimately did, this crap would soon no longer be merely an academic question of management philosophy. Important projects could be brought completely to a standstill by all these idiotic bureaucratic and management procedures.

Now it was finally starting to become evident; we were in the first stages of intentional and total control by people who were pitifully ignorant of the real-world goals and methods of the engineering and construction professions. The process that brought us to this point had been so calculated and so insidious that we hadn't even known what was happening to us until it was too late.

This first meeting continued and Roger then brought up a subject that gave us our first firm indication that there was at least one project 'procedure' about which he seemed not to have even a *basic* understanding. He started by requesting that we not send our Fairbanks office any of our monthly progress/payment estimates until we had given him a chance to review them and check the numbers in detail, comparing them to his own records. We had no objection to letting him check our estimates, but not in such detail that it would delay us in sending the documents to the district office. We tried to tell him of the deadline requirements for invoice submittals and that any significant failure to comply would probably result in a serious delay in payment. Additionally, we pointed out that he had no survey records to support any differences between his excavation/embankment quantities and ours; truckload count records were neither sufficiently accurate nor allowed by specification as a basis for payment.

Roger was obviously distressed about what he termed our

'casual attitude' regarding progress estimates. This resulted in the first of many explanations to him that the monthly (interim) estimate figures were just that, *estimates*, and that the final payment would be based on precise measurements, would be checked and re-checked and would include all the retainage that had been held back during the project.

Roger was an early example of the encroachment, into the real world of construction, of the absurd concept of 'generic' management. We couldn't seem to get the idea through to him that consistent overestimates could well result in low (or in theory even negative) figures on the final estimate. In this instance I have to believe that Roger was sincere; he seemed unable or unwilling to grasp the concept of 'reasonable approximation', or that more precise work in preparation of the final estimate was intended to take care of any minor errors in quantity calculations during the course of the project.

People like that make me nervous. They seem to be the result of some kind of institutionalization wherein they are programmed to react in specific ways to specific stimuli, making it mentally impossible for them to even consider other opinions or points of view. Unhappily, many more of that type would show up as we sank deeper and deeper into the imported bureaucracy.

Henry, Roxy, and I were all present at Roger's introductory meeting, I guess because we all wanted to hear what he had to say. Except for the two subjects above, the meeting was pretty inane, but in my opinion, it was worthwhile both to let Henry get a feeling for the contractor's approach and for all three of us to meet, and 'take the measure of' the *new* Roger. Henry was a pretty intelligent guy, but as we left this meeting I got the sense that he was a little bit puzzled by some of Roger's bizarre remarks.

Of course, I introduced Henry to Don, the superintendent,

and the inspectors introduced him to all the foremen. When Henry asked me what I thought his specific duties should be, all I could say was that he should probably do the same things that I was doing whenever I wasn't doing them. In those days position descriptions for most jobs, even with the state government, weren't nearly as detailed as they are today. I guess we must have figured that if a man/woman was occupying a position of any responsibility, they would have been checked out previously by someone knowledgeable, and they would already know what to do. These days, of course, job descriptions are written out in exhaustive detail, although in reality they are frequently meaningless. They are often written by managers or bureaucrats who are fluent in 'governmentese' because they, or someone just like them, invented it. However, they rarely know anything at all about the details of the job in question.

I went into so much detail with this project description stuff because I want to show how things were handled at that time, and to provide a basis for comparison when we get to some of the more recent jobs.

Sometime between the end of September and the first part of October 1963 the decision was made to convert the entire Denali Highway from Paxson to Cantwell into a residency, which would be another agency administrative tier between the district and the individual Denali Projects. This was another typical example of the creeping bureaucratic effort to keep creating additional organizational and managerial control positions. The dragons were obviously setting us up to become another clone of the gazillion outside agencies charged with similar responsibilities.

Having been involved with every project that had taken place on this highway since 1953, except the actual survey and construction from Cantwell to the Susitna River, I felt that since there was to be such a position, I should unquestionably be the logical choice for the job of resident engineer over the entire highway. The job would involve responsibility for all maintenance and construction operations over the highway from Cantwell to Paxson. I was looking forward to it.

I was bitterly disappointed when the job went to a man named Ed who had been the engineer for the Nome sub-district during the past three or four years. Ed was a very personable fellow, and I found him to be very friendly, but when I was asked to familiarize him with the Denali Highway, it was just too much for me to deal with. He didn't even know where either Paxson or Cantwell were, the condition of the existing road, the soils in the area, the climate, or anything else about the Denali country in general or the highway route in particular. I felt, and still feel, that there was absolutely nothing to justify his being appointed over me as resident engineer for the Denali Highway. On top of all the other considerations, he was neither a college graduate nor a registered engineer – two accomplishments for which Irene and I had worked so hard.

Accordingly, I resigned from the BPR on or about October 15, 1963 and accepted a job as engineer/estimator for Green Construction, headquartered in Fairbanks. The chief engineer, and more or less the local boss, was a man named Mort who I had known from numerous previous jobs. As it turned out, taking the job with Green Construction was probably one of the best career moves I ever made. I was given the opportunity to see things from a contractor's point of view and to appreciate some of the problems *they* were regularly confronted with during the course of a project. I quickly realized that the bureaucratic and managerial crap that had so concerned me with the agency was simply not present within the *company* administration. That sort of thing was too expensive; most of the same tasks that supposedly required whole offices full of administrators, bureaucrats and managers with the agency were handled within the company by no more than two or three people. It was impressive; I took that impression with me when I left the company, and I haven't forgotten it.

The first two months or so I spent with Green Construction were taken up familiarizing myself with some upcoming potential projects and learning the company estimating procedures. Green had estimating 'factors' for just about everything, e.g. for a given number of estimated hours for a specific piece of equipment there were multipliers for tire replacements, engine maintenance, allowable depreciation and so on. Once the estimator decided on the necessary equipment as well as the crew and the number of working hours required for a particular work item on a bid schedule, the rest was pretty much "look up the records from past jobs and do some multiplying." There were records from many, many past jobs of all descriptions to draw from.

I had the opportunity to accompany Mort on several field inspections for jobs that were coming up for bid. The main reason for making such field inspections was to make sure of what sort of equipment might be necessary to do the work, and how long it might take.

There are only three things that I remember about most of these late fall trips: 1) There was only one inspection per job and only two men per inspection. We were expected to gather and agree upon all the information and data we needed during that single field inspection. 2) My estimates of time required were consistently 20% to 30% longer than Mort's, although in the event, mine were sometimes closer than his. 3) It was almost always colder than hell.

I can specifically remember staying in one of the cabins at the Forty-Mile Roadhouse about twenty-five miles south of Tok Junction when the stove stopped working at about eleven o'clock one night. We damn near froze to death before six o'clock the next morning. I think the temperature must have dropped to about twenty below that night, even in the cabin.

On January 13, 1964 Jacqueline Carol came to Irene and me. She was a beautiful baby. In fact, she was so beautiful that when she was a year or two old my mother borrowed her and took her to live in Yreka, California for a year or so. She has progressed from a beautiful baby to a beautiful woman, now with a fine, honorable husband and two little babies, who are no longer babies, of her own. Jacque (not 'Jackie') was a confirmation that God has blessed both Irene and I with intelligent, beautiful and, in so many ways, extraordinary children. Jacque has taken it upon herself to improve her station in life through advanced education, and like all our children, she has done it without help from anyone or anything; driven only by her own desire for self-improvement and her unselfish ambition. I will always be extremely proud of Jacque.

At the time I went to work for Green Construction the company already had a road construction job in progress running along the Alaska Railroad corridor between Lignite and Healy. I was sent there as project engineer for the company.

Lignite is nothing but a named location along the railroad about fifteen or twenty miles south of Nenana. At the time, the train never even stopped there unless someone flagged it down. I've been told that along with too many other things, the practice of allowing individuals to flag down the trains at isolated locations is no longer permitted. I suppose the Alaska Railroad is now about the same as any 'stateside' railroad – God help us.

There is a road at Lignite leading into the mountains west of the railroad; reportedly there had been (maybe still is) some prospecting up there for both coal and gold. There may also be some coal deposits east of the railroad near Lignite, but if there are, I've never heard much about them.

Nobody lived at Lignite, at least nowhere near the railroad.

There was only a sign that said 'LIGNITE' and usually some Scottish highlander cattle hanging around nearby. I don't know where they come from, but considering the horrific weather that descends on that area during the winter, they must be nuts or incredibly stupid to stay there by choice the whole time without hotfooting it someplace further south.

Unlike Lignite, Healy is an actual small community at the north end of the Nenana River Canyon and across the river from the Usibelli coal mine, an operating and I believe lucrative mine. I went to college with young Joe Usibelli, but we were never close friends. He enjoyed marching around and around the gymnasium in his ROTC uniform, which was an activity that never really caught my interest. I think he got a commission and served as an Army officer after his graduation.

The Alaska Railroad owned the whole community of Healy and the property it's built on, including the Healy Hotel, which offered the only lodging in town. I'm not sure, but I think that the restaurant in the hotel was also the only restaurant in town. The hotel had additional housing in an annex right next door and a bunkhouse about 200 feet away. No matter where one stayed in any of those facilities, particularly the annex, there was an all-night next-door symphony of clunking, clanking, banging, bumping, and thumping between railroad cars and engines. Except for Otto Lake about two miles from 'town', the Healy Hotel and its annex were all there was. Besides, the hotel was the outfit with whom the company had a room and board agreement.

Eloise and me at Otto Lake Lodge near Healy

This was not a reconstruction or improvement project. There was no previous real road through or to the area; the job was what we used to call 'pioneer' construction. That particular term makes the project sound a lot more dramatic than it actually was; it just means it was the first road through there. It was pretty routine work, usually with two scraper spreads involving average hauls of about 2000 feet and one or two (moving) excavator/truck operation(s) with haul distances between a half and one or two miles.

Other than relating stories back and forth to one another like the railroad crews did, there were very few distractions in the Healy area during the off hours. There was the bar at the hotel, but it was dark and gloomy most of the time and many of us sought out something a little more interesting at the Clear Sky Lodge bar and dance hall about ten miles north of the project.

The place was really nothing special, but it did have a comfortable bar (a 'lounge' – with tables, no less) and a dance floor. There was always a good and friendly crowd there on weekends. That's something else we can no longer be sure of, especially near a military base, in this case the Clear Air Force facility. Many of the newcomers (often military) who frequented the lodge liked to think that since they were now "legitimate residents of their 'Last Frontier'," they were empowered to wear guns and act like jackasses. After a few drinks, people like that can get really dangerous and the rising rate of violent crime in Alaska testifies to that danger. The rising crime rates is just one more stateside 'blessing' that Americanization, resulting largely from statehood and the oil rush, have brought us.

Even with such an amenity as Clear Sky Lodge, the Healy job was settling into enough of a routine that a change would be, and was, welcome. Providentially, a need arose on the company's Fox to Livengood (Elliot Highway) project, for which I was uniquely qualified among company employees. It was about August 1, and I was to witness firsthand a stark example of the stateside 'expertise' coming north to educate us.

Before meeting the project superintendent at Fox, a small community on the Steese Highway at the junction with the Elliot Highway about twenty miles north of Fairbanks, I reported to Mort at the Fairbanks office to find out what it was that he wanted me to do. Apparently, the state (DOT & PF) survey crew had gotten completely bogged down in the process of setting construction stakes, and as a result our (Green's) construction operations would soon grind to a halt. Mort had already spoken to the state project engineer, a guy named Jim, and gotten the OK for me to step in as a sort of temporary party chief until the slope staking was done far enough ahead of the construction to avoid holding up our operations.

At this point, I should explain that a 'slope stake' is a stake set at the point where the toe of the fill slope or the top of the cut slope will be when the completed road is constructed according to the plans and specifications. Setting them properly requires some field calculations during the progress of the work and a good understanding of the geometrics involved. The slope stakes are set after clearing and prior to earthwork construction on both sides of the proposed road at fifty or hundred-foot centerlines intervals.

Upon arrival at the project, I found out quickly why their survey crew hadn't gotten any further than they had. It was so obvious that, quoting George Patton upon his taking over 2nd Corps in Tunisia, "A blind man could see it in a minute." The story needs a little background to illustrate the problems of the survey crew, and although I'm trying hard to keep these narratives to a minimum, I'm going to relate it here. It shows the problems with imported incompetence that had begun to show up shortly after statehood.

The state's project engineer (Jim) should have been arrested; he would have been if incompetence and inattention to his responsibilities were illegal. He had come to Alaska around the time of statehood, probably as a result of the unfortunate nationwide media attention we were getting at the time; the same reasons that *many* such bozos began showing up at that time. Nobody really knew what his expertise was when he worked 'outside', but apparently he didn't bring it up north with him since up to then no one had been able to identify it. Maybe the new 'Managers' were impressed by his *Curriculum Vitae,* if he wasn't too refined to show it in public.

When I first went to visit him, he started the conversation by telling me that, in an *extremely* liberal interpretation of the specifications, our superintendent had promised to have paneling up, cooking facilities installed and several other improvements completed in his office 'building' (shack) by that time. I could hardly believe what I was hearing. His crew was out there stumbling around in the dirt trying to figure out how to do what they were supposed to do and here was this incompetent jackass jabbering about paneling, plumbing and stuff like that. Any contractor other than Green would have turned him in then and there.

When asked about the procedures and methods being used by his slope staking crew, he didn't seem to know what I was talking about. He kept bringing up the business of finishing his office in accordance with some sort of plan that he had in mind, and he might have even insinuated that if it wasn't done soon, he might find it necessary to hold up our next progress payment. I had observed other examples of malfeasance, incompetence and indifference on the part of agency officials, but this was by far the most blatant I had ever seen. Jim didn't seem to be the slightest bit embarrassed by his obvious incompetence or the slightest bit worried about his glaring misuse of influence to demand things like finishing his office quarters. I've forgotten what state Jim left to come up north, but wherever it was, either they had very low employee standards or he had scooted away under a pretty serious cloud. On the other hand, maybe he was just a born grifter who figured that, Alaska being a relatively new state, he could get away with the kind of behavior he was exhibiting here.

Before I left the project, the slope stake crew had become one of the best that I ever worked with. Within about a month and a half of my arrival we had finished correctly setting out slope stakes for the entire project, and the crew had become really expert at what they did. The key man on any slope staking crew is the rodman, and the man that we had doing that task on this project turned out to be really outstanding. I felt pretty happy, even proud, that I had helped bring out the real capabilities of this crew. I hope they stayed together and that they had the opportunity to demonstrate their collective skill on some other projects and for some other project engineer who understood what they were doing and appreciated how good they were.

The project kept going until late in October, and I stayed with the state survey crew during the entire time, although it got pretty damn cold before we finally left the job and moved back into town. After that, the snowbirds went south and the residents burrowed in for another winter.

During the winter of 1964/65, I made several trips with Mort to look at potential projects that might be coming up for bid within the next year or so. It occurred to me at the time that virtually all the jobs Green was then doing in Alaska were for the DOT & PF (Highway Department). However, the oil boom changed the picture for everyone in the state, including Green Construction. The company eventually became included in some sort of joint venture involving work on the Trans-Alaska Pipeline. I don't recall hearing much about Green Construction in connection with highway work after that.

There were other jobs accomplished during my time with the

company. We were the successful bidder for the reconstruction and pavement overlay of the Alaska Highway from the Little Tok River, about twenty-two miles north to Tok Junction, and I was again assigned as company project engineer for the job. I got down there sometime during the last week in May or the first week in June 1965.

The Tok River country is classic interior Alaska. It is Athabaskan country and the influence of the ancient people can be felt everywhere if one is sensitive to it. I can't really describe what the feeling is, but it was always there, even during a modern construction project.

The last time I went through Tok there didn't seem to be much development going on. Maybe they have so far escaped the creeping changes from down south and if so, I hope they can keep it that way, although I fear that the migrating dragons must eventually triumph.

The contract for the Tok job required the digging out and leveling of frost-heaved sections in the existing asphalt surfacing, removing, processing and relaying the existing pavement where necessary, the widening and paving of shoulders to meet existing standards, and finally a two or three-inch asphalt leveling course over the entire roadway. This was a job tailored for Green Construction, a pioneer in Alaskan paving work. It was no surprise that we were the lowest bidder since we had the largest accumulation of experience in the state in this kind of work, not to mention a large yard full of paving equipment parked at Tok Junction.

The superintendent at Tok was Joe, the same man I had worked for at Healy. I was glad to see him because I knew he was a real expert at what he did, and that he did it without a lot of extra talk or acting like some kind of big shot. Of course, I was also always pleased with the opportunity to work with Joe because of what I could learn from him. I think that Joe, as well as Harvey at the Delta River, were two of the first men to demonstrate for me what being a real expert was all about, not just on their own jobs but in several other instances as well. It definitely had *nothing* to do with meetings, memoranda or meaningless regulations. The value of such expertise can easily be strangled by such things, which were even then becoming more and more pervasive within the state administration.

The Highway Department folks had a nicely equipped soils/materials laboratory on the Tok project, but it was manned by personnel with virtually no experience in soils or materials work. They were devoted, hardworking young people, and they were anxious to learn. However, getting test results might have been a little faster if the agency had sent out someone with more lab experience. I tried to offer as much help as I could. Of course, by then the state folks had adopted regulations limiting the amount of hands-on help that could be accepted from the contractor's engineer. This new 'enlightened' state administration was starting to demonstrate an unfortunate tendency to keep shooting themselves in the foot by adopting new construction policies and regulations written by someone who knew *nothing* about the subject. Our role in helping the survey crew for the Fox-Livengood project was unprecedented and, as far as I know, has never been repeated.

One of the most pleasant and instructive activities (for me) at Tok was accompanying Joe when he was looking for suitable locations to set up the crusher plant or to take gravel. I have to bring Joe into this discussion whenever I can because he was so representative of the Alaskan heavy construction men I deeply admired and respected at the time and who have now virtually disappeared. I really don't know if he took me along with him during those searches because he knew that I had some soils experience or if he just wanted the company. In either case, the result was that I was able to use my knowledge of gravel materials and at the same time learn a great deal about some of the non-academic aspects of construction project operations.

I wonder why there are so few Joes anymore. It seems like the combinations of Americanization, statehood and the loads of administrative crap that came with them, as well as the increasing political and bureaucratic influences and interferences caused those people to just sort of fade away, wraith-like, into the fog of memory.

Sometime during the first week in October, we closed down the Tok job for the winter and went back to town because this was, after all, primarily a paving job and there are practical air-temperature limitations for putting down asphalt.

For some reason Irene and the kids weren't with me while I was on this job; I almost went nuts missing them and drove back into town to see them whenever I could. When I got back to Fairbanks on one such trip I read an ad in the *News-Miner* requesting applications for the position of Fairbanks city engineer. I applied for the job and was accepted.

I remember only one thing in particular about the day I was offered the Fairbanks job. I was in Green's office; Mort was there and so was another company project engineer named Cole (first name). I recall that Cole said something like, "Let's get some company publicity by letting the newspaper know that one of our engineers has accepted the job of city engineer in Fairbanks." He then left for the job where he was working; I think it was at Soldotna on the Kenai Peninsula. On the way, he ran off the road near Harding Lake, about forty-five miles south of Fairbanks, and was killed. We were told later that he had run into a roadside pond. He was apparently knocked out and then restrained from turning toward the surface by his seat belt. I wonder how they could tell all that after he was already dead. He reportedly drowned in less than three feet of water – God rest him. There is such a micro-thin veil between life and death that it sometimes seems incomprehensible.

When I went to work for the City of Fairbanks, the City Engineering Division (a division of the Public Works Department) was located a block or two south of Airport Way on Gillam Street in one of the fire department's district buildings. Through that same old fog of memory, I seem to recall that we occupied just a small portion of the space near the front of the building. It seems like the rest was taken up by a fire department crew or maybe a mobile police unit; I just remember that there were a lot of vehicles parked in and around the back half of the building. I met a lot of people during my tenure as Fairbanks city engineer and many of the Fairbanks old-timers are worth remembering because when they're gone, if they aren't already, it's not likely that today's Alaska can produce any more like them.

I hadn't been in this office more than a week or two before I got a visit from a sanitary engineer named Sage, and he had a guy called LeRoy in tow. Sage was a very distinguished and learned practitioner, and I was honored that he came to see us, although at the time I wasn't sure why. He seemed to want to talk about the city sewage treatment plant, which at that time was fairly new in both concept and construction. I didn't hesitate to tell him that I really hadn't had time to become familiar with most of the city facilities but that in a month or two I would enjoy going into some real detail about the subject.

He also introduced LeRoy, who worked for the uniformed part of the Public Health Service. LeRoy was wearing his uniform, which looked almost identical to a Coast Guard outfit except that there was no shield on the left sleeve. He had a couple of rows of impressive looking service ribbons over his upper left pocket like a genuine combat veteran. I asked him if he had been awarded those ribbons for entering and inspecting some particularly noxious sewage treatment plants. I don't remember what his reply was, if there was one. I only meant it as a passing remark, but Sage really cracked up over it, and it even came up frequently in conversations during the subsequent years I knew him.

Sage was one of the truly remarkable people that I have known over the years. He was superbly intelligent, not only in his chosen field of sanitary engineering, but over a wide range of subjects and disciplines. At one point I started, and almost finished, a graduate sanitary engineering course under his tutelage, but I failed to complete the paper that he required for the final grade. It was a show of complete irresponsibility on my part, and I felt, and still feel, that I really let him down because he really believed that I was capable of much more from an academic standpoint. By that time, however, I was still so fed up with school and graduate school that it gave me a stomachache just to think about it.

Anyway, I am where I am and Sage is where he is, wherever that is. I don't think that he's much older than me, so he's probably still alive. It would be good to see him again.

Sage was another of the extraordinary people who, before all the changes and the undesirable outside immigrants altered Alaska so irreversibly, seemed drawn to the state and who fit in so comfortably while they were there. For some inexplicable reasons, many of *them* also seem to have disappeared. Where do such people go?

Downtown Fairbanks – Fifth and Cushman with City Hall on the left

I guess the fire or police folks must have wanted the rest of the floor space the engineering department was occupying in the building when I went to work. About four months after I started, we were moved to the bottom floor (not quite the basement) of the City Hall at Fifth and Cushman streets. It was a lot closer to downtown but also a lot more cramped Nonetheless, we got used to it, and after a few months we even grew to like it there – at least I did.

Fairbanks is just about at the southern limit of deep permafrost in the lowland interior, although annual frost penetration is often more damaging to underground utilities and surface improvements than permanently frozen ground if the permafrost can be preserved. I have been told that in the Fairbanks area permanently frozen ground will sometimes be established *behind* south facing buildings where there was none previously; demonstrating the marginal nature of the permafrost in the area. Despite such things and despite the periodic extreme cold 'snaps' of the winters, Fairbanks is a city of old, established families and a long-time history to a far greater extent than Anchorage.

Of course, frozen ground is a matter of utmost importance primarily to those concerned with the design, construction and maintenance of both municipal sewer and underground water lines. Very few people are really interested in sewer or water systems until they fail and the sewer backs up into the toilet, or someone turns the faucet and no water comes out. However, it should be noted that both the sewer and water systems in Fairbanks are unusual in many respects and even unique in a few. Nonetheless, even the professionals in the field sometimes forget that except in some villages in the arctic the bulk of the systems in Alaska are underground, and they are rarely seen – out of sight, out of mind, as they say. I'd like to relate one case in point.

It happened that LeRoy, the uniformed Public Health Service LeRoy who had accompanied Sage when they visited my office, had recently bought a new home in a residential development which one of our new sewer line extensions was intended to serve. One day while visiting the project, I saw him mowing his new lawn that he had apparently just planted. I didn't know that he had moved in there, but I was glad to see him because I assumed that since he worked for the PHS he probably knew something about sewer lines and I could elicit his opinion about our project.

I attracted his attention and after all the greetings and the 'how've you been' questions etc., I asked him what he thought of our project. He told me it looked pretty good to him, but added that the little float ball in the back of his toilet kept getting stuck. I couldn't tell if he was joking or not so, in case he wasn't, I let the subject drop.

Although we had been a state for five or six years this was still sort of a transition period between the old Alaska and what was yet to come as a result of a number of factors, *including* statehood and the increasing national interest resulting from it. As I've noted before and probably will again, all the attention and the political vacuum that occurred drew a lot of people north, many of whom were undesirable in that they were opportunistic lawyers, politicians, bureaucrats and 'Management' leeches. Naturally, they brought a lot of their 'baggage' with them in the voluminous form of unnecessary administrative nonsense; the last thing we needed in a new state just getting on our feet, so to speak, from the 'body blow' of statehood. Many of these newcomers acted like they were there to take over and educate the savages (us) and behaved so officiously and imperiously that they immediately antagonized those of us who were long-time residents.

One of these opportunists was a man named Charles. He wasn't Chuck or Charley, he was 'Charles', upon which he insisted if you were privileged enough to use his first name. He was one of the most officious, arrogant horse's asses I have ever met, before or since, and I've met a lot of them. He was the general manager for the Fairbanks utilities system while I was there, and he personified every nasty remark I ever made about 'Managers'. He said some unbelievable things in support of his apparent belief that he was some kind of managerial genius, even though Municipal Utilities was constantly coming to the City of Fairbanks seeking financial bailouts.

At one point, I learned that a lady named Karen in the accounting section of the city administrative staff had earned a bachelor's degree in mathematics, yet here she was sitting at no permanent desk working at a dead-end job along with about fifteen or so of the typical bean-counters for a minimum wage.

A mathematics degree is no small thing, so I immediately began an interdepartmental campaign to have her transferred to engineering at a significantly higher pay scale. There was a lot of opposition, more than I had anticipated. The accounting folks objected to losing her, which I could understand, but Charles also objected, apparently because the city's accounting section also did the rate calculations for Municipal Utilities.

After I had secured Karen's transfer Charles came to me[22] and demanded – demanded yet, I couldn't believe it – that I not offer Karen any more salary than she was already making. I didn't even reply; I just left his office.

Karen was transferred to a position in the engineering division that paid almost twice what she was making in accounting. I suppose Charles was a little upset about the outcome of all that – good! I don't think we had many people like Charles around before statehood and the oil boom. In the old days, Alaskans just didn't put up with people like that.

Charles and his imperious behavior notwithstanding, the city administration in Fairbanks had at that time noticeably but

---

[22] Actually he 'called me to his office' as he put it like some kind of Caesar.

perhaps unconsciously escaped inundation by the absurd and overdone administrative procedures creeping northward. I'm not sure why that was the case then, but since the federal government has become more and more of a participant in municipal affairs, Fairbanks has probably by now also fallen victim to the modern 'Managers' and their bureaucratic fellow dragons.

There were several things I was able to do as Fairbanks city engineer that I still feel pretty good about.

Since seeing some brief demonstrations at a conference in Eastern Washington years ago, I had been anxious to try out the concept of cement-treated base under a chip seal for municipal streets and/or low-volume roads. The Fairbanks city manager, Wally[23], had so far been pretty tolerant of almost all my ideas regarding street improvements because he recognized and understood the local problems. Unlike today's 'Managers', Wally was genuinely concerned with and knowledgeable about the real world of action rather than the non-substantive nonsense that most 'Managers' think drives progress and production. Although the director of public works was at first a little hesitant, he finally came around, and I got the go-ahead to set up a demonstration project.

We looked at several streets as candidates for the first soil cement project and finally settled on Barnette Street, between First and Fifth Avenues, as the first job. We decided to start at Fifth and work north toward First. For our initial effort, we waited for a really dry day following at least three other dry days, cleaned and dried out a twelve-yard dump truck, attached a chip spreader and loaded the truck with dry cement. Obviously we felt that dryness was a critical factor, perhaps to a greater extent than it actually was. Everything finally fell into place and away we went!

---

[23] Not Hickel – God forbid.

Within ten seconds or less of the moment the cement hit the spreader, a *huge* cloud of cement dust billowed out over about a four block area in all directions from our dump truck. We finally got a distributor truck to spray a little water through the cement cloud, but it took almost two hours to do that, and since the technical integrity of the project demanded that we not stop regardless of the dust, the problem got even worse during that period.

The public response to what had happened was far more vocal than justified by the actual event, but it was short-lived. We had the entire dust problem under control within three or four hours of the beginning of the project, and the mixing, compacting and rolling of the street was comfortably completed within the next two days.

The street set up solidly, and I've been told became one of the most stable in the whole city in resisting potholing. Most projects incorporating new concepts and/or techniques encounter more or less spectacular problems with their first attempts, and ours was no exception. At that time there was still a basic difference between the reaction to our problem in Fairbanks and what we would have encountered in the outside states. We had no accusatory demands for explanations, no threatened lawsuits, no claims of respiratory damage and no irate letters to the editor, as would certainly have been the case down there and now probably in Alaska.

Despite the initial public reaction to our efforts, there were still enough of the 'good ol' boys' around Fairbanks to see the humor in the event, and we were soon the object of a lot of good-natured teasing rather than mean-spirited criticism. We laughed along with everyone else, and it was very gratifying to be assured that the Alaskan attitude was still alive in Fairbanks. Alas, we were still too naïve to sense that we would all too soon become swamped with a tidal wave of Charles's (of Municipal

Utilities) clones.

Sometime in the fall of 1966, the City/Borough of Juneau advertised for applications for the position of director of public works. Engineering registration and a college degree were called out as two of the requirements, and it appeared to be primarily an engineering position, although not specifically titled as such, so I traveled down there to talk to the Juneau Council.

My interviews with the folks in Juneau went pretty well and after a day or two of waiting, I was offered the job. I should have accepted immediately, but I wanted to talk to Irene first so before I said OK, I called her and asked her to come down to Juneau so we could talk it over. After all, the education and registration that qualified me for the position were as much a result of her efforts as of mine.

Juneau Airport – Posing with mother-in-law and dead polar bear

Before she got there, I received a call from George, my old night crew boss. He had been appointed director of public works for the state, and he wanted me to think about the job of director of aviation, a position that was second level down from the governor and headquartered in Anchorage. This made the decisions more complicated, and it seemed even *more* critical that I talk to Irene about it, so I called a second time and asked her again to please come down to Juneau without delay.

When she did get there, we discussed the matter at length and decided that it was best for our future to take the director of aviation position. As I look back on it over the years and consider everything that has happened since then, I think that, all things considered, I should have taken the Juneau job.

I will perhaps never escape the feeling (right or wrong) that Irene's thoughts in the matter were influenced by her tendency to seek association with people thought of as big shots, and that she may have seen the Division of Aviation job as falling into that category. I think she gets that from her father. In any case, after she and I reached our decision I called George and told him that I was prepared to take the director of aviation job beginning January 1, 1967.

I want to add a few more words about the City of Fairbanks because I fear that the town I knew then is no longer there, and that many of the people who made it the way it was aren't there anymore either. Much of the soul of the city may also have disappeared with them and others like them.

I must admit that I felt a little bit emotional about leaving my job with the city. Fairbanks is a city of optimists; there are (or were) a surprising number of people there who were involved with what would be called 'crackpot' schemes anywhere else. They were not crackpot schemes, they were dreams; and those who dreamed them were not crackpots, they were dreamers, the kind of people with the guts and imagination to shape our society. They're gone now, sucked up into the shadow world created by over-administration, management, and bureaucracy.

We had a man named Bob in the Engineering Division who had drawn up detailed plans for planting about a gazillion acres of tomatoes and covering them with clear plastic to let in the sun and keep out the cold. He would, he said, then just wait for them to ripen and start raking in the monetary fruits of his labor. I don't know if Bob's dream ever became a reality, but I doubt it. There *are* a lot of sunny days in the Tanana Valley, and if the cold could be filtered out and the heat could be kept in, perhaps the sunlight *could* provide sufficient nutrients for the plants to do whatever plants do with sunlight in the more temperate areas of the country. However, I seriously doubt if the clear plastic could provide enough insulation to keep the plants from freezing solid during the Fairbanks winter when the sunlight is very limited. Maybe I'm wrong, and I hope so for Bob's sake. At the time I started referring to him as 'Tomato Bob' but not to his face. The Tomato Bobs have faded away too, perhaps discouraged by the stateside tendency to abandon projects when faced by undeniable cold, hard facts.

Perhaps that instinctive Alaskan optimism is partly what keeps people staying in Fairbanks. Maybe in deep winter their sub-conscious or heart-of-hearts or whatever, keeps telling them that nothing can really be this bad, and that soon there will surely be a permanent change for the better, even though they *really* know the climate won't actually change much during their lifetime. Still, such observations don't square with the fact that there are a number of families in town who have been there for several generations and wouldn't live anywhere else. Go figure.

Our chief surveyor, party chief and chief of parties for the Engineering Division was a man named Amos. He had been there a long, long time before I got there, probably since before dirt, and he was a damn good surveyor. He was one of the 'old breed' type surveyors – the kind who not only knew all the theories and such, but also how to use the tools, how to do the work and how to make the survey compatible with the project. Sadly, those kinds of surveyors are disappearing fast. Pretty soon, there won't be any real surveyors left at all, only theorists and electronic technicians. Anyway, Amos wasn't restricted to survey duties alone, he was also the building inspector and sometimes acted as inspector on the contract jobs, engendering a certain amount of trepidation on my part.

Amos had a steel rod that he carried with him all the time when inspecting construction jobs. It was approximately six or eight feet long, pointed at one end with a little eight or ten-inch welded-on handle about two or three feet from the other end. He swore up and down that he could determine the percentage compaction of any contractor-placed embankment or backfill merely by pushing the pointed end of his rod into the imported and compacted material. Presumably, it was not necessary that he be informed of the laboratory 'Proctor' densities for any of the materials he tested with his steel rod.

Without going into too much detail, I should explain that the percentage figures result from a comparison of the density (in pounds per cubic foot) of the contractor-placed/compacted material in the field with a standard sample of the same material compacted to optimum ('Proctor' – I think it's named after the originator of the method) density at optimum moisture content in the laboratory. I'm pretty sure that Amos never understood any of that "stuff" (his term), and I'm also pretty sure that he didn't know what the 'percentage' was a percentage of. There are standard methods prescribed for determining these densities because unless everyone is doing it the same, it doesn't mean anything. These methods are written into the specifications for virtually every state or city in the U.S. as well in the standard methods manuals of the ASTM (American Society for Testing Materials). *None* of the accepted methods include poking a steel rod into the embankment.

Amos refused to recognize any of these standard methods. I even loaned him copies of the relevant ASTM manuals from my own library, but although he thanked me very much, I'm sure he never read them. I think he regarded all that "stuff" as just unnecessary nonsense invented by some overeducated jerk who didn't know *anything* about actually working in the field.

I always had this vision of being hauled into court by a lawyer for some contractor that Amos had shut down because his rod told him that the contractor's backfill compaction was inadequate. I could almost hear the contractor's attorney (coached by someone else who actually knew what they were talking about). "And could you tell us, Mr. Harman, how your agency determined that my client was not within the specifications with regard to backfill compaction?"

And me replying, "Well, our inspector poked a steel rod into the backfill and he can tell by how it feels if it's fully compacted or not."

Ah well, thankfully a lawsuit like that never happened, at least not while I was there. I miss Amos because he was so representative of the Alaskan 'irregulars' of the time. Have all the Amoses faded away too?

I can't leave the subject of Fairbanks without mentioning Tommy's Elbow Room again, a bar on the east end of Second Avenue. It was by far the favorite hangout for most of the over twenty-one, or those who could convince Tommy that they were over twenty-one, students at the University of Alaska. Tommy's was the base for our Christmastime antics with Stanley the Barber that I wrote about earlier. That sort of thing was probably a little extreme as an example of the good times we had there, but it was by no means an isolated incident.

Tommy, the owner of the place, had been a mining engineering student at the U. of A., although I don't know if he completed his requirements for a degree. Whenever we asked about it, he would tell us that he had indeed gone into mining and had set up his dredge (meaning the bar/lounge) right there on Second Avenue.

As usual with any of the 'good ol' boy' bars, there was a cadre of regulars who could be found at the Elbow Room whenever they had a spare moment. I was part of that crowd of about eight or ten – maybe a few more from time to time. We had a table that was more or less 'reserved' for us, sort of tucked into a corner near the far end of the bar. The atmosphere was extremely comfortable, sort of a like a very close-knit family. Unfortunately, I was not perceptive or sensitive enough to see how it was already damaging the relationship between Irene and me. Perhaps this was part of the background that may have driven her to seek other companionship, if in fact that was the case.

I've been told that since I lived there, the Elbow Room has turned into sort of a 'dive' with the usual fights and unsavory people who frequent such places. I guess another era must pass, as they always do.

The year I left the city was the centennial year, celebrating a hundred years since the purchase of Alaska; derided at the time as 'Seward's Folly'. In preparation for the event, the City of Fairbanks built a sort of theme park with a small replica of an old-time railroad running from one end to the other, a full-sized reconstruction of part of one street of the old city as it was during the gold rush, and an old riverboat tied up along the banks of the Chena River next to the park. In order to be ready for the centennial celebrations the work was done during the summer and fall of 1966 while I was still there. It was a well-done project. The buildings that were used to reconstruct the old town were actual buildings from various parts of town that had been built during the gold rush and rescued from the urban renewal zealots. They were fixed up and moved to the park, where they looked a lot better than they had for the last seventy-five years. I think that the cost of all this was somewhat offset by generous funding assistance from the state.

'Alaskaland' – Originally Centennial Park in Fairbanks

For Fairbanks, the project sort of served a dual purpose; it was, of course, a very credible memorial project for the centennial, and additionally, moving all those old buildings constituted what amounted to an early de facto urban renewal project, except that no one got moved out of their home. Most of the overall design work was done by architectural consultants who are pretty much like engineering consultants except that they usually don't write dimensions on anything. The project has served as a city run amusement park since the end of the centennial year.

The city engineering division was charged with the responsibility for design and construction inspection of the entire parking facility for the project. I would like to say that I recognized the necessity for some relatively intensive pre-construction sampling and testing of the foundation material under the area, but I didn't. This lapse of engineering judgment was my fault. The end result of my negligence was a catastrophic failure of the parking lot surface with heaving, settlement and 'birdbaths' of up to three inches in depth all over the place. The only redeeming statement that I can offer is that I made no excuses or efforts to place the blame on anyone else. After the failures became evident, I think that I apologized to both Wally, the city manager, and to my previous titular boss Ed, the director of public works, even though I no longer worked there. I'm not sure whether I thought that I was doing the honorable thing or if I just realized that there was no way to get around the responsibility. If my memory is faulty and I didn't actually make those apologies, at least I meant to.

That's another thing that came to Alaska right after statehood, probably imported by the vagrant politicians and 'Managers' who swarmed in. They brought with them an impressive repertoire of verbal gymnastics crafted to escape responsibility for virtually anything that didn't go well, despite any previous predictions or promises of success and benefit. The naïve Alaskans, including me, were not familiar with such legitimate-sounding deceptions and we were duly impressed. No more, we now have our own share of genuine, homegrown political grifters.

Working for the City of Fairbanks began a sort of basic change in my attitude about my profession and where engineers should fit into the overall scheme of things. Prior to this position, my thinking had been almost entirely project-oriented. That is, I looked at events around me only in terms of how they might affect our project. After a year or so with the city, my outlook (somewhat to my surprise) began to change, and I started considering how *our* projects might be affecting the overall picture instead of the other way around. This new attitude has stayed with me ever since and, I hope, has enabled me to see my own profession in a more realistic perspective than one carries out of college. Despite my satisfaction with the Fairbanks job, it was now time to go on to something new and, as it turned out, more challenging in a lot of ways – not all of them susceptible to engineering logic.

During the entire process of job interviews and such with the Juneau Municipality, I had kept the Fairbanks city manager and the director of public works fully informed about what I was doing. I hope that they understood that I was not seeking out these other jobs, but that I was only responding to advertised or offered opportunities for what I hoped was a move up the professional ladder, so to speak. It has become clear to me since then that what we initially think of as a step up may in fact turn out to be something quite different.

In any case, I was now about to embark on a job that opened my eyes to a lot of non-engineering and sometimes unsavory realities and imported political stratagems that were beginning to pollute our traditional Alaskan values and attitudes.

Along the Tok Cutoff (Glenn Highway). Looking at the north side of the Coast Range.

Gastineau Channel/Douglas Island from Juneau Dock

With Ivar on the Alaskan coast

Cooling off – Ivar the dog at Mendenhall Glacier

Totem Park Near Ketchikan

Hammer Slough, downtown Petersburg – Not as bad as it looks

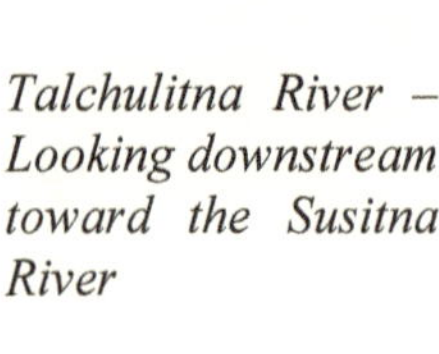

Talchulitna River – Looking downstream toward the Susitna River

Mendenhall Glacier /Mendenhall Lake Sister-in-law Angie

Picnic site and viewpoint south of Cache Creek, B.C.

Glacier Point (Lion head) from the Glenn Highway – 115(+/-) miles east of Anchorage

1964 earthquake damage – Portage

Dawson City/Yukon River

Prince Rupert B.C. From Top of Tram

Deep winter in Valdez – Street scene circa 1937

East side of Wrangell Narrows – four or five miles south of Petersburg

Old mining operation – Klondike region

Yukon River Ferry

Mountain sheep seen from Alaska Highway (Eating AC Pavement perhaps)

Glenn Highway – Approaching Glacier Point (Lion Head) from the east

Denali Highway – MacClaren River Valley, Landmark Gap

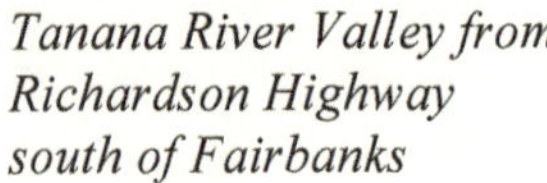

Tanana River Valley from Richardson Highway south of Fairbanks

Shrine of St. Theresa – North of Juneau

MacClaren River Valley, Denali Highway 40 (+/-) miles west of Paxson

Alaska Highway – Watson Lake information sign. Fred's there too.

Watson Lake "Sign Forest" – As mentioned in the sign above

View of frozen Tanana River – South of Fairbanks

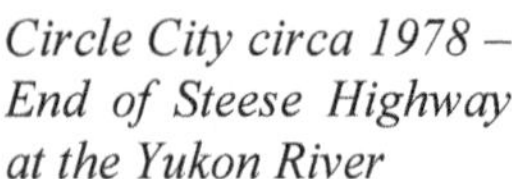

Circle City circa 1978 – End of Steese Highway at the Yukon River

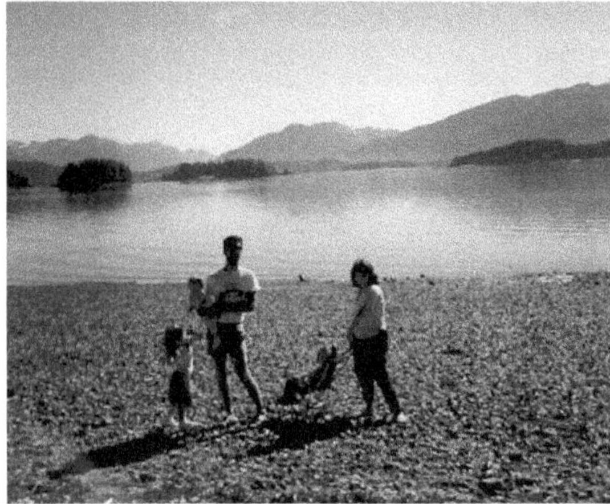

Kids and grandkids at Auke Bay Recreation Area northwest of Juneau

Talchulitna Homestead Survey – Supreme headquarters

Sons of Norway Lodge Meeting/Social Hall – Downtown Petersburg

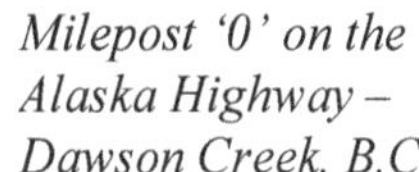

Milepost '0' on the Alaska Highway – Dawson Creek, B.C.

Looking south down Gastineau Channel from downtown Juneau. Mine Tailings Dump (from old Alaska-Juneau [A.J.] Hard-Rock Goldmine) in view.

PART IV
AWAKENINGS

Chapter 1: The Dragon Feeds

Irene and I flew back from Juneau to Anchorage on one of the old twin-tail Constellation airplanes (the 'Connie') that Cordova Airlines was still using at the time. As a matter of fact, I was in the air when there was an incident involving that airplane at the Nome Airport.

An old 'Connie' was parked on the apron right in front of the terminal after unloading some passengers and waiting to take off with a few more. All of a sudden the landing gear collapsed. I was told the airplane just sort of "sat down." Fortunately no one was on board, but suppose it had happened during takeoff or landing? I think the incident prompted at least Cordova Airlines to closely inspect their whole fleet – I hope so.

Thank God I didn't know about it at the time so it didn't concern me during that first flight from Juneau to Anchorage. In fact, not much of anything concerned me because I was pretty well doped up. I didn't like flying even then because it scared the hell out of me, and it still does.

Despite such misgivings, I traveled by air on my way back from Juneau to Anchorage to take up the duties of director of aviation for the State of Alaska. After I got established, and more or less used to and familiar with the division and the inherent problems, I think I must have spent at least a couple of days a week in airplanes of various sizes flying all over Alaska from one airstrip to another. It was necessary to fly around the state to discharge the responsibilities of the job, but I never got used to it or grew to enjoy it as some folks do. In view of such a dislike of flying, the reader might wonder why I had been offered (or had accepted) the job as director of aviation. Contrary to what one might think, the position (or the division) had little to do with airplanes or flying. The agency mission was the construction and maintenance of airports and airport facilities throughout the state.

When I got to Anchorage, George was already there, and he called together all the ADA (Alaska Division of Aviation) people in the Anchorage area, introduced me and said something to the effect that we were going to move ahead to accomplish things that had not been accomplished during the previous administration…blah, blah, blah. It was the kind of bullshit I wasn't used to hearing from George, and it was decidedly out of character for him.

I had no idea what he meant about the things that weren't accomplished during the previous administration; that's how naïve I was at the time. However, I was sure that at some point, the chronic complainers that always infect the ranks of government outfits would let me know about that; along with all their other individual gripes from just about every conceivable point of view.

The whole discussion didn't sound at all like the George that I had known; it was too full of platitudes and rah-rah nonsense to be really genuine. It certainly didn't fit into the mold of our old straightforward Alaskans who, regrettably, were now beginning to fade ever more quickly into the past.

During the meeting, I was still largely under the influence of the sedating medication that I had taken to calm my nerves in preparation for flying to Anchorage. The other attendees must have thought that George had jumped the track in making such a choice as this obviously punch-drunk kid for director of aviation. I was only thirty-two years old; the youngest man ever to hold that position, before or since. I can't be sure, but I think this period may have opened a portal into a new phase of my life. Such things are rarely evident at the time they happen. Irene stayed in Anchorage with me for a few days and then flew back to Fairbanks on some big four-engine airplane that I think was one of the last propeller-driven planes of that size in service.

In those days, Alaska Airlines had a route between Anchorage and Fairbanks that pretty much followed the route of the Alaska Railroad. I believe that they also had a scheduled stop at Cantwell, in the Alaska Range, maybe halfway between Anchorage and Fairbanks, but I don't think that they ever stopped there – maybe because nobody ever went there by air. I only rode on that flight once and noticed that, like the flight between Juneau and Whitehorse, the plane barely had time to reach cruising altitude, maintain that altitude for maybe ten or fifteen minutes and then begin the descent into Fairbanks. That flight was sometime during the Fairbanks flood in 1967 and there was no pretense about stopping at Cantwell – it wasn't even mentioned.

At the time I started with the ADA (Alaska Division of Aviation) the headquarters was located in a one-story building about a quarter-mile south of the terminal building. Since then the ADA has hired a bunch more 'Managers' and administrators and moved into a new two-story building on the other side of Airport Road.

The interior of the old building was divided into numerous small offices of various sizes with the largest ones being assigned to the 'Managers' of this and that who were already multiplying alarmingly. There were a lot of people occupying these offices, and it wasn't really clear to me what each of them was responsible for or why it needed to be done at all.

Although I hate meetings just for the sake of meetings, I called for one during which each of the 'Managers' was to explain to me what they did for the division and why they did it; everyone was notified in advance about the subject to be discussed. I think the action of calling for a meeting reassured everyone then working for the outfit; this meeting business was something they were used to and could understand.

They had no clue how rare and specific I intended to make all our subsequent meetings. If there is a reason for the staff of *any* organization to get together to discuss a problem, it should be an ad hoc sort of thing with only the staff members directly concerned with the problem (or problems) in attendance. There should be a specific agenda prepared and distributed at least one day prior to the meeting to minimize extraneous talk. It has been my experience that there are an *incredible* number of hours wasted in meetings about nothing in particular, but that are held just because they are scheduled on a weekly, monthly, or whatever, basis.

In the course of that particular meeting, I think I made it clear to begin with that all I wanted to know was what responsibilities each staff member was charged with, and what each of them did to discharge these responsibilities. There wasn't to be any discussion beyond that, and there wouldn't be another meeting until it was needed for some specific reason. It was also an opportunity to get some idea about the personalities of each of these principal staff members. I still remember the meeting well.

Perhaps it was because these staff members were Anchorage residents or perhaps it was because they were struggling to fit into the mold that the immigrant dragons[24] were casting and already insinuating into the Alaskan workplaces. In any case, I

[24] Read managers, lawyers, politicians, and bureaucrats.

just didn't feel comfortable with them early on. I had the vague feeling that they really didn't trust me or that they feared I was about to trash the division. Nonetheless, the meeting went ahead and, with only one exception, turned out a lot better than I envisioned.

It finally dawned on me that several of these guys were representative of the generation of technical leaders who were now going to step in and lead our profession, not to mention one of the working arms of the state, into the future. Although I was in the same age group (or younger) as the engineers at the meeting, I somehow felt much older. My background had been closely allied with the long-time Alaskans who were conditioned by reality to think in terms of product over process, and as a result of that background I felt much the same way.

As it turned out, there was only one staff member out of the whole bunch I had any substantive differences with. In fact, he and I were never fully comfortable with one another during much of the time I worked there, although with time he did finally adjust himself to some of my thinking and desired procedures.

His name was Glen, which is ironic because in a later job I ran into another 'Glen' with whom I also had a number of ongoing differences. This Glen was the administrative officer for the headquarters office in Anchorage. After the meeting, he immediately informed me that all these people at the table, and by implication everyone else in the office, actually worked under him, and that if I wished to give them any directions, I was to inform him first. He was a real career government employee, and I don't know whether he cared what I thought of him or not, but what he had just told me was precisely the wrong thing to say. I like to think that I don't anger easily, and that I'm pretty easygoing, but managerially minded people are, in my opinion, mostly useless anyway, and if they must hang around, they should just stay out of the way, keep their mouths shut, and let people get things done.

I was a little taken aback by the bluntness of Glen's remarks, and I didn't know how to respond at first. I finally decided to be just as blunt as he had been, even though it's always been hard for me to speak harshly to people. I told him that his description of who he *had been*, how important he *had been* and how everything *had gone* through him may have been true up to then, but that as of the close of business that day he was going to have a new job description. I went on to say that, from then on, *he* was working *for* all the section bosses (I refused to call them managers) in the office, and he was to take care of only procedural matters for them in response to *their* requests and in accordance with *their* instructions. He was no longer to interfere, or even be involved in, any decision-making or operational matters and particularly not in the formulation of any new regulations or procedural memoranda.

I really didn't know if I could make all that stick, but by now I was beginning to get really annoyed with Glen, and I was determined to put him in his place, as I saw it. This time *he* looked taken aback. I don't think he was used to being talked to like that, but I didn't care. He said something like, "We'll see about that," and, "I was here long before you came and I'll be here long after you leave."

I didn't doubt that for a *minute*, and I think I told him so. Glen was one of the very few long-time Alaskans I ever met who was into that 'Management' gobbledygook and its associated bogus procedural crap before it all began sneaking, and finally flooding, into our workplaces.

Later that same day, he came into my office in what almost seemed to be an apologetic mode and made one of the most bizarre suggestions that I'd ever heard. It bears repeating because it is a peek into the bureaucratic mentality that was then sneaking up on us.

It happened that the west wall of his office was also the east wall of the twelve-foot wide building entryway that led up to the receptionist's desk. Actually she wasn't really a 'receptionist' at all; she was there to give directions to visitors coming in from the parking lot – sort of an indoor traffic director. In fact, each of the 'Managers' had a receptionist of their own, something I was unable to correct during my short tenure there, although I tried. Anyway, Glen described this existing wall configuration and (this is where it gets weird, but I swear it's true) suggested that if we installed a one-way mirror in that common wall, he could see who was walking up to the 'receptionist's' desk and then call and alert me without letting them see him.

I thought he was joking, so I asked if he also thought it would be a good idea to install a button in his office controlling a trap door in front of the 'receptionist's' desk. That way, if the visitor looked undesirable to him he could just press the button, whereupon the questionable visitor would vanish into the basement or mechanical room or whatever was under there. He didn't even chuckle; he just left my office. I really didn't mean to offend him, only to go along with the 'joke'.

Happily, the way it turned out Glen seemed to mellow toward my new policies during the time that I was there. I suppose after I got fired he went back to his old ways just as he had predicted. However, in the interim he behaved pretty much in accordance with my instructions. He regularly helped all the section bosses find their way through the administrative jungle of state and federal bureaucracy and actually made himself pretty useful at times. He made it his task to keep everyone up to date with all the rules and regulations that seemed to change every time a gang of bureaucrats had a meeting. He was no longer at all officious or arrogant, at least while I was still with the division. In fact, unlike most 'Managers', he became a competent and productive employee; that is, as competent and productive as any administrator *can* be given the nature of their chosen 'profession'. Of course, there are some things, mostly involving direct action, that bureaucrats and managers are simply psychosomatically unable to do, but I must give Glen credit, he *did* try. Incidentally, he was correct in his prediction that he would be there long after I was (thankfully) gone. He probably retired in that same job. I wonder if good old Glen is still alive.

Unfortunately, the division was, after all, a government organization and because it was, the ubiquitous 'Managers' began popping up all over the place. They were usually typical unrepentant bureaucrats who constantly invented and proclaimed endless, and mostly irrelevant, impractical, and useless rules and regulations restricting just about any kind of progressive or productive action. Although I suspect there were always a few Glens in the existing organizational underbrush, in the old days, by far the majority of them didn't show up and begin asserting themselves until shortly after statehood. I think they were emboldened by the opportunistic and grasping lawyers and politicians who swarmed in on us to 'smash-and-grab' in a political and maybe a social sense.

There were several incumbent employees of the division who were supportive of my efforts to 'de-emphasize' the administrative, managerial and bureaucratic aspects of division operations. However, despite all our efforts to minimize those characteristics of the organization, we were largely unsuccessful.

Government agency methods always seem to take incredibly firm root in the minds and mentality of most long-term career employees. Unfortunately, many of the younger workers watching the way things are done start thinking that such conduct is normal and acceptable workplace behavior. As an example, Stuart, the Northern Alaska maintenance superintendent, had his secretary send a memo to Bill, the chief design engineer, regarding a gravel outcrop that he (Stuart) had seen near the site of an upcoming runway reconstruction project at one of the remote airstrips. I guess he dictated to her that Bill should send a design engineer out to look at this possibly useful gravel. Evidently, her transcription or the tape was unclear at the point where Stuart was talking about sending out the design engineer. She must have been watching the typical actions of the division over some time so when she transcribed the dictation it came out "…Stuart recommends that you send out a dozen engineers to look over the gravel material." Like many things, engineers are cheaper by the dozen, I guess. I wish I had kept a copy of that memo.

I'm also a little bit proud to say that I kept a relatively low profile while I was working for the state. For some reason, I was once at a meeting[25] in the governor's Juneau office shortly after he had taken over and shortly after I came to work for him. After we all sat down at the conference table, the governor was making small talk with almost everyone around the table until he came to me, where I was trying to look as inconspicuous as possible. This is a badly misunderstood attitude in an administration such as this one where prominence was so much more highly valued than substance. I don't think that I'll ever forget what he said. "Who is he? Is he with us?" It almost sounded like he was searching out enemies – the Joseph Stalin or Richard Nixon syndrome. At least he didn't have everyone shot that he suspected. However, based on my own admittedly minimal knowledge of his personality, he would probably have done just that if he could have gotten away with it. I guess we shouldn't judge him by that characteristic; almost all politicians are driven by the same instinct for personal survival over the public good.

---

[25] GOD, how I hated those meetings.

That particular meeting in the governor's office also highlighted what should have been a clear signal to me regarding where this political game was leading. Perhaps I should have seen that it signaled the administrative and political future of post-statehood Alaska, but I didn't. I was still the naïve Alaska boy from the southeast and the interior with no understanding of the sophisticated arts and artifices of politics and 'Management'. Looking back, I now realize that there were certain eye-opening aspects to the conversation I should have seized upon and taken away with me.

During the entire course of that meeting there was not a *single* mention of what facilities should be built or improved *throughout* the state, or how we could improve the state's own procedures in order to benefit the *people*, particularly those in the remote areas. In fact, the governor himself seemed not to understand what the term 'remote areas' even meant. Throughout the meeting the discussion seemed to center solely on how we could make whatever we did *look good* to the greatest possible percentage of the electorate and how *any* action would reflect on the *current administration* (translates to 'him'), not how the people would be affected. It would be comfortable to say that I immediately saw this meeting for what it was – a gathering of opportunists and a clear indication of the true nature of the administration's lust for power and political gain.

Unfortunately, that wasn't the case. In fact I can't recall that at the time, I thought much of anything about what had been discussed at the meeting, although I did remember it all, and still do. Nonetheless, either then or at some other time, I must have done or said something to piss off the man himself or some of his crowd of suck-up sycophants. Such a thing would have been quite possible because keeping my opinions to myself in public has never been one of my strong points. If that's what happened I'm glad it did because it would have meant that I hadn't been trying to phony myself up and conform to this 'new wave' of administrative behavior. Not that it matters, but the only time that I can remember doing anything that might have offended the governor or his 'court attendants' was when I met one of his people (apparently an aide of some significance) down at the Imperial Poolroom in Juneau. The incident is an illustration of what kind of people were taking over my Alaska.

I remember that I had the next position in line for a pool table when a guy came in who must have recognized me. He wanted the next turn at the table, and he asked if I knew who he was. I didn't, so he told me that he was a close aide to the governor and then said that he was taking my place in line for the table because he had to leave very soon, and he inferred that his business was far more important than mine.

It probably was, and whoever used the table next wasn't really important, but his arrogance and 'more important than you' attitude were so unbearable that I had to tell him to kiss off. I guess he didn't like what I said and when he told me again who he was, I replied that I wasn't interested in what his job was. I wonder if he went back and told his boss (his big daddy who would snuggle and protect him) all about it.

One of the things that bothered me most about this job was being more or less obligated to support a policy that surreptitiously ignored the needs of the bush villages in favor of the 'big vote' areas, although such a policy was never articulated of course. I can't be sure if this was because of some sort of political manipulation to wring the most possible gain from the most politically promising areas and ignore the others. Maybe it was some part of a long-range plan to concentrate on the urban areas and thereby help the most possible people – somehow I doubt that. I have to suspect that Governor Hickel was already taking advantage of statehood and using his position to gain as much national notoriety as possible with very little thought about what was best for the Alaskan people. By this time the fact of the oil deposits on the North Slope was generally known, although the big publicity push had not yet hit the national media. I'm now pretty suspicious that King Wally I (Hickel) was making veiled or implied promises to the big oil companies in return for their influence with Nixon to get him (Wally) a national cabinet position. If all that sounds complicated, it's because it probably was – if it was happening at all. As we all know now, if it was indeed some sort of scheme, it worked. Nixon appointed him as Secretary of the Interior. Maybe someone later discovered that Wally didn't know how to do anything practical so Nixon fired him.

While I worked for him, we always heard a lot of talk about how the governor's plan was calculated to help the people in the remote areas. In fact, I recall a much-publicized trip, supposedly to the remote areas, in order to gauge the needs out there and to "get in touch with the people." He flew to Nome, stayed a few days, and then flew back – no comment.

Personally, my own experience forces me to conclude that the remote areas didn't have enough political clout to be of much concern to Hickel's administration. Every time we tried to implement plans for rural projects using some of the 'discretionary' funds allocated to the division, we were told to redirect our efforts to some areas with either more votes or more publicity potential. At least that was the way it looked to me, and it became increasingly difficult to justify these seemingly politically motivated expenditures when speaking with the representatives from the bush who occasionally came by to ask what had happened to all the promises. After a while, whenever they came to my office with such queries, I began directing them to the governor's office for answers, and in fact once placed a call to some of his aides and let the questioner talk to *them*. I'm sure all they got was a lot of double-talk or 'Hickelese'. Of course that sort of thing did nothing to enhance my popularity with the administration.

I was becoming more and more disgusted and disillusioned with what looked to me like the obvious political motivations of the governor's policies. As a result of my increasing cynicism, I may also have been becoming more and more reckless about what I said, where I said it, and to whom I said it.

Every office above a certain administrative level had an obviously retouched photographic portrait of the governor hanging on the wall. Whenever someone came to visit, I joked that they should be careful what they said because the picture was probably bugged. I wonder sometimes if it really was.

Although perhaps expected to support some sort of administrative or political philosophy, I never pretended or promised to be anything but an engineer; not a Republican, not a Democrat, just an engineer. 'Please leave me alone and let me do my work' was my attitude, and I'm afraid it became pretty obvious as time went on. I was not in the market for any more 'Management' authority, thank you very much. The 'Managers' and the high-rollers don't like to hear that kind of talk because they all seem to have a deep-seated fear that the politicians who are *truly* concerned about progress and product[26] will discover that all this crap about generic management and administrative control is a lot of nonsense.

There were a few inspection trips to some of the remote airstrips that I can remember specifically, although I can't always remember the names of the villages they served. The strips along the coast of the Arctic Ocean always mystified me because whenever the pilot was first circling or, as they say, making his 'downwind leg', there was no one to be seen on the ground. However, once the plane landed, there were people all over the place. I found this to also be true on St. Lawrence Island

[26] There *are* a few – *very* few admittedly.

in the Bering Sea, at some of the strips along the Aleutian Islands, and at a number of other remote places in the interior and the arctic. It's probably just my imagination. Not even good Alaskans can just pop up from nowhere like lawyers, politicians and cockroaches, can they?

Neither the Fairbanks nor the Anchorage International Airports were (are) leased to the cities they serve, as is the case in Juneau, Ketchikan, Sitka, Nenana, Kodiak and a couple of others. I think they aren't leased because they are relatively visible and thus offer attractive possibilities for the politicians in power to make potentially lucrative impressions on people who might become useful to them. Anchorage and Fairbanks are the largest airports in the state, and they are almost always the first public facility that any politician sees when he/she comes to visit us and to get some easy publicity.

The governor was, and probably still is, interested in making the best possible impression on these folks as soon as they set foot in the cities where the 'halls of administrative power' have sway or where some urban area is in reasonably close proximity. That's not just speculation; I was told exactly that.

There wasn't much work done at the Fairbanks terminal while I was there, except when the terminal became just about the only dry spot during the flood – I'll get to that later. Anchorage, however, was another matter. Just about the whole time I was with the division, the terminal was being designed for major re-modeling. The design project was contracted to an architectural firm called Mayer and Associates. I think they had a local office in Anchorage, but their headquarters were 'outside' in someplace like Seattle or Portland, somewhere on the west coast anyway.

There was also a lot of activity at other locations on the airport property, both at Anchorage and Fairbanks during my tenure as director. People were building new hangars, fuel depots, sewer/water extensions, and all sorts of aviation-related improvements. For some reason, the North Slope Native Corporation was permitted to build an 'iglooruk', an anglization of the Eskimo word for 'big house'[27] almost directly across Airport Road from the then location of the ADA. I don't remember the purpose of the structure, but I'm sure that there was some sort of weasel-wording used to make the purpose look aviation-related. It was OK with me, but I was a little worried that the FAA might object because they policed that 'aviation-related' business pretty closely.

I went to at least two meetings at the iglooruk, and although I don't remember the subject of the discussions, I *do* remember that they had employed Fred Pettijohn as one, maybe the only one, of their public relations people. Please recall that I had first met him on the Denali in 1955 or '56 where he had taught many of us young surveyors some of the treasured old songs of the profession. It was good to see Fred again, and we spent several enjoyable hours at various times in various taverns; we were recalling and talking about the days gone by in the Denali country before and after our surveys up there. Even though they could perhaps be more or less morphed into something more compatible with the 'new' Alaska, I'm afraid the real Fred Pettijohns are gone now too.

At the time, it was politically wise to allow as much latitude as possible in dealing with the Native Corporations, and that may have had something to do with the marginal interpretation of 'aviation-related' on behalf of the Eskimo folks who were using this new iglooruk. I was in favor of letting them use airport property, but I couldn't help thinking back to the *bad* old days when the Indian folks weren't even allowed in the bars and only grudgingly in the restaurants. Now they *own* a lot of them. Not *all* the statehood changes were negative. The hypocrisy of the

[27] Or maybe 'big house' is English for 'iglooruk'.

high rollers and politicians who once supported the 'no Indians allowed' policies but are now grasping for their attention (and money) is disgusting.

During this period, there was a phenomenal amount of growth at both the Anchorage and Fairbanks International Airports until they both grew into the imposing and intimidating metropolitan appendages they, like a gazillion other lower 48 airports, are today. Looking back on those times, I feel sure that among the industrial/business community, there must also have been advance information regarding the future North Slope oil boom that was about to happen. If that was the case, it would have been logical for those airplane people who could afford it to set up facilities at the two main airports (Anchorage and Fairbanks) in preparation for servicing oil company development on the slope, and that's what was happening. However, the most significant event during my time with the division was, in my opinion, the 1967 Fairbanks flood. I should describe the flood because there is evidence of a sort of juxtaposition of the old ways and the 'new' Alaska.

In the late spring of that year, a huge ice jam on the Tanana River south of Fairbanks set off a major flood event over the plain between the Tanana and Chena Rivers. As I described earlier, Fairbanks lies right in the middle of that plain and has experienced several past floods to a greater or lesser extent. In 1967, the Corps of Engineers project involving bypass trenches among other hydraulic control devices had already been conceived, and it may have been partially designed, but it was not yet built. The 1967 flood was a big one; it resulted in four to seven feet of muddy water covering the entire city of Fairbanks, as well as the surrounding areas from the Tanana to the base of the hills east of the college, and from the base of college hill to the hills northeast of town. It was a mess.

It was probably more good luck than good planning/design

that resulted in the terminal area of the Fairbanks Airport property being one of the two or three pieces of ground that remained above water across the entire Fairbanks basin.

The Red Cross and the Salvation Army set up shop in the terminal and began doing what they could for the people who had been flooded out and had come to the airport seeking sanctuary from the rising water. The people were crowded into all the floor space in the terminal, and both the relief organizations were distributing blankets, pillows, coffee, hot chocolate and whatever else they could provide to meet the most urgent needs. Somebody told me later that the Red Cross was back-charging people for these services whereas the Salvation Army was not, preferring instead to just concentrate on the immediate problems. That 'accusation' is just hearsay as far as I'm concerned. I personally never saw any evidence that either of these relief agencies were charging anybody for anything.

The whole situation gave the gloomy impression of a refugee camp. It looked like one of those dark pictures from WWII showing people fleeing from advancing armies and resting during their flight.

The appearance of the downtown Fairbanks area was almost surreal, particularly whenever the sun went down. The Eskimo Scouts were then the only National Guard unit that was always on active duty and they had soldiers stationed all over town to keep order and prevent looting. They did an excellent job in the fulfillment of their mission. The Eskimo people are ultimately from the same racial stock that produced Genghis Kahn and his conquering armies, and some of them still have the appearance of those ancient and fierce warriors. In the semi-dusk of a Fairbanks early spring evening, the fierce-looking Eskimo soldiers doing their duty in the flooded downtown area were truly as intimidating as they were intended to be – maybe more so. There was no significant looting, no doubt largely because of the presence of these Scout troops, who had apparently been shipped in from up north. The appearances were of course misleading; the Eskimo people in general are among the kindest, gentlest and most accommodating people on earth.

I think there are two U.S. Corps of Engineers, at least there seemed to be at that time and in those circumstances. One of them is the familiar bureaucratic government agency primarily concerned with stopping any construction projects that your agency or company wishes to pursue. They cite mostly environmental concerns, but if these tactics fail, they can require extensive reviews by their staffs, which can often take an entire year or more to complete. Even then they were becoming worse and worse in those respects and probably intentionally mentoring the juvenile (eight-year-old) Alaska environmental agencies to become the same.

Paradoxically, the other Corps of Engineers is impossible to stop or even delay when there's a job to be done. They quickly evaluate the situation, and within hours they begin awarding contracts for repair and reconstruction projects. This must have been, thank God, the Corps of Engineers who served with our armed forces during WWII.

I don't know how these two organizations co-exist, but fortunately it was the second of the two that showed up to help with the repairs and reconstruction work during and after the Fairbanks flood. They wasted no time. When legitimate problems were brought to their attention, they inspected the field conditions immediately – I mean *immediately*. If any major repair or reconstruction was necessary, they would have the work advertised for bids in hours and a contractor on board no more than two days after that – usually just *one* day. Given all the detestable bureaucracy that infests government procedures and was even then slithering into our own Alaskan agencies, we were astonished (and refreshed) to see how quickly and efficiently this Corps of Engineers did their work. These were real engineers. Maybe they need a few more 'Managers' to slow them down with some more meetings and regulations! If they can operate as efficiently and effectively as they do, how come all these other sluggish and shamefully bureaucratic government agencies can't do the same thing? I wonder why we didn't use this second C. of E. as a model for some of the agencies now infecting Alaska. There are a few anecdotes about events that supposedly happened during the flood, at least one of which might be worth relating.

This one I believe because I know a lot of these Alaskan old-timers who would certainly act just like the protagonist of the story.

It seems that there was an old miner who didn't become overly alarmed by the flood, although he was in one of the residential areas under the deepest water. He may well have been through one of the previous flood events. I heard that when the water started rising, he got all his gear together such as his portable radio, sleeping bags/blankets, dry changes of clothes, Coleman lanterns, camp cooking stove, waterproof tarp with supports, and an adequate supply of canned and dried food. He probably salvaged a liberal supply of whiskey too. He then took everything up to the flat portion of his roof (sort of a deck), put it all in order, turned on the radio and waited for news of what was happening.

After he had been there for ten or twelve hours, a rescue helicopter that had been picking up people all over town came by, reportedly spotted him there, and went in to 'rescue' him. He tried to wave the helicopter off and indicate to the pilot that he didn't need rescuing. The pilot, however, apparently took all the waving to be a distress signal and moved in closer and closer in preparation for landing on the roof and rescuing this evidently stranded person. In the process of doing this, the wind from the blades of the rescuer's helicopter blew most of the old-timer's gear off the roof. He was reportedly furious about this turn of events, but he was now forced to accept the rescue even though he originally neither wanted nor needed it.

I don't know how true this story is, but I believe it. I knew many Fairbanks residents who, under such circumstances, would behave exactly as the man in the story did.

Most of those old miner types are gone now, replaced by the politically correct 'suits' who, in their disgusting similarity, now fill the halls of the government buildings and go forth, with their phony 'P.R.' smiles, from the big new corporation or agency offices that were then springing up all over the place. These are, more often than not, the corporations who coincidentally showed up to 'serve and help' us around the same time the big oil money got there.

Except for providing refuge, the Division of Aviation actually fulfilled only a peripheral role during the Fairbanks flood. We were, however, able to work with the Corps of Engineers just as engineers without any specific reference to the airport. It was pleasant to get back to pure design and construction and to work with an action-oriented outfit like this particular Corps as opposed to the Corps that's dedicated to stopping all construction projects.

Before I went back to Anchorage I was of course obligated to visit someone from Tommy's Elbow Room to see how they had fared during the flood. Frank, the bartender, told me that he had been working that day and as the water rose there were two or three guys who refused to abandon their stools until the water had risen to at least waist level, at which time they finally waded out. They were apparently (according to Frank – a real long-time friend of mine) unconcerned about whatever was going on.

The city officials who were then working under the emergency direction of the State Health Department also told me that Tommy had brought up some sealed bottles of whiskey from downstairs that he had refused to let the officials condemn. I was told that he was giving away free drinks from those bottles, and I'm sure that there were plenty of takers. That's the Elbow Room I remember – independent, and if necessary, defiant. Why have such people and places disappeared?

On June 1, 1967 heaven sent Irene and I our last child – a little boy named Thomas Joseph. He was such a well-behaved and happy baby that it was hard to believe. I can see and hear him, as always these days, through that depressing fog of memory. I can see him toddling toward my outstretched arms during a picnic or something down near Portage. I can hear him asking, "Do you think you could 'llow us to have one of those, Dad?" while holding on to me with one hand and pointing at an ATV with the other. I can hear myself saying, "Those are really dangerous for little boys and I might lose my Tommy. What would I do without my Tommy?" Through long past tears, I can see him standing on the porch of Irene and Chuck's house in Soldotna and waving goodbye to me. I can see him as a fierce young competitor playing hockey in the Sullivan Arena. I can see him in cap and gown taking his bachelor's degree in the Patty Gymnasium at the University of Alaska, and then I can see him rushing over the stage at Oregon State University to receive his master's. I can feel my own agony over his romantic misadventures, and I pray to a merciful God that he will soon find happiness in this respect. He is now a fine grown-up man, but in the shadows of my memory I still see that little toddler reaching out to me at the picnic site.

After inspecting the post-flood conditions, I wrote up my report recommending the rehabilitation and other such work made necessary by the flood damage at the airport. After that, I got all my gear together and flew back to Anchorage.

About two weeks after I returned, I got a call from Juneau

instructing me to report certain planned Fairbanks Airport improvement projects as being damage repair from the flood. I won't say who I got the call from, except to note that it wasn't George. I told the caller that I wouldn't do what he was asking, and if he pursued the matter any further, I would report it to the Attorney General's Office. It seemed to me that obtaining relief funding from the federal government on the basis of such false statements could constitute fraud, and I wanted no part of it. I never heard any more about it. I was told later that the attorney general[28] was also in the governor's pocket, as so many of the administation's appointees and staff members seemed to be. Looking back, I question whether it would have done any good to report to him about anything that cast the existing administration in a bad light.

If such skullduggery was so blatant at the state level, how much more prevalent must it be at the federal level? However, other stuff was on my mind at the moment, and I didn't give the matter much more thought. Certain indications were piling up, and I began to feel that, in the political winds that swirl around the governor and his anointed few, I was becoming sort of *persona-non-grata* for some reason. I had already been alerted that some of the 'palace intrigues' (I like that expression) circulating within the sacred halls of the domain of King Wally had me placed on the 'hit list'.

It was during the last week of December 1967 that I was officially terminated, effective January 15, 1968. My tenure had lasted just fifteen days more than exactly one year. I got the news in a telephone call from George. He told me that news of my 'resignation' had already been released to the Juneau media, and that I should try to support the same story that had appeared in the *Juneau Empire* saying that I had resigned.

It must have been the same day that I got the call from

[28] A man named Ed, and I think he only had one eye.

George when the *Anchorage Times* called and asked why I had resigned. I told them that I hadn't resigned, but that I had been fired, although I didn't know why. As a matter of fact, I never *was* told why; I knew that the job was political, that I served at the pleasure of the administration (the governor) and that I could be terminated "without prejudice" (whatever that means) at any time. On the same day I was fired, the governor appointed a man named Wakefield as the new director of aviation. When asked to comment, the governor said something like, "Harman is strong in his knowledge of engineering, but Wakefield is strong in his knowledge of aviation." Don't they call that "damned by faint praise?" I should probably have felt bad about being fired from the division, but aside from a little embarrassment, it didn't bother me much. In fact, it didn't bother me at all; it was actually sort of a welcome relief. It seemed to distress Irene more than it did me.

Now I had to find something different to do, but still in the engineering field of course. I didn't know how to do anything else, and I didn't feel like going into 'Management'! I also didn't feel like pounding the pavement looking for another salaried job in Anchorage. Anyway, I had become so sick of taking orders from other people that it would probably be obvious to any prospective employer. Established companies are rightfully wary of hiring people who seem as though they don't like to do what they're told to do just because they're told to do it.

I knew that we couldn't afford to move back to Juneau, and besides, even then I had begun to wonder if there might be something more than just an employer/employee relationship between Irene and her lawyers. I was, therefore, just a little doubtful that she would consider leaving her current 'job'. It was only a visceral feeling for which I hadn't (or haven't) the slightest concrete evidence.

It seemed like, all things considered, the only satisfactory solution would be to set up a small engineering company of my own. In view of the impending development on the North Slope and the air of expansion in the Anchorage area, such a decision seemed at the time to offer a certain amount of promise. I contacted a thirty-year friend of mine named Howard, who had also been working for the ADA, and with the confidence of youth that still existed and anticipating the Alaskan attitude which still existed although already decaying around the edges, we set out to become successful consultants.

I didn't relate that little firing story to demonstrate how badly I personally may or may not have been treated. It just seemed to be a good chance to show how the Hickel administration had begun turning into a 'cult of personality' rather than an organization dedicated to working on behalf of the people of Alaska. Sadly, there were other examples to follow with increasing frequency.

By now the old Alaska was in the initial stages of her death throes. Our characteristic freedom of thought and independence of action might survive briefly in the more isolated areas, but formula 'Management' was taking over in the halls of big and little officialdom. Much to the satisfaction of the proliferating bureaucrats and managers, we were starting to *fall into line*.

Chapter 2: Dodging the Dragon

We accidentally named our company *Engineering Services*. When we applied for the business license that was the description we meant to write in the space that asked what kind of work we intended to do. We mistakenly wrote it on the line that said "Company Name." That was the name we went by for the next five years. At the time Howard and I opened our doors, the impact of the oil discoveries on the North Slope was just beginning to become significant.

Most of the optimism and scrambling for rewarding positions at the envisioned financial feeding trough filled with oil money seemed to be taking place in the Anchorage rather than the Fairbanks area. There were, *I think*, two basic reasons for this. 1) Although many of them would deny it, Fairbanks residents, as long-time Alaskans, tended to be a little standoffish or reticent with outsiders and newcomers, whereas many or most of the Anchorage people *were* newcomers themselves. Most of them seemed anxious to make the city as much like where they came from as possible. In general, such a concept was, and is, repellant to most Fairbanks residents. 2) A large percentage of the residents of Fairbanks were fourth, fifth or even more, generation Alaskans. They neither appreciated, liked, nor understood what they often characterized as the 'dubious' practices of outside business. They were therefore often quietly cautious or openly reluctant about dealing with outsiders. Of course, most of this was not overt, but it could be sensed. The people in Anchorage, however, being largely newcomers themselves, as noted, were less resistant in dealing with these opportunistic immigrant companies because they understood the outside business tactics. They had brought a few of their own when they came north not so long ago.

There were numerous landowners around Anchorage who had seen the oil boom coming and wanted to improve their properties in order to make them more attractive to the development speculators they knew would be coming north. It seemed like all the nouveau-rich landowners, entrepreneurs and high rollers around Anchorage expected the country to be suddenly overrun by endless crowds of filthy rich Texans and Oklahomans coming after the oil or seeking to profit from the results of the oil discoveries. In their minds, there was no doubt that these oil folks would soon be throwing huge amounts of money around right and left. Many of the Anchorage people had, in the eyes of the real old timers and others from more traditionally Alaskan parts of the state, never been real Alaskans anyway, and these local landowners were no exception; they often had no family attachment to the land. After all, most of Anchorage itself was only seventy or eighty years old at best.

Whether they were real Alaskans or not, much of the work that Howard and I did during our first year or two in business involved subdividing large tracts of land around Anchorage. The owners said they were confident that when the presumed rush of 'oil-sniffers' and their families showed up, the property could be sold lot by lot at wildly inflated prices, and they would thereby stuff their pockets with bundles and bundles of money.

For us, the job of preparing these tracts of land for lot by lot sale included dealing with the local city or borough to obtain approvals for such things as lot dimensions, street widths, survey accuracy, neighborhood covenants and so on. The requirement for obtaining these approvals was not in itself unreasonable. Most jurisdictions monitor such things to a greater or lesser extent, and it is probably a good idea since it discourages incompetent or sloppy work. The alarming aspect of our efforts in 1968 was the overwhelming bureaucracy that we ran into.

There were a few times early in my limited tenure as director of the ADA when we had occasion to do business with the City or Municipality of Anchorage; mostly with regard to property adjacent to the airport or connections with utilities like sewers and water. At that time, their offices were located on West Fourth Avenue, about a block east of what was then the Chamber of Commerce log cabin. They had even then obviously begun to feel the belated impact of statehood. There were spaces meant for one occupant that were occupied by two, and the paperwork required to do business with them was, although voluminous, doable during the time spent in their offices. It was also notable that their engineering department was still located on the main floor so that technical matters could be quickly dealt with. However, by the time Howard and I began doing property development work, those same offices had expanded to almost comical proportions. Their main building was still in the same location, but the interior office arrangement had become unrecognizable.

It was no longer possible to get single answers to single questions or problems. Each answer seemed to be a matter of concern to at least two, and usually more, reviewers. Even at that, the answers were rarely forthcoming without requiring the gathering of additional obviously extraneous information and a return trip or two. Amazingly, each of these additional people had a functional title: Development Coordinator, Dimensional Reviewer, Utilities Examiner, Code Compliance Officer, Assistant Development Coordinator and so on. I was amused by one title that included the word 'Expeditor'; there was certainly no expediting going on, and I couldn't help remembering the definition of that word as explained to me by Harvey at Donnelly Inn.

As might have been expected, very few of these people had even the slightest bit of technical knowledge regarding the subjects implied by their title. Moreover, at the time we visited less than 50% of them were doing anything; mostly talking, drinking coffee, or drinking coffee *and* talking. To make matters even worse, almost all of them were there just to hand out copies of the instructions and applications to members of the public. Once they received all the completed forms and such, they merely passed it all on to someone at a 'higher level' and the review process began all over again with the higher-level folks.

The seating arrangements had become ludicrous. There were numerous instances of two or more people sharing the same desk and, I swear, some of them even seated in the hallways. The engineering people weren't even on the upper floors anymore. They had been moved into what must have been the dungeons of the lower levels, and those who had been there previously had been moved to some other building somewhere down near Merrill Field, the Municipal Airport. The downtown bureaucracy, in their original building, intoxicated with those sacred principles of formula management had clearly established itself. It was but one cancer of the many then eating at the dying flesh of the Alaskan lifestyle. Happily, there *were* a few holdouts although visiting them was strangely sad because of the inevitability of change.

Early in 1969, we were hired by an outfit called Kodiak Island Homes for retracement of a large subdivision on the north side of the City of Kodiak. Like many such out-of-town jobs, when we got there we found it to be more complicated than it had been described.

It turned out to be necessary to redo the entire boundary

survey, relocate many of the lot lines to fit the corrected boundary and to accommodate the improvements actually on the ground, set new monuments and lot corners, gain approval from the Kodiak planning and zoning folks and file a new subdivision plat with the Kodiak Recorders Office. We also conducted a detailed sub-surface soils survey on a site where the Kodiak campus of the University of Alaska was planning some new buildings. The Kodiak jobs added up to a lot of work and they consumed a lot of elapsed time, happening as they did while we were also engaged in other work around Anchorage.

When we got to Kodiak, we could feel that some of the old Alaskan attitude and lifestyle were still in existence. For starters, Kodiak city and probably the other settled areas and villages on the island were very provincial. No one ever actually told us that they didn't give a damn what was going on anyplace else but the 'feeling' was there. The front page of the *Kodiak Mirror*, the local newspaper, was almost exclusively devoted to local news, which in my opinion was, and is, how it should be.

Both the climate and the spectacular scenery around Kodiak are so attractive that given the nationwide attention generated by statehood as well as the oil strike and the subsequent environmental concerns more and more people are bound to be attracted to the area. As with everywhere else, they will no doubt bring their administrative and bureaucratic baggage with them. I haven't been to Kodiak for many years, but I fear that the administrative malaise that has infected most of the rest of the state has also begun slithering onto the island in the guise of 'Management enlightenment'.

There is also the looming threat of the overzealous environmentalists (the 'rabbit-trackers') who are collectively convinced that as long-time Alaskans, we are not capable of protecting our own environment. This arrogance is supposedly given credence by the tragic example of the *Exxon Valdez* and the massive oils spill in Prince William Sound. The environmentalists seem to ignore the fact that this disaster was *not* caused by Alaskans, nor was any relaxation of environmental standards allowed by Alaskans. The drilling was done with federal sanctions, and there were several examples of 'looking the other way' on the part of both the federal government and the outside so-called protectors of the environment. Perhaps these folks should spend a little more time looking inward and a little less trying to protect us from ourselves. Naturally, we all hope that such a tragic thing as the *Exxon Valdez* never happens again. Perhaps the excess bureaucrats could write some more stringent regulations prohibiting oil tankers from doing stuff like bumping into such things as Bligh Reef. Maybe they're too busy writing up regulations against chewing gum or preventing technical decisions without managerial approvals

Unfortunately, none of such arguments change the fact that these environmental crusaders are almost certain to saturate the coastal areas of Alaska if they haven't done so already. The problem will become much more intense if the Arctic National Wildlife Range is opened to oil exploration. In such an event, Kodiak Island will undoubtedly attract more than its share of these longhaired loonies simply as a result of statewide, unrestricted, opportunistic immigration and normal population increases. One needn't be a wizard to predict that the Alaskan ambiance of Kodiak and the surrounding areas will deteriorate, just as it will throughout the rest of the state. Before leaving the subject of Kodiak, I must describe a friend I met there. He was a true Alaskan.

John Pavlik was a seal hunter, a once brutal and still extremely rigorous profession if it's still allowed at all. Despite his impressive strength and lean but muscular build, John was a very gentle person. Nonetheless, he seemed to be over-concerned with his public image, not as a fighter or tough guy, but as an outdoorsman, showing supreme indifference to the cruelest of sea and weather conditions.

More than once, a few of us less adventurous types watched him making winter crossings of the inner harbor in an open skiff with no coat on. He would simultaneously guide the outboard rudder while breaking accumulated ice off his exposed chest with his free hand. Our vantage point for watching this display was usually across the warm downstairs bar at the Kodiak Inn. After his boat was tied up and secured, John would invariably rush into the bar and huddle shivering by the stove until the chill had been chased away. It wasn't phoniness – John wasn't a phony person. I think it must have just been that John felt that the more sophisticated folks in the upstairs lounge were entitled to something more interesting than the simple sight of an apparently fully protected fisherman returning from a routine fishing trip. There are no more John Pavliks. Perhaps it's because of the more restrictive regulations or prohibitions regarding seal hunting. More likely it's simply because there just isn't any place for them in the new Alaska. I've heard that Kodiak has now been included on the itinerary of some of the cruise ships. I hope it's not true.

Just before completing the Kodiak job, we obtained a subcontract from a contractor who had been awarded a project by the U.S. Air Force to construct an eighteen-hole golf course adjacent to Elmendorf Air Force Base. The golf course had been designed by Robert Trent Jones who, someone told us, was one of the world's foremost golf course designers. Like most architects, apparently even landscape architects, he didn't put dimensions on anything. Fortunately, with the help of some of the base officials and the accurately established and monumented coordinate system, we were able to figure everything out. Our mission was to lay out all the fairways, greens, etc. for the equipment operators.

The golf course (military) property had a common boundary with the east Anchorage suburb called Mountain View, an area containing middle to lower-income family homes. Many of the residents were in the armed forces and this place was a convenient neighborhood to live in because it was so near the bases and relatively inexpensive.

One day, we happened to be working close to that common boundary with some of the heavy brush clearing equipment. Perhaps the noise attracted them, but whatever it was, an engine detachment of the Mountain View Volunteer Fire Department showed up, apparently unaware that we were working on Air Force property. I swear they looked like something from the *Keystone Cops* or *Smokey Stover*. They drove in on an unimproved access road leading across the property line in what must have been some kind of antique fire truck with a profusion of dents all over it and about five different colors of paint. The crew themselves were wearing all sorts of bizarre 'costumes' and helmets – no two of them alike. I can't forget the expression of the apparent chief of this ludicrous display when he said, (referring to the golf course project) "OK, who's in charge of *this* little operation?"

When someone told him that it was the Air Force and that it was on Air Force property, he just seemed to sort of melt. He got all flushed, said something like, "Well, OK, just be careful," turned his equipment and people around and clanked and banged back down the access road with as much dignity as he and his crew could salvage. He may have gone on to talk with someone at an upper command level to explain his actions. If he did, I hope he didn't take his crew and their truck with him. In any case, we never saw or heard from him again.

Although this *was* Anchorage, the Mountain View Fire Department display seemed *very* Alaskan because they obviously didn't care what they looked like to anyone else.

Sadly, People like that are gone now, swallowed up by the conformity brought up north by the 'stateside' management and oil company immigrants. The same old question: where did all the Alaska types go? Did they just wander off into the woods? Did they move somewhere else far away? Or did they just morph into other people?

At one point during the golf course project, the payment from the Air Force was held up. As usual we were short of money and always faced with the continual responsibility for the wages of our surveyors. The contractor wasn't getting his periodic payment either so Howard called Mike Gravel, one of our Alaskan senators at the time, and asked him to look into this payment delay, the result was *electrifying*. Payment for both the contractor and us came through within a week of Howard's phone call, along with an apology and some sort of weak excuse for being late. Since then I have seen similar instances and have become really impressed at how quickly these government agencies will respond to senatorial enquiries. I wish some of the conscientious senators would step in, investigate all the administratively constipated agencies for inefficiencies, and kick ass among all the bureaucrats and 'Managers'.

The golf course project was actually not paid for by any of the portion of the federal military funding that goes to the Air Force. It was independently funded by some sort of auxiliary organization that is responsible for such things as officers' clubs, recreational facilities and apparently golf courses. Evidently the senators have considerable clout with outfits like that as well as with the actual federal agencies.

It must have been sometime around late summer/early fall of 1970 that we were retained by the Alaska Division of Aviation (my old outfit, sans Hickel) to conduct a foundation study and prepare a design report for an extension of the Nome Airport scheduled for award either late in 1971 or early in 1972.

Since this was a soils-related project, I got to go initially while Howard stayed in Anchorage. I think he had a couple of structural jobs going at the time, and he also may have been negotiating for a subdivision project up near Palmer. The crew I left with consisted of a man named Joe (an old friend from Juneau), a young fellow called Ricky, and I think there must have been one other man, although I can't remember his name.

When we got to Nome, our first job was to line up the tractor (truck), lowboy trailer and D6 tractor we needed to conduct our consolidation (plate bearing) tests under load at various locations all over the airport. To begin with, we had a hell of a time finding the guy we had made arrangements with for all the equipment rentals, but we finally chased him down at the Nugget Hotel coffee shop where we reminded him about our rental agreement. He didn't even put down his coffee cup. He just said something like, "Oh yeah, well, we'll take care of it – maybe tomorrow."

This was the laid-back sort of approach that we ran into everywhere in Nome whenever we tried to get anything done that involved interfacing with the local business folks. That sort of attitude is delightfully relaxing, and the only negative aspect of it is that it's infectious, and it isn't long before the 'out-of-towner' begins thinking the same way. Personally, I love it. It's the old Alaskan way, and it was gradually being destroyed by the same outside cultural encroachment that was polluting the whole state. Nome, with the Iditarod race and related events attracting attention, may have succumbed to many of the outside influences, but if it has, we can be sure that the long-time residents didn't give in quietly.

Once we got started on the project there were no further problems, and, in fact, our erstwhile equipment rental guy seemed as anxious to get things done as we were. He became particularly interested in what we were doing, why we were doing it, and what we expected to come up with. At that time the process consisted of placing a set of one-inch thick steel plates (we brought them with us) under a heavy stationary load; in our case a lowboy loaded with a D6 tractor, then using a heavy duty hydraulic jack to push between the stationary load and the plates. The amount of settlement versus time can be measured with a dial or set of dials made specifically for stuff like that. From these measurements, the behavior of the foundation soils under load and over time can be calculated and forecast. The procedure is called a plate-bearing test and it's actually fairly extensive, requiring much more time, equipment and man-hours than almost any other field-testing procedure.

Sadly, I'm sure that nowadays there are much more sophisticated and probably more accurate electronic methods for obtaining the same data. There will no doubt soon be no more need for this old time-honored procedure or for many others as well. No more rigors of lying under the flatbed taking readings while the arctic winds and snow flurries scoot along the ground. Anyway, that's what we were doing with the tractor and lowboy trailer. In addition to these measurements, we also drilled almost fifty test holes to depths of ten to sixteen feet and classified the soils we encountered.

The driller we had on the job was a Texan named Frank Younger. He was a shirttail relative of the Younger brothers who had ridden with the Daltons and Jesse James. He seemed pretty proud of that heritage, although those guys were actually a bunch of thieves and killers who have since been romanticized into latter-day Robin Hoods and folk heroes. Frank wasn't like that at all, at least not during any of our working relationships. Maybe the Younger family heritage had mellowed over the past hundred years or so. Time has that effect on lots of things.

After the fieldwork for the Nome job was over, we went back to Anchorage and prepared a report showing closely calculated probable consolidation rates and mathematical curves illustrating total settlements over time. There was a lot of good information in that report. I hope it didn't just end up on a shelf in some ignoramus bureaucrat's office and dismissed as unimportant because he or she couldn't understand it. Too many potentially valuable data have been lost in exactly that way. If we start discarding everything the bureaucrats and managers don't understand, we'll soon be discarding everything with any substance or requiring any mental exertion.

Our biggest job was probably our contract with the State Department of Natural Resources to conduct feasibility studies and prepare development plans for three wilderness areas in the state: Lake Louise, about 130 miles east of Anchorage and twenty-nine miles north of the Glenn Highway; the old Hatcher Pass mining area; and Kachemak Bay across from Homer. Most of the work and the data-gathering excursions were pretty routine, but I can clearly remember one of the trips that Bill (our business manager, among other things), Seth Yerrington, and I took into the into the backcountry north of Lake Louise.

Seth was the principal architect and owner of Seth Yerrington Architects out of Seattle; one of our joint venture associates. Seth had a bear complex, which every Alaskan he talked to naturally encouraged. I still do that if I get the opportunity (not really – ha, ha). Whenever Seth went anyplace beyond the parking lot of some of those so-called wilderness lodges, he carried a big long-barreled .357 Magnum revoler for what he referred to as "bear protection." The thing was a nice-looking weapon that must have cost him $400 or more.

On this occasion, while we were beginning the return trip from the upper lakes back to the Lake Louise Lodge, we got to about the center of the chain of lakes when a vicious little wind/rain storm blew up. The wind was blowing hard parallel to the long axis of the lake and, being allowed such a long reach, was blowing up some pretty sizable little swells and whitecaps. When loaded with the three of us and our gear, the small skiff that we were in had very little freeboard, even in *calm* water. We thought it best to run up on the beach and wait out the little storm at some sheltered spot, knowing that these minor squalls are common on some of the freshwater lakes and they usually blow over pretty quickly.

It was fairly chilly so when we got on shore, Bill and I built a small fire to keep us a little bit warmer. While we were standing close around the fire, I happened to notice the big hog-leg that Seth had fastened on his belt in a holster tied to his leg John Wayne style. He explained about some of the authentic bear stories that he had heard from various lodge owners, bartenders, etc.; the kind of stories that Alaskans loved to pump the tourists full of.

Noting that he had the holster tied pretty close in against his leg, I asked if he might be worried about blowing a hole in his foot or his leg while trying to draw the weapon. He told me that he had ensured against anything like that by keeping the gun unloaded while it was in the holster. Go figure.

As we expected, the wind dropped to almost nothing within a couple of hours, the lake flattened and we resumed our journey. When we got out to the main body of Lake Louise it was slightly rougher, but nothing we couldn't handle. We headed back to the main Lake Louise Lodge, where we stayed for another night and went over our notes regarding soils and access road/parking lot locations, design, and construction with Howard, who had arrived the previous day. I can't remember for sure, but I think Bill and I went back to Anchorage, and Seth stayed to work with Howard.

At that time, Lake Louise and the connected lakes were truly a wilderness retreat – refreshing to body and soul. Since then, I think the main access road from the Glenn Highway has been straightened, widened and paved. I'm sure that many additional lodges and fishing resorts have moved in and the whole area has probably become a jam-packed tourist Mecca. It's a damn shame, but that's representative of what will ultimately overtake the whole state, and it's now too late to do anything about it.

Of course, Howard and I also worked with the other two park sites as well as Lake Louise, particularly Kachemak Bay, and we had purchased a thirty-foot cabin cruiser in Seward specifically for this project. We went to all the trouble of renting a trailer and hauling the boat over to Homer, right across the bay from where the Kachemak Bay park study was to be conducted. However, as we soon discovered during a series of very unpleasant incidents, none of us was fully competent to operate the boat, particularly if the water got even just a little bit choppy, which it did almost every time we passed the breakwater protecting the small boat harbor. From then on, we chartered with a professional outfit from Homer whenever we went back and forth from town to the job. I remember that Seth (the gun-toting architect) and a forester from the Sacramento office of J.A. Roberts & Assoc. joined us on the Kachemak Bay site for at least a week.

The boundaries for the proposed Kachemak Bay wilderness park took in a roadless and relatively inaccessible community called Halibut Cove – home of ex-Governor Jay Hammond. Living inside a park imposes certain limits on property rights, and I'm sure that if the park became a reality there must have been some vigorous objection from the folks living in that community, perhaps even ex-Governor Hammond himself. Quite a few people in the old Alaska lived in remote places like that precisely because they didn't like, and wouldn't tolerate, having their property rights infringed upon. That's the way it used to be, but perhaps that old Alaskan attitude concerning individual rights has been beaten back by the increasingly oppressive policies and regulations being imported with the rapidly proliferating bureaucratic immigrants.

I don't remember the exact date when we finished up at Kachemak Bay and went up to Hatcher Pass. I *do* remember that we were in kind of a hurry because the pass is pretty high and we wanted to avoid the coming winter snow. Therefore, it must have been sometime in August or early September at the latest. As I recall, we finished our share of the entire park study, including our reports and drawings sometime during the winter of 1970/71.

Old gold mining area in Hatcher Pass – Featuring Cousin Fred in the foreground

It was also sometime during the late winter of 1970 that we were retained by the U.S. Public Health Service (PHS) to conduct a feasibility study for providing community water supply and distribution systems for the villages of Gambell (pop. 600 off and on) and Savoonga (pop. 700 from time to time) on St. Lawrence Island in the Bering Sea, roughly two hundred miles offshore from Nome. At the time we began our work, the villagers had, since time immemorial, been gathering and storing fresh water from the frozen sea ice during winter and the PHS wanted to determine the most feasible way of providing supply and distribution systems for both villages. This project proved to be extremely beneficial for us, both in terms of financial return and of cultural exposure. At least that's the way I felt about it.

I went to Gambell first. Within a day or two, Bill, Howard and a new employee named Randy joined me there and we began the investigations that were necessary to determine where there was a reasonable water source. As the village mayor had suggested, we attended the first available council meeting after Howard arrived.

The council had already been talking to the PHS about our study, so they knew all about it. It looked like we wouldn't have to explain the purpose or theory of the study, only how we planned to go about it and what kind of support or help we might need from the community.

Most of the council discussion was carried on in the Eskimo language, which, of course, none of us visitors could either speak or understand, so we couldn't follow a lot of what was going on. It's not a very pretty language, like Spanish for example, but I guess it's served those people up there quite well for several thousand years, so who are we to criticize? If the ubiquitous managers and bureaucrats who were already moving into Alaska were allowed to protrude into some of the villages, the fact that the councils usually conduct business in Eskimo or Indian would have, hopefully, constituted a major stumbling block. That in itself would be a very useful barrier preventing the interfering 'Managers' from peddling their new-age nonsense. I bet the council members, having a delightful sense of humor, talked and laughed about these intruders, knowing that they couldn't understand. It wouldn't have been the first time the language barrier provided them with an opportunity for a little good-natured fun.

We finally got to our place on the agenda, and since they probably knew as much as we did about the study at this point, we kept our report very short – merely saying where we expected to start, what we expected to do, when we expected to finish, and what we thought they could do to help.

Our study guidelines furnished by the PHS did not specifically address the question of sources, nor were we asked to do so. However, we *did* bring up the subject at several places in the finished report because the matter has to be an essential consideration in the design of any distribution system. Without a competent source, there is nothing for a distribution system to distribute.

Gambell, St. Lawrence Island – forty miles from Russia

Gambell is more exposed than Savoonga, primarily because of the difference in topography between the two. Gambell is located on the top of a low hill at the western end of the island. It is exposed to frequently heavy winds from the north and west, blowing in from both the Arctic Ocean and the Bering Sea. Anytime after sundown when the weather is reasonably clear, one can easily see the lights of buildings and moving vehicles from Providenyia, Mechigmen, Lavrentiya and/or Naukan on the south end of the Chukotsk Peninsula in Russia. I can't be sure if those are the proper Russian names or if we were actually looking at those specific places. All I can say is that we often watched lights across there; we saw a hell of a lot of them over what appeared to be long distances and those Russian names are what I took off a map.

People at Gambell and Savoonga have told me that both they and the Russian Eskimos can usually speak and understand each other's languages because there isn't much difference between the two. They probably spring from the same linguistic roots. I was also told that there have been several instances of people traveling across the winter ice to visit those folks over there. I don't know how much stock to place in such tales because the people on St. Lawrence Island, like all good Alaskans, love to spin as many outlandish yarns as they can get away with.

I recently heard that some goofy studies, based only on contemporary American residential standards, had been prepared by some of those outside experts that we're going to see more and more of. They reportedly recommended that Gambell be relocated to a site less exposed to the weather. I hope it's not true, but if it is, those 'researchers' have certainly not done their homework. Do they actually think these people didn't have sense enough to consider all the factors and find a suitable location for their own village? If they had asked any of the local old-timers, they would have been told that Gambell is located where it is for a reason. The high ground, plus the height gained from the second story decks on the tallest houses, affords a long view out to sea when spotting for both walrus and whales. These people take their livelihood from the sea and every action that contributes to maintaining that livelihood has to be utilized.

Such 'researchers' are perfect examples of one of the most disgusting aspects of what has been happening since just before statehood and has accelerated with the national attention brought by the oil industry. We've been, and are being, swamped by outside 'experts' who before all the attention didn't give a damn about Alaska. Now they're all streaming up there to tell the Alaskans what we've been doing wrong all these years. Some of them even have the unmitigated gall to advise the Eskimo people on matters of cold weather survival. Unfortunately, the Eskimo folks are always so polite that so far I don't think they've told these jerks to just shut up and go home. However, it *is* reassuring to know that after politely thanking such outsiders for the advice the Eskimos will no doubt simply continue doing what they've always done. After we had gathered the data we deemed necessary for the Gambell portion of our study, we moved to Savoonga. Howard flew over there, but Randy and I rode sleds pulled behind snow machines.

Savoonga is somewhat better protected by its topography from the extreme winds than Gambell. There is significantly higher ground just north of the village and somewhat higher ground to the west-southwest. The village is thus relatively well shielded from the wind that blows in off the Bering Sea from the north or the southwest. There is some exposure to winds blowing in from the east and east-northeast, both from the Bering Sea between the island and the mainland and from the seasonal winds that blow southwest through the Bering Straits from the Arctic Ocean. All things considered, my guess is that the wind chill factor during a Savoonga winter is not nearly as severe as it is in Gambell.

Savoonga, St. Lawrence Island – Tim Sloowko, snow machine driver

If you're still with me here, don't take my comments about wind direction as gospel or or as coming from some expert. They're just based on some cursory examination of the maps and assumptions about pressure differences. If you really want to know more about the St. Lawrence winds, call somebody who lives on the island; they *do* have phones up there as well as television, computers, e-mail, 'Blackberries' and all the other 'conveniences' that are so drastically altering their traditional way of life.

It must have been middle or late April 1971 by the time we finished gathering all the data we needed for our report[29] to the PHS, so we gathered everything up and traveled back to Anchorage.

[29] Except for some 'pick-up' things that we went back and got later.

By the time we finished the St. Lawrence job and went home, the business had begun to seriously decline. The local development surge resulting from the big oil 'boom' had begun to fizzle for some reason and lots of the people for whom we had done property survey work were now broke and unable to pay us. Many of our so-called 'legally informed' acquaintances advised us to file mechanic's liens against the properties of the developers as soon as we began working for them. This procedure probably looks pretty good to a lawyer anticipating fees for filing the liens and talking a lot, but it doesn't usually work with engineering or surveying projects like these because most of the developers didn't actually own the property that they were trying to develop. More often than not, they were working with the property owner under some sort of lease option and/or profit-sharing arrangement. In every case, our contracts were with the developer, not the property owner, and a lot of them were outside imports to our state. They thought nothing of just turning and walking out on us. I fear that many of today's Alaska residents have begun to model their business behavior on these intruders.

This practice of just ignoring debts and walking (or flying) away was another phenomenon that came north with the post-statehood dragons. Not one of the real, long-time Alaskans we dealt with even thought of running out on their financial obligations, and all of them eventually paid us. Unfortunately, their honesty and dependability were not sufficient to counterbalance what we suffered from the deadbeat developers who just ignored what they owed us and 'went south' – back home – with our money. It thus became obvious to both Howard and me that, in view of the collapse of many of our projects and the bleak financial outlook for the immediate future, we should divide up what we had left and go out separately to do the best we could.

After suffering the "slings and arrows of outrageous fortune" that I suppose accompany the sad closure of any enjoyable business because of financial failure, I decided to look for a change of scenery. With some references from Jim Roberts of JAR, one of our joint venture associates for the Alaskan park study, and a few others, I headed out on a stateside odyssey. I was looking for a job that would be both professionally challenging and personally satisfying and one that I wouldn't feel deceitful about leaving when my wounds from our company's Alaskan failure had healed. After looking at three possibilities, I accepted a job in Irvine, Orange County, California – just south of Los Angeles.

Chapter 3: The Source – Strange Behavior

If you've never been to Southern California, you cannot imagine what I walked into. I want to describe it in some detail because everything about it was so foreign to my Alaskan upbringing. What it *did* do was to help me understand why most of the immigrants who had begun swamping Alaska in recent years behaved the way they did.

Orange County, California is not part of the real world. In 1972, when we first moved there, we saw a lot of orange groves all over the place, but I guess that nowadays they've been pretty much replaced by commercial and residential development. That's what I've been told, but I sure as hell don't want to go down there to see for myself. All that development seemed like an almost eerie preview of our ultimate fate in Alaska.

Even then, I should have noticed that there was plenty of evidence around to indicate that the folks down there were more concerned with shadow than with substance. By this I mean that the average Southern Californian seems to judge others by what they *appear* to be and makes no real effort to understand the actual person or to truly gauge their talents and skills. Of course, the result is an entire population more interested in impressing each other than with creating any physical product of real value. It was somewhat puzzling that otherwise intelligent people would keep up that kind of pretense when they all knew that it was as phony as a three-dollar bill, and that whoever they were talking to was doing the same thing they were, i.e. putting out a lot of bullshit. I suppose they thought of it as 'positive thinking' or some other form of self-delusion. Later I realized that I was living in and witnessing a truly representative example of the kind of places where many of the opportunistic phonies then coming north and polluting our Alaskan workplaces and destroying the atmosphere and attitudes were coming from.

It seems like when some of those engineers down there read about a project in the newspaper, they somehow identify with it and are able to convince themselves that they're involved. My prospective new boss (Ed) somehow gave me the impression that he was supposedly 'on top of' these existing infrastructure projects, and that we would soon begin working on them. He seemed to be familiar with much of the detailed project information, the full names of the jobs, and even some of the people responsible for them; but nothing, I finally realized, that he couldn't have gotten out of the newspaper. He said I would be more or less free to pursue these phantom projects in accordance with my own abilities and judgment. Of course, he didn't call them phantom projects.

It all sounded pretty good to a young naïve Alaskan boy like me. It was a new company, thus supposedly offering rapid advancement, and it was located close to the coast, an environment that I thought both Eloise and I were accustomed to, so I accepted the position.

I had already turned down an offer in Denver, and I called the ski resort where I had also interviewed for a job to tell the head man there that I had accepted the job in Orange County. I now know that my decision was a big mistake. I don't recall that *any* of the big jobs that I was to "pursue in accordance with my own abilities and judgment" ever showed up in Ed's office. In fact, even at the time it struck me as a little strange that those jobs he had spoken of seemed to be sort of ethereal. It wasn't long after going to work for Ed that I began to wonder whether *everything* he had told me about upcoming or ongoing projects, etc. was wishful thinking or maybe just outright lying.

The only projects he had going were a couple of dinky little subdivisions. About two months after I came to work, he *did* manage to get a minor mapping or drafting job from the military at the El-something-or-other military base. He acted like that little job was a major defense contract direct from the Pentagon, arranging all sorts of meetings with base officials wherein we discussed such sensitive national security issues as the weight of the ink and the size of the lettering to be used. I did all the work and got none of the credit, which was fine with me, but I didn't like taking the blame for some of the faulty decisions regarding the map details after being told by Ed to do it that way.

After working there a few months and watching both Ed and his colleagues in action, it dawned on me that the supply of these people was inexhaustible; unchecked, they would continue to leak into Alaska until they were in a position to take complete control. That's what was happening, and it still is unless the takeover is complete.

The first professional organization meeting or conference Ed took me to was in Los Angeles – also a weird little world of its own. He introduced me to a lot of his friends, saying that I had "closed a private practice" in Anchorage just to come to a milder climate. Even that was bullshit.

When some of his friends asked me about the details of this private practice closure, I told them that it wasn't really as coldly professional as it sounded. I admitted that my leaving my business was partly because of depression over my divorce and, more importantly, because the work had slowed down and we were damn near broke. When asked what jobs I thought Ed had going in the Irvine area, I said I didn't think he had any.

Ed happened to overhear the conversation, and he hastened

to interrupt and hurriedly interject that he actually had many projects in the works that I wasn't aware of. I was dumfounded; *everything* he was telling this guy was absolute crap. What I didn't fully appreciate at the time was that since the fellow Ed was talking to was also a Southern Californian, he probably recognized Ed's B.S. for what it was. He was no doubt pumping out the same kind of nonsense when talking about his own business. It seemed like some sort of bizarre game of verbal one-upmanship.

By now I had become reasonably sure that this area was a major contributor to the seemingly endless supply of phonies now infecting Alaska. It was like those folks down there were living in some weird parallel universe where nothing was actually what it appeared to be.

Although I stayed with Ed's outfit for a little over a year, I always felt like an outsider, perhaps because Southern California and its people were so alien to my upbringing. Maybe it was only because, in my heart of hearts, I just wanted to go home to Alaska. I still feel that way whenever I go away from there – even where I am now.

My discontent must have been felt by other people, most particularly Ed. In early June 1973 he fired me; maybe because he felt I was too independent and just wouldn't pay any real attention to instructions, which were usually fuzzy and noncommittal if not impossible to implement. There was also the demonstrated fact that if I did what he said to do and it turned out to be wrong, I'd get blamed for it. Frankly, I actually felt good about being fired because it freed me from the risk of taking any responsibility for, or acting upon, some of Ed's stupid decisions. Some (not all) of his ideas were really unorthodox; I wish I could remember a few in detail. I often wondered if he had forgotten that he was supposed to be mainly an engineer and not just a politician or 'Manager'.

I must not have been too horrible because Ed gave me a few good references as well as some free time to look for another job. The firing also helped me work toward escaping from Ed's almost surreal Southern California world. I interviewed for several jobs, including one for the position of public works director for the City of Garden Grove; another of those ubiquitous little carbon-copy towns surrounding Los Angeles.

The best-paying and most interesting job offer was with the huge Los Angeles firm of Daniels, Mann, Johnson and Mendenhall (DMJM) based in LA. They were, they said, most interested in my extensive experience with heavy-duty dirt shifting work. I think they called it "earthwork construction" using some more professional sounding word than 'dirt'. They were the principal engineering firm for two big simultaneous airport construction jobs, one in Hong Kong and one in Florida. I would, I was told, be expected to visit each job at least once every two to three weeks or so. After about a week of review and interviews, they offered me a position as project engineer for both of these two major projects. A *lot* of very long-distance flying.

While I was sitting around in our rented Huntington Beach house studying up on DMJM's policies, projects and so on, I got a call from an old Anchorage friend named Gerry who owned a company called BB&S Construction in Anchorage. He offered me a job, I accepted immediately and I WAS GOING HOME! Or at least to Anchorage, which was close to home.

Chapter 4: The New Young Dragons

Of course, I was aware of the changes that had transformed Alaska since statehood, and I knew that conditions in the state were nothing like they had been in 'the old days'. I was nonetheless prepared to go back up north and try to come to terms with the new Alaska. It wasn't to be a simple transformation for me because the state had become so polluted with 'outside' ideas and attitudes which by now permeated almost all activity; not just that connected with federal matters. Knowing this, I nonetheless went back up north to work for Gerry at BB&S.

Gerry had decided, for whatever reasons, to expand his company's scope of business to include property development. I suppose he felt he could control the whole project that way, from inception through construction and marketing. Like most Alaskans, he never did really seem to like doing work under someone else's direction. Gerry was an intelligent guy, and after he joined the ranks of the 'movers and shakers', he did remarkably well. What surprised me most was that he seemed to adapt so well to the politically controlled and favor-driven atmosphere that was now noticeably suffusing Alaskan competitive construction.

Apparently, I was to fit into this picture as the company's principal engineer. My duties were to include, in addition to the normal technical aspects (e.g. surveys, quantity calculations, ground layout, etc.), gaining planning, zoning and technical approvals from whatever city and/or borough agencies thought they should be involved in the property development process; there were plenty of them, stiflingly more than necessary.

At the time, there was a lot of confusion arising out of the merger between the city and the borough, which, if carried out by any organization interested in getting things done, might have been a good idea. In comparison to the disgusting state agency's adjustment to the 'way they did it outside', the problems of the borough were a tempest-in-a-teapot. However, they were no less overwhelming for the local bean counters, administrators and mini-bureaucrats; some of whom had been feeding from the city or borough trough since statehood. Now they would have to recognize – as we all would – that we had become just one of (prior to Hawaiian statehood) forty-nine states. Under penalty of fiscal strangulation, we would now have to fall into line with the rest of Uncle Sam's 'children'.

I think the plan around Anchorage was to combine as many agencies as possible and thereby eliminate a lot of duplication. Although that sounds good in theory, in the end it didn't work out as cleanly as everyone thought it would, or should. As it is with all government agencies, they were bureaucracy-choked and highly inefficient. Since all bureaucrats view such mergers with suspicion, fearing loss of authority (or even jobs), there is always a lot of opposition. In this case, the opposition resulted in crippling project delays and a great many duplicate approvals.

Ludicrous though it seems, since the agencies couldn't decide which of them (city or borough) should be responsible for a given approval or review of private development, they decided to compromise and require approvals from both of them. Of course, this meant that the poor developer (or his agent) had to spend a bunch of time running back and forth, trying to satisfy them both, one at a time. Despite the managerial quagmire, we managed to start and finish three or four medium to large-sized subdivisions, including grading and underground utilities. I still think that much of the confusion and the proliferation of nonsensical requirements resulted in large part from the 'managerial' ideas brought north by the opportunistic dragons who had by now pretty well saturated the Alaskan governmental workplace.

Over time, the bureaucracy that creeps into any government organization becomes so ingrained in the employees, from directors to receptionists, that compliance with the detailed requirements becomes automatic – usually without the slightest concept of the original purpose behind them. This is usually the case even though the purpose is more often than not merely to justify more managerial and bureaucratic oversight. Unfortunately, the people interfacing with the public rarely realize this, and even if they did, they couldn't do anything about it. Here's an example.

We planned and constructed a medium-sized subdivision development on the north side of Sand Lake Road, about seven miles from downtown Anchorage. There were a limited number of lots, but the irregular topography required some pretty heavy earthwork construction to meet the borough requirements for minimum street dimensions, maximum gradients and so on. Of course, there were also borough maximum and/or minimum requirements for sewer and waterline extensions. For some reason, I was dealing with the city/borough folks who manned the reception desk and, thankfully, not the so-called 'engineers' who had by now morphed into some sort of scary hybrid mix of manager, bureaucrat and engineer.

Someone had apparently told the receptionist that she *must* require a construction hauling *plan* before issuing a permit for us to go ahead with the work. It didn't seem to matter to her how often and how detailed I verbally explained what we were doing or how simple the work was; she continued to demand a drawing of some kind.

We had managed to obtain permission to deposit waste excavation on private property about two miles east of the project, so I asked her for a blank piece of paper. When she gave me one, I drew a straight line and labeled it Sand Lake Road. I then drew a square at one end, wrote in a street name and a note saying 'Dig Here' and another square (with a street name) at the other end labeled 'Dump Here'. To make it look a little more complete, I drew an approximate north arrow and put arrows pointing both ways along my 'Sand Lake Road' line. I also added a dimension between the 'Dig' and 'Dump' sites showing approximately two miles between the two. The whole thing took about five minutes; less time than it takes to describe it. When I gave it to the receptionist, she seemed *very* pleased. I would have done it sooner if I'd known that was all she needed.

We also did the first 'Zero Lot Line' development I had ever seen. I think maybe this was also a concept brought up from the outside. It seems like an idiotic idea in a state as large and with as much space as Alaska. I guess I'm a little bit naïve about the legal ramifications, but it seemed to me to be nothing more than a series of duplexes with every other one being built over the lot line. Personally, I have never been able to see any advantage to that kind of development for the buyer, but it must have brought some benefits to the bankers, the lawyers, the developers and so on, or it would never have been suggested as an alternate to the old 'one lot – one residence' concept. I'm sure there were frequent arguments over property rights and so on between owners, each of whom owned half of one of the buildings straddling lot lines. These could naturally be settled in favor of whoever had enough money to hire the best lawyers.[30] Those guys (the lawyers) were probably hanging around like flies over

[30] In this context 'best' means the most devious or the least reluctant to lie.

an open cesspool where there was such a potential for dispute between the property owners. This was only one of the many 'outside' ideas brought north to educate the unenlightened Alaskans in how things are done in the more sophisticated parts of the world.

While I was still working for Gerry, I had been talking with the ANB (Alaska Native Brotherhood) about some of the PHS (Public Health Service) projects in northern (Arctic) Alaska – specifically in Kotzebue. These conversations were, of course, subsequent to gaining Gerry's approval (as the boss) to do a little consulting work whenever his needs didn't require my presence.

I was to travel to Kotzebue and come back with a detailed technical report about the deficiencies of the water and sewer projects that the PHS had recently built there. It meant some more flying, which I didn't like, but I thought I could probably put up with it for the sake of the project (but mostly, of course, the money).

I got to Kotzebue pretty early in the day, maybe three or four p.m. It was mid to late spring, and by that time sunset came pretty late so I could check into the hotel (Iglooruk) and still have time for a preliminary walkover of the aboveground utilidor. That's what I did; so the following morning I knew where to go, and I had a notebook full of things that I wanted to look into.

My own personal observations during this trip to Kotzebue confirmed what I've always considered to be the most damaging of all aspects of government administration. There is an insistent, pervasive, and apparently unshakeable habit of government managers and bureaucrats to concentrate more on the *process* of doing things than on the *product* desired. In my view, this is a very basic administrative flaw, and one that I know is becoming, or has become, a seriously damaging 'import' brought into Alaska by the northbound bureaucratic immigrants. This was evident on the Kotzebue project. The effect could be easily seen in the burdensome administrative demands imposed on the PHS representative; some apparently urgent enough to require occasional trips back to Anchorage. There was *no* project pipe being installed in Anchorage. While I was in Kotzebue, a friend of mine named Jack the Mormon[31] contacted Gerry with a proposal to split any profits gained on an 'open-to-entry' (OTE) survey for a set of lots in Bear Cove on the west side of Kachemak Bay.

When I got back to town, Gerry asked me about the job, whether I thought we could do it, how long I thought it might take, and whether or not I wanted to go down there. Of course we could do it, and whether or not I wanted to was irrelevant. I reminded Gerry that I had been on many jobs that were far more remote than this one, so he called Jack and told him that he'd back the job.

One of the conditions that I put on my agreement to participate in the project was that I be allowed to hire a man named Ray who I had known since childhood in Juneau. I wanted Ray to be on the job with me because I knew him to be an extremely proficient woodsman, fisherman, and so on. Because we had known and worked with each other for many years, we shared a genuine mutual trust. This job would be out of reach of any help if one got 'in trouble', and I wanted to be out there with someone I knew I could count on. At the time I wasn't aware of the administrative complications inherent in this new (OTE) program.

I don't know where the original idea for the OTE program came from. However, I wouldn't be surprised if it were proposed by some well-meaning nouveau Alaskan recently up from Iowa or Kansas or someplace similar where such a program had proven to be an efficient and fair method for distribution of

[31] My nickname for him – but not to his face.

public land. If that was the case, it's probable that the proposer was not familiar with Alaskan conditions. For example, they might not have appreciated the extreme remoteness of many, if not most, of these proposed open-to-entry locations or the paucity and/or inaccessibility of the official survey control system that the applicant (through his surveyor) was required to tie into. If that wasn't the case, the Alaskan who proposed it must have been from Anchorage.

After the program had been in effect for a year or two, it became obvious that in many cases, particularly where two lots were intended to adjoin, the extremely heavy vegetation made it virtually impossible to find the previously set corners in order to avoid overlaps, hiatuses, etc.

All the practical problems notwithstanding, the OTE laws, regulations, required procedures, etc. remained in effect over large portions of the state; maybe they still are, although I hope not. However, the large percentage of immigrant administrators and the subsequent deterioration of technical knowledge in the ranks of the 'Managers' has probably diverted attention from the substantial concerns about the difficulties inherent in the program.

The law allowed any Alaskan resident who wanted to stake out some property along certain (open-to-entry) of the state's rivers, lakes and probably ocean beaches to set out initial stakes at each of two points along the water's edge. These were defined to be the front corners (beachfront) of the property that the applicant wished to claim, and the rules prescribed maximum and minimum distances between the front corners.

The Alaska Department of Natural Resources (DNR) was the agency administering the program, and I'm sure they were heavily influenced by some misguided federal oversight. They (I must admit) were happy to provide free detailed and accurate public domain maps for any of the innumerable designated OTE areas in the state in which the hopeful beachfront property owner might be interested.

The first step in the process couldn't have been simpler for the applicant. All that was required was that they drive and mark a stake (or re-bar, or pipe or whatever) where they wanted one of the proposed beachfront corners, measure the prescribed distance in either direction and drive another one. The applicant could then make any improvements that they wished, like a cabin or a garden or something like that, on the upland property that they wanted to claim, as long as they didn't encroach onto any adjacent property that already had someone else's corner stakes in place.

This is where the likely 'outside' influence becomes most evident. The hopeful landowner frequently didn't see any previous stakes because they had become completely hidden by the brush that had grown up since they were set. Of course, largely because of the administrative backlog and the intervening growth of concealing vegetation, none of the surveyors had any idea where previous surveyors had set any controlled corners, and they had a hell of a time finding them because the agency was still holding most of the survey records. Worse, most of the agency functionaries wouldn't even let us look at any of the survey records they had in their in-baskets because they were "under review," whatever that meant.

Some of the prospective property owners became disgusted with the agency procrastination and went ahead with the individual surveys for their own projects. A number of survey firms were contracted for location and surveys (as well as construction layout) of many of these properties, two or three of which I did a fair amount of work on as an independent surveyor at the time when a professional engineering license included authorization of land surveying for the licensee. However, the result of all these confusions and other problems surrounding the

OTE program became very serious and often didn't surface until much later.

It was a well-intentioned program, and after (if) all the problems were straightened out a few years later, one would have to conclude that ultimately it probably served Alaska reasonably well; opening up many of the remote areas for development. There were, however, at least two negative aspects of the program: 1) The difficulties of locating previously set corners resulted in a number of disputes over hiatuses and overlaps. 2) The Alaska residency requirement was probably minimal and a lot of opportunists with nothing except a desire to become landowners were drawn north. Regardless of the positive or negative aspects, the State of Alaska would do well to devote more time to pre-program analyses before pursuing another concept brought in from outside – if that's what it was.

Some of the work that Gerry went after in the early 1970's was directly related to the oil recovery efforts on the North Slope. As I recall the events of that time, things went somewhat as described in the following few paragraphs.

It was in 1968 when the massive oil discoveries on the North Slope hit the newspapers. I don't think it was such a big surprise to anyone who had witnessed the increased activity up there or noted the attention being focused on the area by the big oil companies. I suppose that there were a few politicians and lawyers who knew what was going on too but felt that it was in their own personal best interest not to reveal much about it prematurely.

Although many Alaskans were happy about it because of the anticipated, and hopefully beneficial, economic impact on the state, I may have been a little more skeptical than most. Having closely observed the effects of statehood, it was easy to foresee that the rush to exploit this newly found resource and its peripheral effects would spark a new exodus to our state. I for one was acutely aware of the potential for social disruption such a movement would inevitably bring with it, and I'm sure I wasn't alone in such a concern. However, both statehood and the oil discoveries had become *facts*, and the high-powered corporate executives, the high rollers, and the cowboys who were to follow would very soon become just as real.

No one was more aware than the actual working people with the big oil companies that oil in the ground way up on the arctic coast wasn't the same as oil in the tankers at the docks of the refineries. The company movers and shakers, with their planners and engineers in tow, therefore began trying to figure out how to get all that oil down there. Today, we all know that a pipeline from 'the slope' to Valdez – Valdez being the logical and the closest location as the port of choice – followed by a tanker haul from Valdez to the appropriate refinery was settled on as the solution. The transportation operations, just as with anything new, particularly something as huge and complex as moving the oil from Alaska to an outside destination, was not without its initial problems. I think I recall at least two attacks on some pipeline pumping stations by a couple of environmental whackos, and all manner of political grandstanding with long-winded ignorance-based discussions in support of absurd propositions. I also think we all remember the incident when Captain Hazelwood got drunk and bumped into Bligh Reef in Valdez Arm, spilling huge quantities of oil into the ocean, killing thousands of innocent marine critters and just generally making a big mess of the whole Prince William Sound area.

The oil conglomerates have deep pockets, and at the urging of some of our now overpopulation of ever alert, opportunistic lawyers, every fisherman who had so much as seen Prince William Sound in photographs or on a map sued the oil companies for killing all those fish and allegedly destroying fishing forever as a viable occupation in the sound. The oil companies own a bunch of lawyers too, and although many of the fisherman won their lawsuits, and although their lawyers had gotten, or stood to get, obscenely rich from their exorbitant contingent fees, as of this writing the companies have so far, through continual appeals, avoided paying anybody anything – except their own lawyers of course.

Those big companies have lots of money, and they're not accustomed to giving it away, regardless of the justice of the cause. That's probably one reason why they still have so much. There is no doubt that many of the fishermen deserve some very substantial recompense, but the way these goings-on are being handled is so typical of the way people behave 'outside', and so un-Alaskan that the whole thing is absolutely sickening.

The most expensive and challenging effort of the whole concern was without question the construction of the pipeline from the North Slope to Valdez. There had never been such a major petroleum pipeline built under the conditions, over the terrain extremities, or through as much frozen ground as was anticipated along the proposed route. The big companies recognized the difficulties that would have to be overcome, the major costs involved, and the logic of sharing these difficulties and costs among all the oil corporations involved in exploiting the resource. In response to these considerations, they formed another corporation and named it *Alyeska Pipeline Incorporated.*

Alyeska pipeline

This new outfit was to bear the responsibly for completing the pipeline, and to their credit, they did come up with some very innovative solutions to some unique problems. However, I can testify from personal observation to the shamefully inefficient, wasteful and 'spare-no-expense' attitude with which they approached the project, and the casual, overstaffed manner in which they did the work. Any Alaskan observing all this had to wonder if *this* was the way 'they did it outside'. They seemed to have won the battle against the environment, but it had to have been an obscenely expensive victory.

Interestingly, I happened to attend a meeting between Gerry and a man named Patton in the Alyeska Anchorage office. I don't remember what sort of functionary Patton was, but I do remember that at the time of pipeline design and planning he had some responsibility for deciding on the choice of specialized consultant selection, construction methods and so on. Gerry was there to see what sort of work we could get out of the pipeline consortium. I'm not accustomed to functioning as a salesman for my services, so I'm not really sure why Gerry asked me to go to the meeting with him.

During the conversation, Patton mentioned several times that he was very concerned about the difficulties that would undoubtedly be encountered when attempting to trench for and bury the pipeline in the long sections through seasonally frozen ground and permafrost. There was also an almost certain probability of damage to the permafrost because of the high temperature of the product to be pumped through the line. I had some experience with the use of 'thermo-piles' for constructing both building foundations and village utility lines above ground with several feet of clearance between ground level and the facility. A 'thermo-pile' is really nothing more than an ordinary pipe pile modified to incorporate a little heat pump and channeled to accommodate the necessary airflow. Anyway, after listening to Patton bellyaching about all his woes concerning pipe burial for about half an hour, I asked why he didn't use some of this thermo-pile technology and set the pipeline above ground. He looked at me like I was nuts and said, "Nobody builds petroleum pipelines above ground." Perhaps he was referring to the potential for damage from vandalism, which would probably be a legitimate concern under normal circumstances, but certainly not a serious one in the roadless areas of the arctic. There just aren't that many potential vandals wandering around up there. When I pointed this out, it 'cut no ice'[32] with him.

This was typical of the sort of outside arrogance that Alaskans have traditionally put up with since long before statehood, and after that it became even worse. I don't pretend to be any kind of prophet, but I swear the story is true, and to my subsequent satisfaction, a lot of the line did in fact, get installed above ground. Although I don't think Gerry got any actual pipeline work, he did finally do some work for them that I think was pretty profitable for him.

I don't know if the problem was anticipated by Alyeska prior to construction, but they soon discovered that in the swampy areas the pipe would often float out of the ground unless weighted down. As a result of this discovery, and I suppose some negotiation, BB&S Construction got into the concrete block business, selling them to Alyeska as weights to keep the pipe from floating up.

The 'Monster' up close

There wasn't much engineering involved in the casting of concrete blocks of specified weight, so this was really the

[32] No pun intended; or maybe there was.

beginning of the end of my association with the company. We had a couple of subdivision projects left to final out, and we were waiting for some kind of design approval from the borough, but at the time most of the company effort had been redirected to the Alyeska block project. The two last sub-divisions went smoothly although because of the still prevalent overlap in authority between the borough and the city, both projects were smothered in official reviews, approvals and discussion.

Even while still working for BB&S I had been doing some minor amounts of estimating for Tommy Cleveland of Cleveland Trucking and Excavating. After it became obvious that Gerry no longer needed a full-time engineer, I went to work for Tommy as an estimator. He and I agreed that I could also do some independent consulting work provided none of it was for any of his competitors.

It had been some time since I had been directly involved in competitive construction estimating and bidding, and there were two main aspects of the work that came as something of a surprise, if not a shock, for me. The first of these was the phenomenal increases in costs for everything, including materials, equipment rental rates, supplies and everything else needed for pursuing and completing heavy earthwork construction projects. Of course, this was to be expected in an expanding economy, and since statehood and the oil discovery such an economy was what we seemed to have. I was also surprised by the extremely strong and growing influence of the labor unions in every phase of construction contracting. This may or may not have been an indirect result of statehood, but it was definitely a change from the days when the main concern was to get the work done.

Although they were instrumental in gaining many increased benefits for laboring folks, the unions were creating an adversarial relationship between the workers and the company owners. There had no doubt been cases where the company owners were taking unfair advantage of the workers in both working conditions and wages, and I suppose the unions were helpful in changing such things. However, most of these infractions were being committed by the contractors who had swarmed north, either as a result of statehood or the riches to be 'scooped up' in the wake of the oil companies and the relative activity. We were growing up, and a lot of us didn't like it.

The most interesting of the jobs we did while I was with Tommy was a grading and paving project at the Quartz Creek Campground along the Sterling Highway (the road to Kenai, Soldotna and Homer) about seventy-five miles south of Anchorage. Our bid was under the aegis of a man named Jesse who owned a utilities construction company in Anchorage called Kayak Construction.

It was a paving contract for the U.S. Forest Service at one of their campgrounds. It turned out that the agency project engineer was a man called 'Skip' (presumably a nickname) with whom I had gone to college almost fifteen years previously. During his professional career with the Forest Service, Skip had changed from a full-blooded engineer into sort of cross between an engineer and a 'rabbit-tracker'. The protection of the environment seemed to have become his primary concern. No one would argue that this wasn't (or isn't) a legitimate concern, but it was increasingly becoming a rabidly overzealous 'cause' and so ridiculously overdone that it was wreaking havoc within the construction industry.

The job called for reconstruction, re-grading and AC paving of about six miles of eighteen-foot roadway winding in and out between the large (sixteen to twenty-four-inch diameter) spruce, or fir, or hemlock trees that covered the whole campground at about eight to ten feet on center. There was an existing road there, but it was only about fourteen feet wide and the pavement was badly deteriorated. It was obvious from the beginning that using the necessary equipment, and maneuvering it around all the tight curves and through the trees, would require some masterful operating techniques. It was not so obvious that the USFS (in the person of Skip) would be so much more concerned about the dangers of scraping off tree bark, etc. than they were about such things as AC quality, compaction, gravel gradations and other such construction-related matters. Every time a tree got bumped, regardless of how minimal the damage, we had to suspend operations at that location, clean up the damaged bark and paint it with some kind of coal tar mixture. We also had to stay constantly alert for signs of any kind of little (or big) woodland critter, and if we saw any, we had to take special and expensive measures to ensure their safety and comfort. I don't recall seeing the agency folks taking a single paving mix sample for testing or performing a single on-site quality control test.

Skip wasn't alone in his environmental enthusiasm. At times he reminded me a little of one of those 'born-again' Christians who had reportedly 'seen the light' and wanted to share the joy with anyone they could catch. This over-concern about such things was another of the exaggerated issues brought north after statehood by the folks who came up to 'save' us from ourselves. Interestingly, such concern on the part of 'outside' folks was minimal or non-existent before statehood and the oil discoveries.

These two events were the major factors that had drawn national attention to Alaska up to this point. I think statehood made a lot of people curious about the territory, and since we had traditionally been characterized as 'The Last Frontier', maybe some of them wanted to come up to see if statehood was having any effect – who knows? Alaskans have always cordially welcomed visitors, whatever their reasons for coming. The concern about all the lifestyle changes arose when the visitors began turning into residents.

When the oil strike hit the headlines, many of the outside environmentalists, having had their attention captured by statehood, sort of adopted the preservation of Alaska as their cause for a personal crusade, although most of them had never even been there. After the actual North Slope development began, thousands of them traveled up north in little blue Volkswagens, presumably to protect 'their' Alaskan environment from those of us who lived there. I always resented those people a little; firstly because they rarely had any idea what the hell they were talking about, and secondly because they seemed to think that they were somehow authorized to tell us what to do in our own country.

While I was working with Tommy, I also contracted for some additional estimating when it was clear there was no conflict of interest, and even then only with Tommy's approval. This kind of working agreement has the potential for some really sticky problems because all the contractors (particularly the sub-contractors) typically play their cards so close to the vest that it's difficult to know who's competing with whom.

Kotzebue: Driving corners in frozen ground – no fun at all

I also did numerous lot/boundary surveys, including a layout for a subdivision in Kotzebue, although I can't remember the name of the client; isn't that awful? What I *do* remember about that Kotzebue job was that it was extremely cold the whole time we were there and that the ground was usually frozen so hard we had to use a blowtorch to thaw it before driving the corners. However, it wasn't all bad. Eloise came with me on that job despite her often-expressed distaste for cold weather, and I think she was pleased with certain aspects of the trip.

Kotzebue friends

The people in Kotzebue are mostly Eskimo and their traditional warmth and friendliness was there in abundance. We attended a number of parties and enjoyed numerous home visits, during which Eloise had ample opportunity to experience the Eskimo geniality which I had tried to describe to her many times. I think we were there for a little over a week.

Although it was certainly one of the coldest surveys I've ever been involved with, Kotzebue wasn't the only subdivision-related work I was able to do while working for Tommy. Shortly after finishing the work at Kotzebue I obtained a commission for the street and utilities design and layout in a major new subdivision called Equestrian Acres north of Palmer and along the road to Wasilla. That subdivision is worth a few words here, mostly because of the screwball who owned it. Regardless of all that, he was an Alaskan screwball so I sort of mentally excused his behavior. I doubt if he would survive very long in the conventional business environment now engulfing Alaska. If he hasn't changed his approach, he's probably no longer in business in the 'new' Alaska. We've always had more than our share of that type of person; it was one of the things that once made the place so interesting to live in.

The screwball's nickname was 'Cappie'; apparently because at one time in his career he had been the captain of something. He was a strange man. He seemed to have no qualms whatever about proclaiming his opinions to be absolute fact. If I tried to contradict or correct him, he would angrily remind me that he was paying me, as if that somehow obligated me to agree with everything he said regardless of how farfetched or goofy his remarks might be. He also had a number of questionable personal habits, one of which was particularly repugnant to me. Cappie customarily got up very early every day and he seemed to delight in telephoning everyone who worked with him or had ever worked for him just to wake them up. Even at that time, I was already in the disgusting habit of getting up at four or four thirty every morning, and I think it irritated him that I was always already awake whenever he called.

Failing to wake me up, he started making these early morning calls to some of the other contractors and developers for whom I was also doing work in addition to his subdivision. He began telling them some really bizarre things; he would say that I was sick, or drunk or something and couldn't help them during the upcoming day. Alternatively, he might say that I had been working for him, but he had to fire me for incompetence and all sorts of weird stuff like that. I found all this out because many of my clients that he was calling were also friends of mine. They always called me right away, mostly to find out who this apparent crackpot was and to ask about my relationship with him. I still looked at him as a fellow Alaskan, but I decided that I'd have to say something for my own protection.

When I first began hearing about these things he was doing, I couldn't believe it. Why would a man do things like that? What could he gain by such behavior? Was he hoping to hurt my reputation? Was he trying to keep me from working on any jobs but his? I confronted him with all these questions, called him a few names that were decidedly uncomplimentary, and threatened to sue him for defamation of character or libel, or whatever might be applicable. I also told him that no matter what his response to my insults and accusations, I intended to end our business relationship immediately. I gave him a written statement to that effect, asking him to sign just below my own signature.

His reaction was astonishing. It was as though I hadn't said a word. He ignored my written document and my verbal statement of intent to sever our business relationship. My uncomplimentary remarks about him, his project, his character and his behavior elicited no rejoinders whatever. He just kept on talking about what remained to be done with Equestrian Acres. Even when I repeated that I intended to leave the project, he still kept going on as though I hadn't said anything about my complaints or intentions. It finally became obvious to me that the man was mentally unbalanced, and that he was actually *incapable* of controlling or moderating his behavior. At that point I became a little bit more sympathetic, but I made it clear to him that unless he stopped doing what he was doing, I still intended to sever our business relationship and just leave.

In Cappie's favor, however, I must say that he always paid my billings promptly. I should also note that after I made it clear I would no longer put up with his aberrant behavior and would walk away with no further notice the next time it happened, his antics stopped, and it never happened again, his refusal or inability to even acknowledge anything I had said notwithstanding. Although he seemed not to have heard any of my rejoinders to his despicable attempts to discredit me, apparently some sense of my outrage had gotten through to him.

In any case, Equestrian Acres was successfully completed, and it actually turned out to be a pleasant and very livable development. I wonder if Cappie is still alive. If he is, he's probably pretty proud of 'his' subdivision, although it seemed like he was doing everything he could to torpedo the project during the development phase. I wonder what's happened to all the Cappies.

Much of the property development work around Anchorage really slowed down after the Alyeska pipeline was completed. Despite the slowdown, there was still a lot of financial optimism around town. The oil companies were building big buildings in both Anchorage and Fairbanks, setting up permanent maintenance and pumping stations along the new line and just screwing up the country in general. I jest; actually they did a remarkably good job in keeping the country as pristine as possible.

The real problem was that the oil industry employees and executives from outside were bringing their own attitudes and values up north with them. They weren't at all reluctant to tell us what was wrong with *our* values and attitudes either. It wasn't long before they began moving in permanently, becoming council people, local movers and shakers and so on. In short, they were soon beginning to take over our country and apparently trying to make it just like where they had recently come from. Alaska wasn't and isn't just like where they came from, and most *real* Alaskans don't want it to be.

The highway that was built running along the pipeline corridor from Livengood north was, and will remain, a scar on the face of the land, no matter how necessary it may have been. This was the main permanent damage that the pipeline project inflicted and the resultant traffic continues to pollute the country in many ways, only one of which is the poisoning of the air and the rivers. Roads in themselves do not change lifestyles and attitudes, but by providing access they allow such changes. The road to Prudhoe Bay is no exception. Americanization is coming to the arctic. It may take a while to get there, but get there it will; it's inevitable and there are plenty of historical precedents to serve as examples. Social relationships and inter-person attitudes have also changed and are continuing to change throughout the state, even in much of the remote country. In fairness, not all the results of this new northward migration have been as negative as many Alaskans predicted. Nor has it created the arctic wasteland that the suddenly interested outside environmental 'experts' who, previously never even having *looked* at a map of Alaska, felt qualified to warn us about and to instruct us in how to avoid such things.

Before the line was built there were many dire predictions that the aboveground pipe would cause such stress to the various animals in the area they would suffer the equivalent of human nervous breakdowns or post-traumatic stress syndrome. Maybe so, but I have personally witnessed bears denned in directly below the pipe, and I think that most of the other critters can pass under the raised line without much difficulty at many locations. They don't seem to be aware of, or stressed over, which side of the pipe they're on. I have seen both caribou and moose grazing contentedly on the grass or the willows planted on both sides of the pipe along the pipeline corridor. I think that, in many cases, the line was deliberately elevated high enough to provide clearance for all the native critters to walk easily under it, which they did (and probably still do) with comfortable regularity.

Contrary to what the rabbit-tracking extremists would have us believe, construction of new facilities in the wilderness does not, in the long run, materially affect the area wildlife. I know this to be true because I have personally witnessed such natural adjustment. After the 'improvement' has been in place a year or two, the resident critters seem to accept it as a normal part of their surroundings, and after that they simply ignore it. I can't speak to the problem, if there is one, of mental adjustment, but from what I've seen they seem just as happy with the improvement being there as they were before it was built.

No matter the realities, from what I read in the newspapers it seems that the rabbit trackers are still determined to impose their ideas of what *they* think is best for Alaska. They are the self-appointed guardians of the environment – *our* environment and, by implication, everyone else's. Never mind that at least 95% of them have never even *been* to Alaska, much less to the high arctic. Anyway, it's irreversible now; many of them have moved up north to make it (mostly Anchorage) their home. If it hasn't started already, it won't be long until they begin forming clubs, discussion groups and so on in order to consolidate their ignorance-based efforts.

In truth, saving the environment is an admirable cause and one worthy of pursuing. However, mouthing stupid slogans and marching around with little hand-lettered cardboard signs is not the way to do it. In many, if not most, of the protest cases, it isn't clear exactly what the protesters are protesting against. If the majority of their specific remarks are taken at face value, most of them are embarrassingly wide of the mark. Perhaps the most perceptive of these groups should actually go out into the woods and see exactly what aspect of the wilderness is most vulnerable, why it is the most vulnerable, and how its vulnerability can be recognized and compensated for. It would be interesting to turn a bunch of them loose somewhere along an uncharted stretch of the Colville River in the winter with a minimum of survival gear, pick them up in two or three weeks and *then* ask them about the sensitivity of the country.

At the time, and maybe before, the pipeline construction was in progress, builders and/or developers in the Anchorage 'Municipality' (combined city and borough) were required to retain a professional engineer and furnish their own design and inspection for all their proposed street, sewer and waterline extensions. Those were the rules, but for some reason, increasing numbers of influential property owners could somehow get the borough to do all that for them. I suppose some sort of local politics was involved, but since I had plenty of work, I wasn't interested in looking into it. Local or any other kind of politics or political maneuvering were rarely interesting enough to me to investigate in any depth, particularly after such activities became so pervasive they were accepted as the normal way of doing business.

Even then, and even in Anchorage, someone openly calling themselves a 'management consultant' was pretty rare. Over the past twenty or thirty years they have multiplied like supercharged rabbits, even advertising without embarrassment. I wonder what they consult about or what they advise their clients to do. As it turned out, these 'management' people were not guided by the same principles as the real Alaskans who had been there since the days when a handshake was as unbreakable a bond as any piece of lawyer-written paper. That may sound naively trite, but it was absolutely true.

Although it sounded like a good idea at the time, the move to the new office turned out to be a real mistake. For one thing, the promoters didn't seem to be in serious contact with the actual building managers/maintenance people, I never saw, much less used, any secretarial 'pool', and the cleaning services were sporadic at best – they seemed to forget about my office more often than not. Whenever I called the guy who talked me into this office relocation, he seemed disinterested in the ongoing operational problems with the offices. He just kept asking me if I knew of anyone else who might be looking for office space; I didn't. These were the kind of people who were becoming more and more common in Alaska in general and in Anchorage in particular.

For some reason, while I was in this new office complex, the clients began to pay more and more irregularly. In fact, some of them who had so far been the most reliable for on-time payment during our previous dealings now began to stall more and more frequently. In some cases, my billings were ignored altogether. Maybe they sort of assumed that moving into a real office indicated that my financial affairs were more stable than they had been, and that consequently it wasn't as important to me to collect my accounts as quickly as it had been previously. Since I was never very far above water with regard to 'cash flow' (whatever that is), this slowdown in cash receipts was really crippling. I could usually meet the payroll for any surveyors, technicians and such that I had to hire to complete certain projects, but after that there was damn little left for Eloise and me to live on.

Eloise rarely complained (and she still doesn't) about such things, but during this period, she too was feeling the financial stress. She even went personally to a couple of the non-paying (long overdue) clients and demanded immediate payment, haranguing on them until they paid. To my surprise, it actually worked in a couple of instances, although it really ticked off the clients in question. A few of them swore that they would never again do business with me as long as Eloise was involved – a testimony to her effectiveness. Their attitude didn't bother me at all. After all, who needs business from clients who don't pay?

I have just one more story about this new office. It's worth telling because it demonstrates both the kind of people who were becoming more and more numerous in Alaska as well as the duplicity that I've often found to be present within the legal profession.

About three or four months after I got there, a lawyer happened to move into 'our' complex. After we became reasonably friendly, something that has since become very difficult for me to do with lawyers, I mentioned in passing that I was having some trouble collecting money for completed work. He told me not to worry about it. He suggested that after the billings were thirty days or more overdue, I should just turn them over to him, and he would guarantee to collect the money or he wouldn't ask for any attorney fees.

Despite his arrogant self-assurance, I never saw *any* subsequent increase in collections. In fact, contrary to what I thought was our agreement, I started getting some substantial periodic billings from the lawyer himself. When I took these billings over to his office and reminded him of his promises not to ask for any fees unless his collection efforts were successful, he said that his promises referred only to 'fees'. His charges against me were, he said, just for 'expenses'. If those were truly his expenses, he must have been living pretty high on the hog so to speak, eating caviar, drinking expensive French wines and driving a big new Rolls Royce around to see my "dead-beat clients" (his term). Also, he was apparently spending twenty-four hours a day trying to collect these outstanding billings for me to the exclusion of any of his other work, if he indeed had (or, as it were, needed) any other work. I don't remember that he brought in *any* money from any of my errant clients. Anyway, I'm certain he never collected enough to pay for the bills he kept sending me. After about four months, I stopped using his services.

I heard later[33] that this lawyer had somehow gotten himself named as one of the creditors in several of the cases where my former clients had been forced into bankruptcy. Reportedly, he had thus been able to seat himself at the vulture's table where the remaining personal and real properties of the unfortunate developer were disbursed, although he had suffered absolutely no losses of his own. Naturally, I heard nothing of this at the time, if in fact it actually happened. My experience with such people tells me that he might well have (and gleefully would have) pulled off some stunt exactly like the one I heard about. If he did, he no doubt sprained his arm patting himself on the back over having pulled off such a clever ruse and helping to ruin those unfortunate developers. The financial losses and personal tragedy suffered by my former clients, many of whom had become personal and sincere friends of mine, would have meant nothing whatsoever to this scumbag lawyer. Perhaps he used part of these ill-gotten gains in entertaining some of his other

[33] Just hearsay – but from some pretty reliable sources.

arrogant lawyer friends over drinks in one of Anchorage's high-end watering holes. It's pretty humorous being able to spin tales and share yucks about how you helped to destroy someone, don't you think?

Somehow, people like that guy, and a lot of other dragons, had sneaked in 'under the tent flap' to take advantage of the political vacuum right after statehood back in 1959. Or maybe they had been drawn north by what they saw as easy money coming off the feeding frenzy after the oil discoveries. Looking back over a lot of years, I'm strongly, and unpleasantly, reminded of the phoniness and duplicity of many of the lawyers that I've run into during half a century of actually working for a living and helping to support these social parasites.

In early 1980, the business outlook for me was becoming so bleak that I decided to once more seek a temporary change of scenery, even though I knew it would mean leaving Alaska for a few years. The sorrow was mitigated to some extent by the realization that the Alaska I was leaving was nothing like the one I had originally moved to some thirty-five years previously.

Sometime in April or May of that year, an ad appeared in the *Anchorage Times* seeking applications for the job of "Deputy Director of Public Works" for Grays Harbor County, Washington. I applied for the position, traveled south for a personal interview and was subsequently offered the job.

Since I hoped to return to Alaska as soon as we could get our finances in order and a suitable job up there became available, I hoped to learn something about the way engineering offices in Washington State did business. We had been brought up to believe that the folks down there knew more than we did about almost everything, including how to design and build things. Maybe I could pick up a few pointers to take back up north with me. I was not prepared to find a working environment that was even more casual than the old Alaska.

Chapter 5: An Established Dragon Pit

My first impressions of the Grays Harbor County job made it seem like the county office crew were pursuing objectives that had nothing to do with getting things designed or built. The program structure they were operating under was not oriented that way. Being just an Alaska boy, with none of the 'stateside' sophistication I had been brought up to expect, I was sure I must have been missing something. As it turned out I wasn't really missing anything at all – there wasn't anything to miss.

My first impressions were pretty accurate; they *weren't* pursuing objectives that had anything to do with getting jobs designed or built. Their whole effort was aimed at completing a one-at-a-time series of mini-objectives, most of which arose out of non-technical regulations or policies of the state and federal agencies administering the jobs, and not from pragmatic project technical needs. These mini-objectives apparently constituted a package they had been programmed to believe was a legitimate and standard part of real-world road design and construction. Whatever the reason, someone at the county level got the idea that it was necessary after the completion of each of these irrelevant tasks, to wait for a signed document (letter) of approval before going on to the next administrative 'step'. This was nonsense, and I began to see an example of a complete workplace victory for formula 'Management' and bureaucracy. The designer could wait weeks (or maybe even months) for some of these meaningless approvals, and from a real world perspective, the project might not be able to tolerate such delays. I wanted to stop this state control of our progress. Accordingly, I instructed the designers to make the submittals as required but then to immediately continue with the design without waiting for state approval at each of these artificial bureaucratic "phases" (their term). I reasoned that, from a project standpoint, apologies are far less expensive and damaging than extensive delays.

Before this, everyone had been working in accordance with some sort of oddly phased scheduling that was both stupid and ineffective as a project guidance tool. For one thing, the so-called 'phases' were rarely based on the completion of construction tasks; they were almost all management defined with no significance whatever from a construction perspective. I tried to impress on them that all this stuff the state demanded was unimportant from the standpoint of the physical job. It may have been rude to be so critical about the practices of my new outfit, but what was happening here was ridiculous by anyone's definition. I didn't know it then, but I may have been getting a glimpse into the administrative future of my Alaskan home. These procedures were far from what I had expected and were certainly nothing I wanted to take home with me.

At the risk of seeming to be a blaspheming, ignorant cretin, I was finally able to convince the engineers that these little administrative requirements were not part of any ordinary and accepted process of design and construction. As a further attempt to get them to accept my ideas, I reminded them that the only two really important parts of any project were the beginning and the end. That point could be supported by the fact that any or all of those ephemeral administrative paperwork tasks could be eliminated or completely altered at the whim of any bureaucratic dragon who knew less than nothing about real construction but had the misplaced authority to intervene. In such a case, the amount of dirt to be moved, asphalt to be laid down or concrete to be poured would not change one iota. The effort to convince our engineers and technicians of these things again awakened my fear that the regulation/policy writers might someday be heading north. As events were already showing, it was not an unreasonable fear.

When projects are partly funded by the state or federal government, record keeping and form filling become more important than actually doing the work. Of course records are important but sadly, the invented processes of record-keeping and format have grown to completely unjustified gargantuan proportions and have given superficial and unjustified legitimacy to many non-producing bureaucratic and management positions. Grays Harbor County didn't seem irretrievably infected with the 'Management' virus when I first went to work there but, watching the state and federal bureaucrats interfering in the projects, it was easy to see that it wouldn't be long in coming.

For me, seeing this created a very real apprehension that, since statehood had arrived in Alaska twenty-one years previously, such bureaucracy would soon creep into even the remotest of our projects up there. In fact, the administrative 'Dragon' was overdue up north, and fearing the potential consequences of being overlooked and found to be superfluous, the ranks of 'Management' were not idle. They were furiously inventing and codifying useless rules, regulations and policies to ensure their appearance of necessity. God forbid that major projects should ever be successfully completed without their interference. I feared that their attempts to take over the technical Alaskan workplace would soon be largely successful and I was to see evidence of that fact soon enough.

Part of the design crew at the county also served as construction project engineers and inspectors during the construction season if the workload demanded, which it usually didn't. Bob, the chief construction engineer, had a full time inspector/technician named Dave (not me) working for him as a sort of assistant who, incidentally, moved into Bob's position after Bob left the county and went to work for the City of Everett. There were two full-time graduate design engineers, named Russ and Fred, and a couple of design technicians who were also supposed to double as inspectors or survey technicians as needed. Neither of the graduates ever filled in at such technical positions as drafting or surveying, which was probably a good thing considering their actual work capabilities at the time.

In fact, I was completely bamboozled by the apparent functions of these two design engineers. They didn't seem to know how to actually do *anything* except calculate and think about stuff. This might be OK in an organization where there was constantly enough work to allow the staff to be organized in such a way that a given person might perform only certain tasks for a continuous flow of projects. However, there just weren't enough projects to allow the county staff to be set up like that. Accordingly, I attempted to expand the duties of the full-time design engineers to include both technician work as well as the more professionally demanding tasks that are usually minimal and accomplished fairly quickly for most road design and construction projects.

I don't think I'll ever forget looking at some drawings that these two design engineers had attempted to prepare for a couple of road extensions in the northeast part of the county. The drawings were terrible, and I mean *really* awful. They resembled something done for a third or fourth grade science project. It looked like they hadn't even used a straightedge or any other kind of drafting tool. The 'drawings' were done in ink, but there were smudges and ink blobs all over them, and the lettering (obviously done freehand) was barely legible. I told both of these 'designers' (truthfully) that I had never seen anything so sloppy and unprofessional as these so-called 'drawings'. I recall that one of the guys responded by saying, in a sarcastic tone of voice, "*Well*, we're *not* draftsmen," as though a draftsman was some lower form of life. I think that my response was something like, "That's *really* obvious."

I must add here that both Russ and Fred, the two graduates, have gone on to become extremely competent in what they do. I also note with satisfaction that neither of them still has that indefinable (and almost intolerable) air of superiority that so many inexperienced graduate engineers carry away from their graduation ceremonies. In fact, Russ has become the county road engineer, Fred is his assistant and they no longer seem particularly impressed with themselves. I don't know if either one of them ever learned to draw, but it doesn't matter because today's electronic gadgetry does most of those technician tasks anyway.

In May of 1962, the man who had been both director of public works and county engineer for more than twenty years retired. I don't remember exactly what happened immediately after that, but I *do* remember that his assistant, who had previously been following the director around like a little lap dog, somehow got himself appointed as the new director of public works. He was unregistered as an engineer so he couldn't (by law) also act as county engineer. He, therefore, asked me if I would accept the county engineer position, and I agreed.

What follows is a more detailed account of how all this went down. The personal aspects of the job are not important to my story. However, the things that I learned, some of which I took back to Alaska with me, may have changed my outlook. I may have become better able to recognize the nature of the changes that were, by now, seriously altering Alaska and the Alaskan lifestyle. Although it was hard to accept, my frequent trips back up north while living in Washington State made it sadly obvious to me that living in most places in Alaska would never be the same again.

Prior to 1982, the position of both county engineer and director of public works had traditionally been vested in one man. In 1982, the man in that position was nicknamed 'Tod' – Christian name Charles. Tod retired during the latter half of 1982, leaving a void in both the positions of director of public works and county engineer. It happened that there was a man named Gary who had somehow maneuvered himself into an unofficial position as Tod's trusted alter ego. In this 'position', he managed to set himself up in the guise of a sort of de facto chief of staff (without a staff) for Tod, and as such he offered to attend all the commissioner's meetings as Tod's representative. Tod was not overly impressed by meetings, the people who went to them, or the results that came out of them.

All this apparent effort of Gary's in the guise of loyalty seemed to actually be part of an overall plan to increase his visibility with the Board of Commissioners. I suspect, although I have no real knowledge of it, that he frequently took, or at least implied, credit for some of the good ideas coming out of the Engineering Department that he actually knew nothing about or had no part in formulating.

When Tod retired, Gary was almost desperate to get the job as director of public works for the county. The main stumbling block for Gary was that the county engineer position, which had previously been combined with that of the director, required that the incumbent be registered as a professional engineer in the State of Washington. I know that Gary was registered as a professional land surveyor but not as an engineer. Because of the registration problem, Gary asked me if I would accept the job of county engineer with all the authority (and responsibility) that the WAC (Washington Administrative Code) conferred under that specific title.

The professional certification requirements for the specific position of director of public works were left sort of ambiguously defined. This was the title that Gary really wanted, and because of all his previous lobbying, as well as some influential friends, he expected to get it – and he did.

I can only remember two conditions that I placed on my acceptance of Gary's job offer. I wanted the official job title to be changed to county road engineer because that was the way it was worded in the WAC, and I wanted a salary increase commensurate with the increased workload and legal responsibility. There was no problem with my conditions, so I took the job, not fully realizing the administrative nature of the work.

After becoming county road engineer I became subjected to an almost constant stream of meetings covering almost every conceivable subject even remotely (sometimes *very* remotely) connected with county roads. Many of these meetings seemed to me to be almost frivolous and had little or nothing to do with design or construction of county (or any other) roads. This was a problem not only with me, but also with other members of the engineering staff from project engineer up. It was finally necessary to make it clear to all the engineering staff that none of us was going to attend any more of these meetings unless they were obviously and specifically project related and intended to address specific technical subjects and/or problems. It was not a popular decision at first. I think some of the staff actually enjoyed going to those time-wasting gatherings for some reason.

Even though it's jumping ahead a little, I should note here that in 1988 Gary was fired from his position by the Board of County Commissioners. I never did find out specifically why he got the axe, but I must conclude that it was probably more because of internal politics than for lack of technical ability.

Gary *did* have an extremely irritating habit of interfering with the details of everybody else's work, and it was very annoying to a lot of both the engineering people and the maintenance supervisors. I suppose someone (or a lot of someones) complained to the commissioners, and they went after Gary to appease the complainers. Anyway, who knows? There may have been a lot more to it than that. After I heard about the firing, I called Gary from Alaska[34] and suggested that he just tell the commissioners to stick it in their collective ear, walk away and start up his own survey outfit. For some reason, he was unable to do that, and he went to work for the State of Washington Department of Transportation (WSDOT) as a survey party chief. It wasn't long until he moved up the 'corporate' ladder into some sort of bureaucratic advisory position. He enjoyed that sort of thing because it gave him the chance to interfere with the details of other people's jobs.

I liked Gary. We got along fine, but (for me anyway) he was a little bit difficult to talk to about specific subjects. It always seemed like he was kind of talking 'at right angles' to the subject of any conversation. Maybe other people didn't get the same impression when they talked to him. Anyway, Gary died in late 1992 (God rest him), and that was the end of that. He's probably 'up there' interfering, reviewing, and advising as he enjoyed doing while he was down here.

I like to think that I was able to accomplish a few worthwhile things while serving as county road engineer. One of these was the development of a maintenance management program which is (in part) still in use today. The program was originally designed to serve as a scheduling mechanism flexible enough to change crew make-ups and sizes to achieve optimum production and productivity. The intention was to track these operational factors from the information supplied by the

[34] I was in Petersburg by then.

supervisors on their daily reports. The program also provided methods for tracking costs and for adjusting budget figures on the basis of rational analyses of all the variables. There were also a few more technical things that I'm proud of having accomplished, and although pride is indeed a sin that "goeth before a fall," surely a few remarks about these things are not too far out of line.

During my five years with the county, a lot of statewide attention was being directed toward development of priorities for road reconstruction projects within designated classifications (e.g. primary roads, secondary roads, feeders, collectors and so on). I devised a system of relative evaluations of the structural capacity based on deflection analyses that also predicted rates of reduction of such capacities over both short and long-term use, given reasonable traffic counts and predictions. Of course, such predictions depend on a lot of assumptions for imponderables like gasoline prices, unforeseeable events such as storms, earthquakes, economic fluctuations and things like that. However, we did the best we could and hopefully left enough flexibility in the predictions to allow for anything short of the apocalypse. I still believe the deflection approach is by far the best available. I recall that, with the state's help, we accumulated a lot of data for use with the empirical equations relating deflections, traffic volumes and deterioration of the roadway structure. Whether the county ever did (or will do) anything with them is a separate question, and one that I can't answer. This was another good idea that might well have been useful in the planning for Alaska's highway system, but the administrative jungle I ran into when I got back to Juneau made such technically feasible and potentially valuable planning programs impossible to implement.

The county administrative folks were also attempting to devise some rational method for charging the timber companies in advance for using some of the remote (and some not so remote) county roads for hauling out cut logs to the sawmills. In response to the perceived need, I prepared a paper proposing a method of advance charging for hauling out from a specific resource area. My proposal was based on estimated total loads and hauling dates supplied by the timber companies, equivalent axle loadings and initial roadway structural conditions. The method required almost no physical effort on our part except for a few initial deflection measurements before the work started.

I may be wrong, but I believe Gary tried to explain this proposed advance fee charging mechanism to the timber haulers and got no meaningful response at all. Actually, I don't think he understood it either, but he liked to be seen as the major man in the department with regard to public contact, which didn't bother me at all; I hate that sort of thing. As in a few other cases, my memory fails me and I can't recall whether or not this method was ever used as a basis for charging the timber haulers, although I doubt it. The timber companies have a lot of clout in Grays Harbor County, both economically and politically. If the local government bodies propose something these companies don't like, it usually doesn't happen.

There was one other thing I like to feel I had some influence over. Here again, I felt that Alaska could benefit from such predictive programs as this, but again I found that the imported 'Management' tangle-up in Juneau had become impenetrable by the time I got back there.

Development of the road system in Grays Harbor County seems to have been driven by two separate motivators. Chronologically speaking, the purpose of the first of these was to provide access up the river valleys where the soil was rich for farming, and the game was plentiful because of the easy access to water. The original wagon roads up the valleys probably followed Indian hunting trails, which were no doubt previously routed along the ancient game trails. The second driving force for road development must have begun with the prominence of the timber companies. They seemed dedicated to cutting down every potentially lucrative timber growth area in the country, and to do so they were forced to build access roads to get to the trees. When the trees were gone, it wasn't long before the timber companies were gone too, but the roads remained and eventually people began to settle along these ad hoc routes. Pretty soon, there were enough people living up in the woods to put pressure on the politicians and get the access roads accepted by the county for maintenance, and, as traffic and population increased, for reconstruction as needed. Eventually, the state and the federal government (each of them with their own myriad of agencies and bureaus) also got involved. The result of all this is the administrative morass we now find ourselves (including Alaska) in, supporting about two managers, three bureaucrats and four administrators for every engineer or dirt shifter actually doing any work – a slight (but only slight) exaggeration.

Many of the roads in the county, particularly those in the hills originally intended for resource extraction, are built along side-hills; usually un-benched and often underlain by material that had, in the distant past, sloughed downhill from higher up the slope. Although these roads, originating as logging roads, constitute a significant portion of the county network, it is the ones running up the river valleys that are mostly characteristic of the system and are dominant enough to define it as 'Riverine'. An example of such a system in nature can be easily seen by examining a large tree leaf (such as a maple leaf), observing the central vein and the way the tributary veins feed into it. Most of the systems feeding major rivers are laid out (by nature) pretty much the same way. The result of placing all these roads along the slopes adjacent to the rivers and tributaries is that most roads in the county want to slide into the water. Given the lack of benching and the absence of keyways to buttress the fill slopes, this is not a surprising result. I was, if not disillusioned, at least disappointed that the graduate engineers on the staff did not have enough knowledge of soil mechanics to analyze these slide situations and figure out what was happening. When I introduced the basic undergraduate methods of slope stability analyses, they seemed totally nonplussed. Maybe they were just being polite. Most of the more sophisticated principles of slope stability stuff that I had learned during my brief time in graduate courses were not necessary here. I felt that if I started spouting off about such things, particularly in view of what appeared to be a sad lack of understanding about the basics, it would look like I was showing off.

In any case, I was able to successfully evaluate and analyze a couple of slope areas that had begun to move and looked like they were in imminent danger of complete collapse. In response to the concerns of the maintenance folks, I suggested that we design most slide prevention projects to unload the upslope portions of the failure surfaces and buttress the lower portions, adding supplementary drainage accommodations. Perhaps as a result of our work, none of the suspect areas failed, at least not before I went back up north.

Rightly or wrongly, our design was sometimes given credit for preventing what some others thought would surely be future slope failures. There were, of course, critics who felt that the slopes would have remained stable with or without our designed improvements. Maybe the critics were right, but since most of the projects have been built, neither of us can prove our contentions, can we? Better to have the projects built and not need them than to need them and not have them, isn't it?

As time went by, my memories of Southeast Alaska began to occupy more and more of my thoughts. Every time there was an Alaskan story in the newspaper or a show on television, the pain of homesickness pierced me deeper and deeper.

Suddenly, like an answer to a prayer, an advertisement in the Seattle Times appeared soliciting applications for the position of city engineer in the City of Petersburg, Alaska. I applied for the job, and after a personal interview with the Petersburg City Council (they paid for a roundtrip up and back), I was offered the job at what must have been a satisfactory salary, and I accepted. I don't remember how much money was involved, but if it was only reasonably acceptable, I would have taken the job – it was time to go home.

Chapter 6: The Dragon at Bay

It was now 1985; twenty-six years since statehood and eighteen years since the beginning of the oil boom, but in spite of all that, Petersburg had managed to maintain its Alaskan ambiance and escape the insidious influences of 'outside'.

People genuinely trusted and enjoyed one another; at least 75% of the residents got their mail at post office boxes because they liked seeing each other when they went to pick up the mail. The good 'ol boys met regularly every morning at their favorite coffee shops to solve most of the world's problems, and the bars were places of enjoyment – no shootings and rarely any fights. There was even a big sign in one of the restaurants proclaiming, "WE DON'T GIVE A *DAMN* HOW THEY DO IT OUTSIDE." I hope it's still there and I hope Petersburg is still the Petersburg I knew and grew to be very comfortable with. Unfortunately, my remembrances of Petersburg may be much like childhood dreams. They arise like treasured images from the mist of memory and then seem to fade away under the cruel attack of reality.

Frederick Sound: LeConte Glacier near Petersburg

I found Petersburg to be a very pleasant place to both work and live. I sometimes feel an almost sickening fear that the cowboys, the 'Managers', the executives and the other migrant 'movers and shakers' of little substance will soon begin to move in and change everything – if they haven't already arrived.

Petersburg is the only town on Mitkof Island. There are a number of things that make such towns different from similar places in the lower 48. In the Southeast Alaska (Alexander) Archipelago, there are five relatively large towns and about the same number of smaller towns/villages. They are all served, directly or indirectly, by the Alaska Ferry System, but other than that, there is no direct inter-town access. One of the results of such isolation (considered up there to be a benefit, not a handicap) is the necessity for these towns to be self-sufficient; to provide for such things as medical facilities, police/fire protection needs and public works capabilities for themselves. I believe there is some state financial assistance available to help with the cost of these services, but I doubt if it is enough to cover all the expenses incurred by the towns in providing them. Petersburg is one of such towns, so that in many respects it is much like a larger community as far as municipal service autonomy is concerned.

Petersburg simplicity – Hammer Slough Boardwalk

In general, I personally felt that the situation was like a dream come true. My administrative duties were minimal, there was only one staff meeting a week, and if there was a corps of bureaucrats and managers downtown, I never spoke with or even met them. At last I was free to just be an engineer; not a manager, not a director, not an administrator, just an engineer – as I had been trained to be. I hope that the current Petersburg city engineer enjoys the same autonomous benefits, but I fear that the nature of such jobs has changed to the extent that they are not really even engineering jobs anymore. Like everywhere else, even in my Alaska, I suppose Petersburg must eventually surrender to the frustrating concept of *process* over *product* that has crippled so much of Alaska's productivity.

Most of the other cities, counties and states throughout the nation have become habituated to such a concept because they depend on the federal government for funding and for certain public services. In return for this federal benevolence, they are required to follow the nonsensical bureaucratic and administrative policies invented by the innumerable agency 'Managers' who depend on the proliferation of such counterproductive policies to maintain their authority and their myth of importance.

When I got there, the director of public works was a man named Eli. He had lived in Petersburg most of his life and had acquired a comprehensive understanding of the recurring maintenance problems confronting the city. I seem to recall hearing that at some time in his past Eli had also spent considerable time working in various construction crafts, including heavy equipment operator, mechanic, foreman and several others. Private sector experience is a valuable asset for anyone working in construction-related jobs. I don't know how long he had been in his position as director, but it was obvious that he was an excellent choice for the job. I'm sure that, if asked, he would have agreed that bureaucrats and excess administrators are largely useless. He kept the objectives of his department firmly fixed on *production*, not *process*.

In Petersburg, the Engineering and Public Works

Departments are separate; an arrangement that I for one have never favored. I think it was shortly before I got there that the city utilities (water and sewer) had also been removed from Public Works and raised to departmental status as the Petersburg Utilities Department. It must have been before I arrived because I know I would have strongly advised against such a move. The fragmenting of municipal services is never a good idea. All it really does is to create more management duplication (and jobs) and make it more difficult to respond to a need for action. It leads to more administration rather than less – a definite step in the *wrong* direction.

The creation of additional administrative complexity may account for the increasing popularity of such an organizational framework. The management and the bureaucratic dragons have by now achieved majority in most agencies, and they naturally favor the proliferation of positions that support the aura of legitimacy essential to their own survival. In fact, the bureaucratic poison may by now have even beaten the traditional Alaskan mistrust of excessive government control that was still prevalent in Petersburg. A man named Bruce, a long time Petersburg resident, was named director of the new City Utilities Department created at, or just prior to, the time I got there. Bruce was, and no doubt still is, a very capable guy. I had no objection to his appointment as director of the new department. My objection was to the *creation* of such a new department, or for that matter to the creation of *any* new department.

During the time I served as city engineer in Petersburg we satisfactorily completed at least five major projects and numerous smaller ones ranging in size from the remodeling of the high school to reconstruction of the sewage treatment plant, a couple of street improvement projects and several sewer extension jobs. I felt that the engineering department was able to play a major role in both the design and construction of all these jobs largely because we kept our 'Management Structure' simple; we didn't have one. At that time it was a joy to work there, but I'm afraid it couldn't last.

My tenure in the Petersburg job made it even clearer to me how wasteful, expensive and dangerous the current trend toward heavily 'Managed' projects and agency departments truly is. Such organizational trends are invariably attended by a glut of bureaucrats and administrators who insist on all the irrelevant meetings, memoranda and regulations that serve as justification for their own jobs; they would otherwise be revealed as the parasitic burden they really are. Our 'Management Philosophy' in Petersburg (if we even had one) was to forget about all that peripheral nonsense and just get the work done.

Downtown Petersburg

During the four years I was there, we initiated and completed a public works capital improvement program that was greater than in several much larger administrations where I have served. The fact that we got all this done without administrative interference was largely due to the enlightened policies of the city manager who was there during a large part of that time. His name was Ed – certainly not the Southern California Ed or anything like that. He understood and made use of the principle of delegation (not abandonment) of authority, while maintaining overall control without being officious and overbearing, better than any other 'Manager' I ever worked under. If they were all like Ed, a lot more work would get done rather than discussed *ad infinitum*. Even when the government anointed regulators and their accomplices jumped us, we were able to truncate much of the phony con game they tried on us. The following describes their ploys and our counterstrokes. It is an example of how these grifters can slime in under the cover of new or altered regulations and take serious financial advantage of a small city like Petersburg.

Unfortunately (or maybe fortunately), I was in Petersburg when asbestos reached the peak of its recognition as a major causative agent, if allowed to fragment, of lung cancer. This was a development that turned out to be a real cash cow for a lot of conmen and grifters who recognized and exploited the administrative naivety of many of the smaller Alaskan towns.

As is the case with all such revelations, two things happened: 1) All the 'Managers' and bureaucrats immediately saw an opportunity to begin writing regulations and to set themselves up as enforcers. Although most of them had a wealth of knowledge about how the bureaucracy works and how to take advantage of it, very few (if any) had even the slightest comprehension of the technical matters involved with the burgeoning and exaggerated asbestos problem. Most bureaucratic government 'Managers' understand well that if enough administrative gibberish is used to garble the facts and their own sad ignorance, the technical aspects can be made to appear to the public to be under control, thus magnifying their own role. The 'Managers' count on their ability to bamboozle the public in order to move ahead in building their own little empires. Maybe they could even get a "staff" of their own; an extremely ego-boosting eventuality in the eyes of any of these jerks. 2) Many, many conmen rushed to get themselves registered as "asbestos abatement contractors," the early applications for which required that the applicant know how to spell and pronounce both 'abatement' and 'asbestos', and that was about all. They then rushed out into the world, ostensibly to protect the public from the horrors of demon asbestos but actually to grab as much money as possible from asbestos removal contracts which, in many cases, were actually unnecessary from a practical standpoint. The spokesmen for most such companies had a real gift for making it sound like they were actually sacrificing much of their profit because of genuine concern for the safety and/or legal protection of the client.

It should be noted here that there were also many (perhaps most) of these companies who were sincere and were legitimately trained in the asbestos-removal procedures at first thought to be necessary. In Petersburg, however, we were nearly victimized by a group of the 'conmen company' types.

It all started while we were tearing down part of the old hospital and the high school. We learned later that someone who had been working for the contractor on one of these jobs had a relative in Juneau who had recently become licensed as a supposedly legitimate 'asbestos abatement contractor'. We also later learned that the local informer reported to his Juneau relative that we were tearing these things down without taking the elaborate protective measures against asbestos inhalation that he thought were prescribed by the new regulations. It should be remembered that these were knee-jerk regulations, and like all such reactionary procedures, they were subsequently later shown to have been highly over-conservative, and in many cases unnecessary. Nonetheless, there were a number of unscrupulous little companies who insisted that all these requirements remained in effect until they were shown something official in writing to prove that the regulations had been eased, which they often knew all along.

Anyway, when this guy's relative in Juneau became aware of what we were doing, he called the interim city manager (Patty), and I think he scared her, implying that all sorts of penalties and punishments would befall us unless we hired his firm to initiate the 'proper' asbestos-removal procedures. After talking to the city council about it, she called these phony bastards back and asked them to come down and straighten us out.[35] By then I had been in the engineering field long enough to be able to spot such con games as this one, and I wished (still do) that she had referred that first call to me.

The upshot of all this conversation was that after getting their claws into the city, they moved down and began removing all the asbestos they thought they saw or claimed to see on our two demolition jobs. They put on their impressive-looking masks, set up their clear plastic 'tents' over the work areas, donned their white (supposedly airtight) coveralls, boots and gloves and began putting on their show. They kept at it even after the jobs were completed and all the rubble had been removed and hauled away, claiming they were removing asbestos that had either been dislodged before they got there or missed while they were working under the stress of completion deadlines – nonsense.

Since I had some authority over city projects, I told them their work was over, and they should pack up their gear and go back to Juneau. They didn't want to hear this, so I think they went directly to the city council (even over Patty's head) and told them that there was undoubtedly a lot of asbestos in all the city buildings. The council was told of these trumped-up dangers, not to mention the penalties for violation of the legal requirements, and that it (the council) should give this company a contract to go through all the city buildings and identify the existing asbestos; including, of all things, asbestos tile, which is now recognized as benign. The council was given dire warnings by these phony bastards and their opportunistic, self-serving lawyers that unless they took decisive proactive steps to remove even suspected asbestos, they would also be open to drastic and destructive legal action. Of course, such warnings were later

[35] She probably didn't use those terms; Patty was far too circumspect, polite and charming to use terms like that.

proven to be absolute rubbish, and I'm reasonably sure that these conmen and their lawyer accomplices knew that at the time.

The council bit, and the little company was told to go ahead with the identification work. For them and their lawyers it was a cash cow, and they must have been laughing up their sleeves as they left the council chambers. It seems to me that Dennis, the Petersburg power and light superintendent, jumped on the bandwagon too and wanted his utilities buildings included in the survey. I guess he knew a good thing when he saw it, so to speak. Of course, these grifters began finding asbestos all over the place and immediately got busy writing up agreements to go in and remove it.

Shortly after the council had given these opportunistic phonies the OK to go ahead and begin inspecting the buildings, I managed to get some copies of the most current EPA regulations. It was gratifying to see that the requirements had been greatly modified. Total (city-wide) asbestos inspections had never been required, as these so-called asbestos guys had led the council to believe. Moreover, the requirement to remove it at all had been relaxed to include only 'loose' asbestos; i.e. asbestos that was not secured by some binding agent or was not encapsulated or otherwise prevented from shredding and becoming airborne. It gave me a great deal of satisfaction to send this group of two-bit conmen a letter telling them to go home attached to copies of the newly modified regulations. They were not at all pleased by this turn of events, and I think they may have written to the EPA claiming that before they had gotten to our hospital and high school projects, we had hauled a huge amount of unsecured asbestos to our disposal site. They no doubt hoped for a lucrative contract to go check it out; an act consistent with their previous behaviors.

Shortly after they left, we got a letter from that agency telling us that we had been reported for hauling away a large amount of asbestos-laden debris without taking the precautions prescribed by the applicable regulations. We were advised that we would therefore have to hire an approved asbestos removal contractor to institute all the proper precautionary procedures and test all the hauled-away debris, now deposited at our waste site, for loose asbestos.

By now any asbestos that might be there had been completely covered up by wet stripping (vegetation) waste from other projects, as well as just plain mud and other assorted debris. The EPA letter went to Patty. I don't know if she was as unnerved as she had been by the last warning about asbestos, but, in any case, this time she brought the letter to me for response. Accordingly, I prepared a response for her signature.

Our reply stated that it was our position that there was no asbestos in the waste pile, but if the agency was determined to pursue the matter, they were welcome to send up some of their own experts to investigate the material themselves. We even offered to provide room and board while they were in town and excavating equipment (at reasonable rental rates) to assist them with the digging. We never heard from them again about asbestos in the waste pile, or anyplace else for that matter.

This incident was one of the most self-satisfying experiences of my professional career. In one magnificent move we had foiled a bunch of crooks who thought they could fool us, and we had beaten one of the most bureaucratic of government agencies at their own game. It was probably more likely that my letter to them ended up in the in-basket of some lower-level functionary, but it's more satisfying to believe that we outsmarted them.

As my employment there came to an end, I was becoming apprehensive that Petersburg, like so many other Alaskan towns, had just in the previous four years seen their own 'Childhood's End' approaching without recognizing the signs. Perhaps Petersburg must now also sink into the malaise accompanying the sad Americanization of Alaska. Petersburg was for me a matter of particular concern because during the time I spent there I saw several disquieting events, both from within the city administration itself and from outside agencies or companies that to me seemed like veiled indications of changes to come. Perhaps I was oversensitive because of experiences in other parts of the state – I hope that was the case.

In about July or August 1989, the Municipality of Juneau advertised to fill a vacancy for the job of municipal director of engineering. It sounded enough like 'city engineer' to interest me, so I sent in an application. I was to be seriously disappointed with the nature of the work, but I didn't know that at the time. For many years it had been my one unwavering dream to return to Juneau and, although I really enjoyed the Petersburg job and was saddened to leave, it looked like this might be my opportunity to realize my long-held dream.

There was a big going-away dinner party for me at the Beachcomber Inn and Nightclub about ten miles south of town. This was where Patty made an extremely kind remark about my having "treated Petersburg well." I think (I hope) that she was sincere, but in any case it was a remark that I'll keep in my heart until it's time for me to go away permanently. This was also the occasion when the city presented me with a Norwegian elkhound puppy that we named Ivar, after my young associate in the local engineering department. I grew to love Ivar the dog intensely, and when he died

Downtown Petersburg – Me (right) with two friends named Ivar

of bladder cancer about ten or eleven years later, I actually wept during most of my waking hours for at least three days. And I couldn't bring myself to even mention his death for almost a year. I could write about it, but I couldn't say it. It was emotionally crippling for me, even more so than my divorce. It took two new huskies to ease the pain of his passing. He will never, never be replaced in my heart. Even now, four or five years later, the thought of his death brings tears to my eyes. I had always told him to be a "big brave boy" whenever he seemed upset about things, and these were the last words he heard me say after the vet had given him the shot that ended his life. I don't want to write any more about Ivar.

The Municipality of Juneau paid all my expenses to travel up there and stay a few days to participate in a series of question and answer sessions and general interviews. As I recall, there was no one-on-one interview with the city manager. I should have noted that peculiarity as an indication of his fear of making unilateral decisions, but I didn't. He had hired some 'Management' outfit from someplace outside. They dreamed up a bunch of little screwball scenarios for role-playing schemes into which the applicants were inserted, given an imaginary problem to work out and, during the progress of the role-playing, the applicants and their actions were observed by these consultant folks. The whole thing seemed ridiculous to me, and I felt foolish about performing under the scrutiny of these people. It sort of reminded me of when I was a little kid running around in a Superman cape trying to get it to 'flow' on the wind behind me while explaining to anyone watching that I was really Superman embarking on a mission to save the underdog. The municipal process resembled nothing so much as a 'show and tell' demonstration in grade school. I thought the whole thing was a bunch of overzealous 'generic management' crap. Surely these 'Management' consultants weren't naïve enough to believe that the applicants would act normally when they knew they were being watched and tightly evaluated. More likely, the reviewers had discovered a good source of lots of consultant money from such technical morons as the city manager. In fact, one of the applicants backed off from the whole thing, pleading conflicting obligations that had arisen after he began this foolishness. I suspect that he just saw the whole thing for what it was; a contrived charade intended to lend legitimacy to the concept of 'generic management'. I was to find out soon enough that in Juneau the concept had gone completely berserk. I probably should have withdrawn my application right then; if I had known what was to come, I certainly would have. However, I did the best I could under these absurd conditions. I was, somewhat to my own surprise, able to get through the exercise while still retaining a certain amount of personal dignity and not just laughing out loud. In truth, the whole thing appealed more to my sense of humor than to my command of professional judgment.

If the dream of returning to Juneau hadn't clouded my judgment, I would probably have seen that the whole administrative structure of the Juneau Municipal Government was seriously warped. Everyone except the engineers and the public works people spoke in the vague and non-committal language of the professional 'Manager'.

I don't know whether I did well in the municipality's goofy evaluation process, or if my performance just wasn't as bad as all the other applicants. Any ranking of the applicants in such a bizarre competition would have to have been totally subjective.

I went back to Petersburg with serious doubts about my chances. Nonetheless, I was offered the position and I decided to accept – a decision that I was to regret and I still do. In retrospect, maybe it *wasn't* such a bad decision. At the time I left Petersburg, a new city manager was just coming to work.

He left under a cloud after about a year or two and was subsequently appointed to a position as assistant city manager in Juneau, where I came to know him as a real toady masquerading as a genuine 'Management' horse's ass. He said that he held an MBA, which says something about his grasp of real logic as well as technical matters. I'll include more details about him later.

I left Petersburg, feeling very sad about going, sometime during the first week in September 1989. Although the many proud and truly Alaskan residents of the town may delay the inevitable takeover for some years, the local ambience must eventually give way to the outside pressure and presence. It will be one more tragic commentary on the final demise of the *real* Alaska.

Chapter 7: The Dragon in Control

Please note that I refer to my supervisors (not superiors, by any means) by their job titles in this chapter. You might also note that my comments about them are, in most cases, decidedly uncomplimentary. For this reason and to maintain privacy, I am not using their names, which wouldn't be recognized anyway. If, as the story unfolds, you think you know who these people are because of dates, job descriptions, etc., be aware that you are wrong. Additionally, I am going to go into considerable detail about the Juneau administration because to me it represents exactly what had happened and was happening to so many Alaskan cities following statehood and what is probably inevitable for those still clinging to Alaskan attitudes and lifestyles. In a very real sense, this chapter encapsulates the crux of what this book is all about.

Juneau from Mt. Roberts Trail – Older residential area center right.

The country around Juneau was, of course, the same as it had always been, that is where it wasn't covered with pavement, lawns and houses. The population had expanded exponentially, filling the Mendenhall Valley and turning it into neighborhoods identical to those surrounding any medium-sized city in the 'Lower 48'. The same was true of North Douglas, the fringes of the forests all along the Glacier Highway, the Loop Road, Montana Creek and all the other areas that had been beautifully and peacefully uninhabited when I was last in Juneau. Nonetheless, the mountains, the streams, the smell of wet spruce and that wispy, ragged and almost mystic fog along the edges of the forest were all still there. The strangely captivating odor of old, permanently soaked buildings along the downtown waterfront was still there too and, all things considered, there was much to reawaken some long-past memories and to arouse some hope that I had at last come 'home' after all. I was not prepared for the shock that awaited me upon introduction into the workings of the so-called 'Engineering' Department of the Juneau City/Borough.

The worst aspect of my introduction to the new Juneau was coming to terms with how the city administrators had twisted the local government around. What I walked into was astonishing, and from the very beginning I began silently praying that the rest of Alaska wasn't doomed to become anything like the new municipal government in Juneau.

Downtown Juneau – distance tends to hide management failure.

The Juneau Government seemed to be a squirming nest of managers, bureaucrats, administrators and a lot of people whose functions and responsibilities were very vague and impossible to understand. The Municipal Government of Juneau had become representative of all that was wrong with what all larger Alaskan municipal governments were soon to be faced with or had already succumbed to. As far as the 'engineering' department was concerned, it was a glaring demonstration of exactly how an engineering organization should not be run.

In Juneau I saw a tragic example of what happens when the management theorists are given free rein and allowed to ignore the social and productive responsibilities of a people's local government. It had become a cesspool of everything I feared from the statehood opportunists; the politicians, the lawyers, the cowboys, and the environmentalists who had apparently come to save us from ourselves. Nonetheless, I had accepted the job, and until I left it would be my duty to do the best I possibly could, regardless of the circumstances.

From the day I first went to work for the City/Borough of Juneau, it was obvious to me that this was an organization completely submerged in a kind of surreal atmosphere wherein, as with many jurisdictions in the 'Lower 48', product had long ago taken a back seat to the insubstantial world of process. In Juneau what was done had become much less important than how it was being done administratively. It was deeply depressing.

Managers and their attendant bureaucrats seem unable (or perhaps just unwilling) to understand that if an organization means to accomplish anything, real process must be adjusted and tailored to achieve a specific product objective. Today, far too many organizations take an approach to project accomplishment that is the exact opposite. Placing the emphasis on process rather than product plays directly into the hands of the bureaucratically minded managers. It encourages them to believe that all projects are the same in many respects and thus address these imaginary similarities without having to know anything about the technical or professional aspects – the true elements involved in all project completions. Any competent engineer knows that there are certain administrative processes and procedures common to all projects, particularly within government organizations. However, most engineers will also recognize that these commonalities are of minimum importance as the 'drivers' of project progress because they are purely administrative and have no real-world substance. It is a sad but true fact that Alaskan organizations are falling fast, or have already fallen, into the insidious trap of process over product.

Someone once said: "Managers do things right; leaders do the right things." Although there may have been plenty of 'managers', 'leaders' were thin on the ground in the Juneau municipal organizational structure in late 1989. It didn't take long to see that the city manager was a man of little consequence. He seemed to believe in 'management by consensus'. Every time there was an important decision to be made requiring some positive leadership, he would pass the buck by appointing some ad hoc committee and leaving them to decide the question by majority vote. These committees, incidentally, were rarely made up of people with any particular expertise in the matter to be decided. His method did ensure that whenever he was asked who had made a particularly controversial decision, he could simply reply, "No one in particular." At times, he would even ask for group votes on what to do in response to technical problems. He really should have been working under someone with the guts to make critical decisions and then tell him what to do.

For almost three years I listened to his nonsense and to his so-called rationale regarding problems confronting him; his lack of decisiveness and dearth of specific knowledge about anything was, it seemed, appalling. On the very few occasions he asked for my opinion on something and I gave my thoughts, he would usually say something like, "No, no, no, this is this way and that way blah, blah, blah," a truly dictatorial response to things that he didn't understand and answers he didn't want to hear. It always came across like he didn't really want my opinion but rather just confirmation of some opinion he had already formed based upon his rather unconventional reasoning process. He would have done well to heed the old adage that it is 'far better to keep your mouth shut and let people think you're stupid than to open it and remove all doubt.' He was always impatient with, and irritated by, opinions that didn't support some preconceived idea he had evidently concocted out of thin air.

However, as stated, I had taken the job, and I was thus obligated to support him to the extent I was able, regardless of how wacky and unscientific his ideas appeared, unless I believed there was a real danger or disservice to the public.

I would never have expressed the opinions I have written here while this city manager (CM) was my supervisor – such is loyalty, however misplaced. I could only hope that he didn't represent some sort of vanguard for this bizarre management style that would ultimately become a cancerous management growth metastasizing to engulf the entire state.

Although I had heard (and joked) about such things, this was my first serious exposure to the practice of forcing facts to fit preset conclusions rather than reaching conclusions based upon unbiased analyses of established and proven fact, field data and research. Since then, I have been more sensitive to this strange approach to problem solving and have noted that the CM's behavior in this regard wasn't, and isn't, unique. The increasingly popular concept of 'generic management' seems to be based upon these methods to an alarming extent, and our beloved Alaska must ultimately fall victim to such things.

As mentioned previously, the Juneau Engineering Department was not really an engineering department at all. The administration at that time seemed totally committed to supporting private enterprise by contracting with private consulting firms for both design and construction inspection on all but the most infinitesimal projects. Supporting private enterprise in the engineering profession is an admirable practice, but not to the point that the engineering department loses control. We had only one real draftsman in the office, and he, by the nature of the organizational setup, rarely prepared contract drawings of any consequence. His name was Joe, and more often than not, he was only called upon to prepare small interdepartmental display drawings for one department head or another in support of some idiotic 'management' concept. The engineering department in general had become nothing more than a collection of bureaucratic overseers, expected to keep looking over the shoulders of the consultants.

The basic role that the CM seemed to envision for the engineering department was to act as a sort of consulting service for the other departments – 'client departments', as he usually referred to them. Engineering was theoretically to administer the projects that the 'client departments' wished to build in pursuit of their individual 'missions'. In fact, a similar mission for the engineering department was actually called out and described in the city code. This is a concept that sounds good in theory, but given the tendency of the CM to agree with whoever got to him first and to interfere with everyone else's work, it was unworkable in practice. If he had been even moderately experienced, he would have known that charging one department with the responsibility for independently monitoring the interests of other departments with equal project authority was a flawed concept.

The reality was that the engineering department actually had no control at all over the projects – neither during the design nor the construction phases. The consultants and the contractors knew this, and so did the individual department heads. There was always direct communication between the 'client department' representatives and the consultant or contractor that the engineering department was often not even aware of. We were often not 'in the loop' as they say. This is a condition that is bound to have serious consequences on any project.

I have experienced just exactly such problems many times. It makes it difficult for the 'client' because they often do not fully understand the technical aspects of either the design or the construction, although they usually think they do. This almost always leads to later problems either in completed project function or contractor relations during construction. It makes it difficult for the so-called 'responsible engineer' because he (or she) is often not informed of any instructions or directions that the client department representative or some equally empowered management supervisor may have given the designer, inspector or contractor. Thus, the supposedly responsible engineering department representative completely loses control of the job. In most cases, it also makes it difficult for both the consultant and any reputable contractor because there is no clear line of responsibility or authority, and they don't know who to turn to for clarification of the owner's wishes or for contract specifications interpretation. In the case of unscrupulous contractors (there are a few, but not nearly as many as most agency representatives seem to think), this kind of setup may be a benefit. They can consult the engineer, the client representative and a 'manager' looking for the answer they want to hear; and they often do. In our case, whenever the project engineer or our department tried to point out such working relationship problems, we were accused of trying to magnify our own role and of keeping the 'client department' away from the designers/contractors, denying them any project input. Nothing could have been further from the truth. Our only concern was to establish and maintain a clear and single line of communication in the interest of project control; not in the interest of aggrandizement for the engineering department, myself, or the project engineer – a fairly meaningless title under the circumstances. We were always trying to control the projects, but with such a muddled, muddied and unenforceable communication setup, we were usually thwarted in our efforts.

I could never understand what made the CM so terrified of making decisions on his own. Maybe he was afraid of any possible political repercussions that might result from taking responsibility for an important decision. He may have felt that it would be less self-incriminating to simply shift the blame to a committee or to some department head he had badgered into supporting his own preconceived notion. This shifting of blame was one of his most despicable (albeit successful) practices.

Regrettably, in the ranks of management and among the politically obligated sycophants, this CM's type is not rare. In fact, they are all too common, and becoming more so. The truly tragic consequence of this phenomenon, particularly noticeable in the 'new' Alaska, is the impact that such people have on genuinely dedicated professionals who are unfortunate enough to fall under their supervision. Of course, I have mostly noted this sad trend in Alaska because that's what this book is all about, but I suspect it abounds outside as well since that's where it seems to have come from.

The CM did have an assistant to help him with whatever work he actually did. His behavior was far easier to understand than that of the CM. For one thing, he never responded to my explanations with "No, no, no – it's this and that," the infuriating response that I often got from his boss. The most refreshing characteristics of the ACM's (assistant city manager) behavior were his refreshing openness, his willingness to admit to technical ignorance, and the refusal to try shifting blame to others. I guess maybe he finally got fed up with the CM's questionable ethics and abysmal but un-admitted ignorance. Sometime in about mid-1991, he quit Juneau and accepted the position of parks and recreation director in Boise, Idaho. I hated to see him go, but his decision was certainly understandable. In my opinion, he represented the last vestige of real intelligence and skill with real-world rationale left in the manager's office.

Anyway, the CM finally got what he considered a suitable replacement for his assistant. He was a former short-term Petersburg city manager. He had been strongly encouraged to go into some other line of work by the mayor, most members of the city council, and a majority of the local citizenry. Petersburg may be a small town, but the average citizen there is apparently more intelligent than in most other places I have worked. It doesn't take them long to spot a phony, and that's obviously what happened to our new ACM. I don't know if he and the other candidates (if there were any) for the Juneau ACM job ever went through the childish show-and-tell procedure that I did before getting the municipal engineering job, but whatever the testing process, the CM seemed pleased with the choice. For the new ACM's part, it didn't take long for him to move in and plant his nose firmly up the CM's backside.

Early in his tenure, the ACM said that he would be attending all our staff meetings, presumably to make sure we were doing things in the way he thought they should be done, even though he was ignorant of the status of any projects, and despite his obvious technical incompetence. I told him that if he did this, I would either cancel all the subsequent meetings or, if he countermanded such an order, I would refuse to attend. He may have been offended, but at that point I had already become disgusted with the municipality as well as with the CM and now his new lap dog, so I didn't really care if it offended him or not. I never actually had any direct confrontations with the ACM over our differences of opinion, but I always had the feeling he knew I had little interest in, or respect for, his opinions regarding anything technical.

I recall once, during a conversation about something I had no interest in, or knowledge of, he asked my opinion – maybe thinking that the engineering department should be involved. I told him that considering my ignorance of the subject, I really had no opinion. He replied that I had to adopt one.

I think maybe the connection between serious opinions and knowledge escaped him, much as it seemed to escape the CM, and as I have since learned, almost the entire new breed of generic 'managers'. Perhaps he resented my attitude, but he was never honest enough to just say so. However, I suspect he often went back to the CM's office, put his head on his master's shoulder and whined about how everyone was being mean to him.

Finally, our differences and my obvious contempt for the whole organization must have become apparent to the ruling twins. One day the CM and his disciple came to my office and told me that I should "look for a job in engineering." I think a statement like that is management talk for, "You're fired." I think I responded by asking if it might be possible to modify my behavior and change the things they found objectionable. It sounds like a silly question and it probably was considering my thinly disguised contempt for both of them. Maybe I was just trying to be polite. Of course they both said, "No," and after that I had no further comment.

The ACM said something about how he knew I wasn't inclined to express my inner feelings outwardly, and asked if I wished to say anything further. I told him that I didn't have any inner feelings about the matter (I really didn't), and that I was actually relieved to be taken out of the department's head position (which I really was). My concern had absolutely nothing to do with loss of status, prestige or anything like that. A genuine lack of interest in such things is incomprehensible to technically incompetent political hacks like the CM and the ACM. I was only concerned with keeping a paycheck coming in while looking for another position, which, at the age of fifty-seven, would not be particularly easy to find.

These two 'managers', and many others just like them, were typical examples of what statehood brought to Alaska. They had, between the two of them, practically destroyed the Alaskan workplace ambiance in Juneau. When they or their clones manage to infiltrate other Alaskan government organizations, the consequences will be irreversible. At the moment, there's little worry of them slithering into private enterprise, at least not in the construction business. Their lack of ability to produce anything would assure very limited tenure in the private sector.

I must honestly admit that I was grateful when the CM and his lap dog offered me an interim position as project engineer and inspector for the new elementary school just east of the old Glacier Highway.[36] I moved into a twenty-five-foot on-site trailer and it served as my project office until I left the municipality altogether.

I think I came to the project before any of the structural work began, so I was mostly concerned with site preparation. This was an assignment that I truly enjoyed, and one that the visiting school officials and other such big shots did not understand at all. This meant that I could tell them almost anything, swoop them with such terms as "soil bearing capacity, shear resistance, plasticity, Atterberg limits," and so on. Most

[36] The school has a Tlingit name which I thought was a great idea, but I can neither pronounce nor spell it, so I'm not even going to try.

people just nodded as if they understood what I was talking about, but every now and then some truly honest (Alaskan?) person would ask, "What the hell does all that mean?" I like people like that, and in such cases, I always did my best to explain these technical terms in non-technical language. Such terms are not really that difficult to explain. Those are the kind of people who were and are disappearing from Alaska. Where do they all go?

The contractor was a local outfit called Dulin Inc. Old man Dulin had one or two sons, and I think they ran most of the company's projects. One of them was the superintendent on our school job, and he seemed to be a very astute and conscientious young man. He told me once that I should be sure to include my firing by the CM on any future résumés because for anyone who knew the CM the firing would serve as a very good recommendation.

One of my biggest sources of resentment toward the CM was the fact that he and his toadies allowed and encouraged the change of my hometown from a comfortable, down-to-earth little city into a nightmare of nothing but tourist-oriented façades and the local government into a disgusting spectacle of 'generic management' masquerading as expertise. His remarks and statements of opinion meant *nothing*. Regardless of how many of the local citizens (for whom he often privately expressed his disdain) were affected; he would change his 'official' opinion or intentions at any time he thought his own interest could be better served. Thank God I'm retired, and I'm not in danger of ever having to humor or pretend to respect some jackass like him again. You can't really hate someone like the CM any more than you can hate a chicken for being as stupid as a chicken. However, if you find yourself being supervised by a chicken, something is seriously out of whack. Maybe the 'chickens' are taking over in large parts of Alaska rather than the 'dragons'.

Shortly after the CM and his 'suck-up' lap dog fired me, I began looking for another position. By this time, I was beginning to get a little older, so although I might not have realized it myself at the time, I was probably looking for something with a government agency. Such jobs demand far less personal commitment than jobs with a private company/corporation or any private construction outfit.

During the process of my job search, I spoke with an old friend named Joe who at that time was the top man with the Gold Belt Corporation – a Tlingit corporation based in Juneau. He said that although he would like to hire me as an engineer, he couldn't do it unilaterally; he had to clear it with his board, and that might take quite a while. They were rapidly learning such bureaucratic obfuscation from the BIA (Federal Bureau of Indian Affairs).

In the meantime, I was in contact with Grays Harbor County in Washington, where I had previously served as county road engineer. A friend of mine named Mike had risen to the position of public works director after the departure and subsequent death of Gary, and he said he could offer me the position of county traffic engineer. I tried to explain to him that I had very little specific training in traffic engineering, and that I actually didn't like what little I knew about it. Mike explained to me that this was the only position on the roster that was unfilled, and that if I couldn't accept that particular position, perhaps I should look someplace else. I agreed to apply for the position and in May I was offered the job, so I took it.

PART V
EXILE

Chapter 1: The Established Dragon

It was painful to leave Juneau, particularly since I had hoped that our move there in 1989 would be permanent. For me, it was supposed to have been a return home, which was what Juneau was and still is, even though I certainly would never want to work under that city manager there again; or anyone like him anywhere. Anyway, we moved back to Grays Harbor County and Ivar the elkhound came happily along with us, trying all the while to keep wagging his tightly rolled up little tail.

Leaving Juneau – Mayflower Island (Douglas) on the left

The traffic engineering position, into which I was hired that spring, supposedly required training in a discipline in which I had only the undergraduate training included in the standard civil engineering curriculum. As a matter of fact, I had always harbored a certain amount of disdain for the more routine aspects of the field because it seemed to me to be decidedly subjective – presenting opinion and observation as scientific fact. I once teased the traffic engineer who was with the county during the last time I worked there by reading four pages from one of his traffic engineering textbooks explaining that drivers could see better at night if they kept the car lights on. He became both angry and embarrassed, and he was probably justified in feeling that way. He died in 2007 when he was only about fifty years old. God rest him.

At a subsequent traffic-engineering seminar, I discovered that there was a whole lot more to the subject than I'd realized, including mathematical solutions to high-volume traffic flow problems and the effect of geometric parameters. Those mathematical approaches are very, very impressive on blackboards at traffic seminars, and the conclusions appear to be unassailable. For some reason, however, whenever all the conditions are suitable and the proper parameters are in place to provide values for the variables and to facilitate the construction of the relative equations, observed results rarely verify those that are mathematically predicted. That's a sort of convoluted way of saying that theory and practice, more often than not, do not agree. This is a fact that many nouveau Alaskan engineers now working within today's 'Management' nightmare will have to recognize and come to terms with, and worse, try to explain to their technically illiterate 'Managers'.

In the days before statehood, we more or less relied on empirical data gathered over a span of several years to predict future traffic patterns and behaviors and to thus define governing design parameters. I still feel that this procedure for Alaska is preferable to any generalized mathematical approach because, in the first place, solutions to the accepted equations as traffic predictions are almost always wrong, even with the more controlled traffic conditions in the 'lower 48'. Up north, such an inherent error is magnified by the wide variety of environmental conditions not ordinarily accounted for as variables in the accepted equations. Nonetheless, I fear that the lure of federal financing will eventually force Alaskan designers to apply these mathematical methods regardless of how bogus the results may prove to be. It certainly wouldn't be the first time such completely unsuitable demands were forced on Alaskan engineers. This has traditionally required a lot of project change orders to accommodate the actual conditions encountered. Oh well, the federal government has lots of money, right?

In Grays Harbor County, I was lucky in that Don, the major assistant to the previous traffic engineer, was still working for the county. He knew a lot more about the field practices of traffic engineering than I did, so I more or less left all the signing decisions and control to him and just tried to look supervisory! In fact, most of my traffic engineering efforts consisted of not much more than riding around with Don or his helper, Chuck, while they checked on sign placement, maintenance, pavement markings or new traffic control devices placed during construction. Much of *his* time was taken up explaining to *me* why certain traffic control devices were necessary under the conditions that he pointed out to me. This is the first time I have ever admitted it, and I hope Don won't be offended if he ever reads this, but I really didn't care much about all the stuff he kept pointing out to me. I was satisfied that he knew what he was doing and what he was talking about. Anyway, I intended to blame him if anything turned out wrong; a little 'Management' ploy that I learned from the city manager in Juneau. Just kidding.

Somehow, we also got fairly heavily involved in a statewide program about something called 'pavement management'. I should describe the program as well as its strong and weak aspects because I suspect that the federal folks will soon impose a requirement for such a program on Alaska if they haven't done so already.

The so-called 'Pavement Management Program' was an effort spearheaded by the County Road Administration Board (CRAB). This is an organization sponsored and paid for by the state, ostensibly intended to help the county folks translate all the bureaucratic gibberish that the state uses to tell the counties what to do. It is an organization that started with only one or two permanent technical employees and a secretary about twenty-five to thirty years ago with what was then a sort of vague mission. When we first started working with them we were getting into the age of acronyms, and I have since wondered many times what acronym the CRAB folks would have used if their organization had been titled the 'County Road Administration Panel'.

I guess that the assumption is that for some reason the engineers working for the counties are less capable than those with the state. I never really understood that attitude. Nor could I understand how some of the county engineers that I personally knew to be far more competent and more experienced than most of these younger state 'advisors' could sit still and listen to stuff that they knew to be a lot of crap. It must have had something to do with the fact that the state, with CRAB in an advisory role, controlled the disbursement of the federal funding.

All that checking and reviewing between the counties and the state is another example of a totally unnecessary duplication of effort. It is probably rooted in the uncontrollable and ridiculous empire-building instinct built into the genetic makeup of all government bureaucrats. I once asked one of them if he thought maybe what he was doing might be considered 'empire-building', and he responded that it was indeed just that, and that he hoped he would be successful. He answered like he was proud of it and thought that it was what he was supposed to do. I never held any ill feelings toward these people in the states because, for the most part, they just don't know any better, and besides, it's probably too late to change such deeply ingrained attitudes and mindsets. They are usually sincere but misguided and rarely in the mold of someone like the Juneau city manager, who I believe knew that a lot of what he did was unjustifiable bullshit and was just plain self-serving. I doubt if he really cared whether anyone else was hurt or not.

The CRAB folks have now expanded to include a staff of at least ten or fifteen engineers, probably many more administrative technicians than that, probably ten or more engineering technicians, and God only knows how many 'Managers'. The engineers also probably have a number of engineering technicians (draftsman, designers, computer folks, maybe surveyors, etc.) working for them too since today's young graduate engineers are almost never capable of performing those technical tasks themselves. They usually seem to think that they should only be called upon to do engineer stuff (whatever that is).

My true fear concerning all this burgeoning bureaucracy is that the current explosion of such stuff will further infiltrate and infect my beloved Alaska. I'm not totally unaware of the direction all this 'Management' nonsense is taking in the 'lower 48', and I realize that Alaska cannot forever remain immune to further inroads into the more remote areas by this insidious administrative pollution. In fact, as I pointed out earlier, there are a significant number of Alaskan jurisdictions that have already succumbed to the carefully crafted managerial arguments and the bureaucratic saturation of the workplace. However, I still hope that there are enough of the 'good 'ol boy' Alaskans to fight such a thing down to the last true working person. Maybe I'm just dreaming; maybe I'm already too late.

I should now go back to the pavement management concept that I mentioned earlier. I recall that participation in the 'program' by all the counties was encouraged by tying such participation to funding from one of the state administered improvement programs. I think each county was required to conduct a countywide pavement condition survey once or twice a year, and if it weren't done, the non-participating county would be excluded from certain funding sources.

The statewide program was based on the premise that roadway structural life could be predicted by extrapolating pavement structure conditions based on a series of past annual condition measurements. The concept is good, but problems arise when trying to decide how to measure these conditions in some quantitative way.

Personally, I always thought (and still think) that the only really meaningful evaluation of sub-grade and pavement structure capacity was by means of deflection measurements. Of course, such measurement methods must prescribe precisely the same equipment, loadings and methods for all the evaluators so that the comparisons from one place to another for relative priority determination and from one year to another are meaningful. This was really the only measurement necessary for these determinations. However, the collective judgment of some sort of 'Pavement Management Control Group' held that additional evaluation was a good idea. Here is an example where the sensible and quantitative methods of measurement were polluted by the useless and subjective evaluation procedures favored by the MBA-type managers.

It was, in large part, these administrative morons who came up with a rating sheet that provided for entering the name of the road being evaluated, the mile point, and the 'condition rating' in terms of 'good', 'fair', or 'poor' – a thoroughly ridiculous procedure. It was obviously far too subjective, so the geniuses who came up with the first rating sheet added stuff like 'number of patches per mile', 'length of cracks per mile', and so on. It would have taken months (maybe even years considering seasonal restrictions) to accurately measure all these additional parameters so almost all the county evaluators just guessed at the numbers, thus introducing yet another degree of subjectivity and almost certain inaccuracy.

The results of these so-called pavement condition surveys were, in many cases, really bizarre. Because of the fairly frequent changes in personnel doing the evaluating, a lot of road sections showed up as having improved over the years without any reconstruction effort on the part of the county. This says a lot about the 'good, fair, poor' and measuring cracks, etc. evaluations.

Once, during a meeting of pavement evaluators in Chehalis, when I pointed out the uselessness of these kinds of rating terms, someone further back in the room said jokingly, "I agree; we need something more objective. Couldn't we say one, two or three instead?" I *hope* they were joking.

The program went ahead, and our county road engineer[37] finally said that we were no longer going to make a 'program' out of it. After that I lost track of the statewide goings on. They may still be at it for all I know, but I doubt it – at least not with the same dedication.

Since I retired, I have (driven by curiosity) actually plotted up some of the numerical translations of the subjective evaluations against time. The plotted results do indeed show that many of the Grays Harbor County roads improved from year to year without having any maintenance or construction effort devoted to them – just as described above. In fact, the whole package of accumulated data from the aborted pavement

[37] By then Russ had been elevated to that position after I left in 1985.

management program using such subjective evaluations exhibited enough inconsistencies and aberrations to render the whole body of data useless.

Such a program would be totally unsuitable for Alaska because of the widely varying environmental conditions and the lack of (so far) a means of quantitatively classifying or evaluating the innumerable different parameters that arise out of each of these conditions. I suppose such a program could be initiated up there, but I doubt if the return for the effort invested would be worth it. Nonetheless, I wouldn't be surprised if some Johnny-come-lately stateside egghead decided to work up a program like that even though it would probably turn out just like the one in the lower 48, or worse.

In my new position with the county, I was somehow able to shift my title to read 'Traffic and *Planning* Engineer' so that I could then concentrate my efforts almost exclusively on planning for potential future improvements, which I found much more rewarding than chasing signs around and so on. Besides, as I said, Don knew a lot more about that sign stuff than I did, and he seemed to enjoy doing it. Grays Harbor County never really had a need for much technically rigorous work in traffic engineering, simply because there wasn't a whole lot of traffic on most of the county roads. Long-term road system planning, on the other hand, was an area that had never received much attention, and I found it challenging. It was much like the sort of work I had done sometime in the 1950's or 1960's when serving as Location Engineer for the Fairbanks District of the Alaska Road Commission. Before I left the county in 2000, I was able to locate at least fifteen possibilities for road re-alignments of various lengths, and I understand that several of them have been built, and that a few others are in the project pre-design and/or design phase. That has to be a little bit satisfying for an old location/design highway engineer.

The concept of traffic 'roundabout' intersections was another idea that was introduced into American highway design engineering about the time that I was with the county between 1992 and 2000. On a worldwide basis, this sort of intersection treatment is nothing new. I had first been impressed with the idea while visiting an uncle in England in the early 1970's. My appreciation of the concept has been further enhanced after seeing such a thing in operation in Dawson Creek, British Columbia during numerous trips up the Alaska Highway. The major advantage of the idea is the relatively small amount of space required compared to that needed for the usual American freeway interchange, thus dramatically reducing the necessary amount of right-of-way. It's obviously also a lot cheaper to build. If the need can be justified by traffic count, a 'roundabout' is a very good option both from the standpoint of cost and safety.

The concept of traffic circles is being increasingly adopted by the American traffic engineering community. It's a good idea, and we shouldn't give it short shrift just because some other country came up with it first. As a matter of fact, there is now such a 'roundabout' at the west end of the Juneau-Douglas Bridge. I've watched it in operation during rush hours and have been very favorably impressed. This adoption of an 'outside' idea is the sort of thing which might convince Alaskans that not everything from outside has negative effects on the country. However, I still think we were better off before statehood, and I know I'm not alone in that opinion. In fact, I think some Alaskans who initially favored statehood have since changed their minds – too late now.

After an additional eight years with Grays Harbor County, I celebrated (maybe 'endured' is a better word) my 65th birthday on May 30, 2000. I retired from the county on June 1. No sense wasting any time.

Chapter 2: Retirement

I hear a lot of whining from retired people saying that they wish they were still working. Not me; I can now sleep until noon whenever I wish, and I don't have to be at any particular place at any particular time unless I want to. I must admit that it's a bit of a bummer to keep being faced with the fact that death is only a few years away, but it comes to everyone; and anyway, there's nothing I can do about it.

Fortunately, the guys at the county engineering division seem to think that I still have something to offer, so I commit to a personal services contract every year and do some consulting with them concerning what to do about situations they run into with respect to slides, slope stability, and so on. I like to think I've come up with some pretty good solutions to their problems, but to date I don't think they've acted on many of them, although they do plan to build the last one I did.

Actually, I don't really care whether they use my solutions or not because they always pay my billings with satisfying regularity. A little extra money always helps. Personally, I rarely think much about money, but Eloise always likes to get some, so I just give it all to her because it pleases her. So that's how this career ends.

Chapter 3: Questions

Now the questions return. What *has* happened to the Alaska we grew up with and why did it happen? Are our memories really just old dreams, wishful thinking about a past that never really existed? Have we forgotten all the pain, the heartaches and the losses we can never recover? Maybe the bittersweet memories are just as precious a part of our past as our visions of happier times now long gone. Maybe the mix of memories is all the more poignant for the variety and the still remembered emotional roller coaster of life intensified by youth. Or maybe the memories just seem more intense because they arise from youthful recollections of a home that has undergone so many changes during the past half century.

I'll try to restate and then answer the questions that I wanted to address when I started this book.

1. *Where* <u>*did*</u> *that sea of compromise and conformity – the one that swallowed up our Alaska – come from?*

It's no mystery. We, in the persons of our politicians, lobbyists, lawyers and other *homegrown* opportunists, went 'outside' and begged for it, campaigned for it, and brought it home with us accompanied by lot of contrived and programmed praise and celebration. At first we didn't recognize what was going on. In our naivety we didn't see all these self-serving actions for what they really were. By the time we woke up to the reality, it was too late. Our own 'in-house' corps of dragons had brought us statehood, dreams of unparalleled economic development and federal support, the seeds of the so-called 'benefits' of an outside lifestyle and promises of greater things to come. So who was ultimately to blame for all the unhappy lifestyle, professional and administrative changes that flowed from the greed-driven efforts of the few self-appointed Alaskan 'ambassadors' who started the whole thing? It was us! To paraphrase that immortal twentieth century philosopher *Pogo*: "We had met the enemy, and it was *us*."

2. *What then of official statehood; of the oil discoveries on the North Slope and of the burgeoning tourist trade?*

These were not causative factors in the 'Americanization of Alaska', the pronouncements of the social scientists notwithstanding. These were *events*. They were events that *followed* the planting of the seeds of change. It is undeniably true that a lot of opportunistic immigrant bureaucrats, politicians and lawyers flowed north to take advantage of the political vacuum following statehood. It is equally true that the oil discoveries brought many jobseekers as well as oil industry executives and workers. However, in my view none of these population increases brought about any basic *lifestyle* changes – at least none that could be observed or felt at the time. The seeds of such changes had already been sown through the greedy and self-serving efforts of the persistent statehood pushers, many of them long-time residents and many of them Anchorage based. Why would these 'sideshow barkers' do such a thing? Although self-interest was unquestionably a primary motivation, it's doubtful if there was a conscious effort to promote outside attitudes.

It was natural on the part of the Anchorageites to assume that a stateside lifestyle would accompany statehood and to behave accordingly. There had been at least a submerged stateside attitude (albeit disguised – maybe for the sake of appearance) around Anchorage almost since the Alaska Railroad had established a base of operations there.

It was also unavoidable that the unelected statehood pushers would prefer to operate in an atmosphere of stateside ambience because that was where they were pursuing their questionable promotional activities. They brought it all home with them and, unnoticed by average Alaskans who were content, even happy, with the way it was, they planted the seeds among us. In a manner of speaking, the subsequent migrations watered and nourished these seeds. The official anointing as the forty-ninth state and the oil rush that followed eight years later should be viewed as catalysts accelerating the process. On top of all the other increasingly influential factors, the onset of the communications age with its accelerated exchange of information obviously pushed us further and further away from the once unique Alaskan values and practices. Additionally, the jet airliners and the consequent convenience of long-distance travel didn't help any. I suppose, all things considered, the transformation of Alaska was and is inevitable regardless of how much a few of us may resist or have resisted in the past.

Alaska could, to a greater or lesser extent, be said to have always enjoyed a robust tourist trade, particularly if the gold-rush years are considered part of the 'always'. Even in those days, ladies and gents in Victorian get-up were riding steamboats up and down the Alaska coast and the Yukon River, probably looking at the same things the folks on the decks of the cruise ships look at today. The difference now is that the numbers of these people have increased by tens of thousands and improved transportation allows access to many places that couldn't be reached until relatively recently.

Although tourism has proven to be a lucrative industry for Alaska, there can be no doubt that the massive influx of visitors has affected the lifestyle of the state. In the case of the tourists, however, the influence doesn't tend to push that lifestyle toward a stateside ambience. In fact, in many cases, the Alaskan entrepreneurs who make a living off those visitors are frantically trying to recreate an Alaska that hasn't existed for about a hundred years or more. I guess that's OK except that the state is becoming cluttered with a bunch of phony rebuilt old buildings, mining sites, etc. and a lot of Alaskan businessmen looking silly dressed up as bearded old sourdoughs.

3. *Can we deny the influence of a dynamic body of technology? Of course not! Can we pretend that all the aspects of these advances have been negative? Of course not! However, can we* ignore *the negatives? Not unless we are prepared to abandon the concept of the supremacy of man over machine. What have been the effects of this technological 'tsunami' vis-à-vis our unique Alaskan workplace conditions?*

Alaska is not alone in feeling the impact of advanced electronic technology in the workplace. Personally I can only address the profound changes that have occurred in the civil engineering disciplines, but I'm sure most other professions have been affected equally if not more. In many, perhaps most, cases the changes have resulted in increased productivity and in improved ease of training in use of the 'tools'. However, there is a trade-off here.

Traditionally, engineers in charge of detailed field and design operations were familiar not only with methods, but with purpose and ultimate objectives as well. This has changed, and is continuing to change – almost to an alarming extent. There are more and more young surveyors and field engineers showing up who are superbly skilled in the use of all the modern tools, including (but not limited to) the now ubiquitous electronic instruments.

Skill in anything is a form of knowledge and is therefore inherently beneficial if properly applied. However, skill without knowledge and understanding of the ultimate objective can be, and frequently is, skill *mis*applied, often wasted, and sometimes even detrimental.

Whatever the reason, many of today's field technicians, surveyors and engineers in the construction industry, while able to quickly overwhelm the designers with voluminous data, sometimes seem not to fully understand that the fieldwork and the data are not ends in themselves. As an old engineer with many years of experience, I've worked with a lot of surveyors and other engineers – some good, some not so good – and I may appear overly critical. Nonetheless, there is an almost subliminal impression that the traditional surveyor's instinct for the nature of the existing topography, and its potential compatibility with the completed project, is missing or submerged in the operational aspects of the modern equipment (tools). I know that these effects of today's dynamic technology are not unique to Alaska. However, the impact in *our* state, taken with the other changes attendant to our 'Americanization', has had an influence that ripples beyond the workplace.

Additionally, there seems to be a growing class of well-educated young designers and supervisory engineers who *completely* lack any of the traditional engineering skills such as design drawing, surveying or any of the associated technical tasks. It is, therefore, extremely hard or impossible for these engineers to recognize or understand the problems that arise in the performance of such tasks. Nonetheless, it often becomes their responsibility to supervise or direct the efforts of technicians who *are* performing such sub-professional work. This naturally gives rise to a lot of misunderstandings and misinterpretations. For some reason Alaska is frequently a destination for many of these overeducated and under-experienced young engineers; the type who quickly and innocently fall prey to the conniving 'Managers' and bureaucrats whose influence is becoming more and more evident up north.

In summary, there is today in Alaska a dearth of hands-on ability and/or technical experience among both the field and office supervisory engineering practitioners. It's been many years since I've worked as a field surveyor or a design draftsman, but I place a great deal of value on the experience because it has unquestionably made me a much better supervisor.

4. *How did Alaska fall victim to the management crisis that has engulfed the state and turned the workplaces into little administrative clones of the agencies and corporations in the 'lower 48'? How did Alaskans fall into the trap of 'process over product' and is the current condition irreversible?*

Statehood affected us in a lot of ways. One of the most insidious of these arose out of the preparation of a state administrative code. The idea was probably to establish uniform bureaucratic and administrative procedures for the entire body of minutia perceived to be necessary for running a state government and exercising as much control as possible over the citizens' daily lives. Just the *idea* of state interference in personal affairs was (and I hope still is) strongly repugnant to real Alaskans, and the politicians knew it, so the preparation of this code was probably conducted with a minimum of publicity. At the time, I felt that the Alaskans on all the boards and commissions would have enough influence to represent our interests. I think most other Alaskans held out the same hope. I think we knew instinctively that we would need protection from the overzealous bureaucrats and 'Managers', many of whom had, even by then, already rushed in from outside to suck up to the 'right' politicians and fill what seemed like the hundreds of newly created jobs. Alas, ours was to prove a forlorn hope. My views regarding generic management and bureaucracy are well documented throughout the text of this book, so I won't repeat them here. Instead, I'll try to analyze how we were overtaken by these outside concepts and to examine the possibility of a reversal of the current overdone administrative procedures.

The document that was born of all the deliberations immediately following official statehood was probably called the 'Alaska Administrative Code'. Like a lot of other pronouncements, proclamations, rules and regulations, this one was presumably based on an amalgam of similar codes adopted by other states. Such codes are prepared almost exclusively by administrative people or 'Managers' and their ubiquitous bureaucrats vassals. They very rarely include pragmatic provisions addressing technical matters. In my own view, based on past experience, they primarily serve to provide authority and justification for the very people who wrote them. In effect, this is administratively comparable to allowing someone full freedom to write his or her own position description before going to work. From what little detail I know, the whole process from concept to implementation seems ludicrous. It would be comical except that the effect of it all is to place authority over technical matters in the hands of those who are not competent to judge them and to allow such people to administer with an emphasis on *process* rather than *product* – the old procedural enemy of progress. Such thinking, as any experienced construction engineer knows, produces project and program procedures and strictures that at best result in prohibitive operational costs, and at worst causes project slowdowns and interruptions for no sensible reason.

So how should we deal with an imported management structure that allows, indeed encourages, such administrative interference in technical matters.

Obviously, we must first recognize where the authority for this interference comes from and, if we can, attack the source of the practice and not the practitioners. If the subject was brought up to folks like that, they wouldn't even understand what they were being told, much less why it was a problem.

As tax-paying citizens, we should have access to a governmental mechanism whereby we can point out specific faults in the administrative code, explain our concerns and seek changes. There is little doubt that, with some research, any really competent and concerned engineer could find a trail through all the arcane government gobbledygook and come up with a logical and doable plan for pursuing those changes. This would of course, take a lot of time, and since most engineers are busy with other matters, it might be a good idea to hire a lawyer – God help us. There are some lawyers who specialize in things governmental and they often have a lot of that kind of stuff memorized; a practice frequently resorted to by those who feel that rationale and reasoning are too rigorous.

That would be one way to deal with the intrusion of the 'Managers' into technical decision-making. It has the advantage of clipping their wings and making it official, at least until they start kissing up to the politicians and political hacks who actually control things. Would it work? Probably not. We need to remember that in seeking changes to the administrative code, one would be attacking the sole source of sustenance for these people. They have neither the training nor, in most cases, the common sense to equip them for doing anything else or for performing any useful physical task. It is certain that they would resort to both political and personal measures to fight any changes to the code that would diminish either their authority or their image. Unfortunately, most engineers are not really sophisticated enough to counter the tactics that would probably be resorted to by the 'Managers'. The lawyer would probably be useful here too if he or she could be made to understand that they were merely ad hoc consultants hired for a specific purpose; not to act as guidance counselors. There are ways that management authority for technical decision-making and interference might be unofficially limited.

Most 'Managers' are surrounded by people like bookkeepers, secretaries, receptionists, para-something or others, and numerous other fledgling administrative 'camp followers'. They (the 'Managers') rarely know anything about the technical details of what's going on with construction or survey projects under their jurisdiction and must therefore depend on reports or word-of-mouth coming through this screen of subordinates to get any project information. Since they can't interfere to alter or otherwise modify decisions they haven't heard about, responsible project and program engineers could simply neglect to tell them anything. This plan would obviously work best in an organization with a large number of projects in progress simultaneously. One could also resort to feeding the 'Managers' bogus information to the extent that any technical decisions they made would be outlandish, thus ultimately destroying their credibility. Finally, one might seek a written declaration from management to the effect that engineering and technical matters requiring decisions would be handled strictly by the engineer(s) with absolutely no 'Management' interference. Unfortunately, this option requires decisions as to which matters fall under which definition. In a bureaucratically controlled organization, decisions require meetings, meetings require conclusions, conclusions require recommendations and here we go again – forget it!

Tragically, it may be too late to change the situation regarding 'Management' vis-à-vis engineering. Largely because of the events of the oil strike and statehood, we are simply outnumbered by the immigrants who moved in and took over the workplaces. We allowed it to happen, and although it hurts to admit it, we have only ourselves to blame for all the initially implied political encouragement. Anyway, many of the old-timers who were vital to the Alaskan attitude of 'Get 'er done' have retired or fled – a sad end to a robust and productive work ethic.

Given that the stateside attitudes and practices are now so pervasive in Alaska, it is very, very doubtful that any action on the part of the few production-minded engineers still up there could change things. This becomes even more evident when one recognizes that many of the people now in control were among the immigrants, and their professional experience was in large part gained under the management systems now polluting the Alaskan workplace.

In closing, I can only look back and wonder what happened to the Russian Mikes, the Pigshit Burns, the Tomato Bobs, Joe Voglers, John Pavliks, the Dukes and the Harveys and all the others who made Alaska what it was? Are we truly doomed to accept mediocrity and anonymity as just another member of the union of the United States?

In the old days, when signing in at a guest register for a museum, an art exhibition or a hotel, I took a great deal of pride in naming 'Alaska' as my place of residence, knowing that others would be impressed when they saw it. I guess such pride is no longer justified, or it won't be when it becomes common knowledge that Alaska is just like anyplace else. It's sad, isn't it? My *Camelot* has faded away like the morning mist in the forest of Southeast Alaska.

Chapter 4: Reflections at Seventy-Three

Someone once told me that the kind of writing I'm about to begin here was called "stream of consciousness" writing. She was my youngest son Tom's first wife, Michelle – a psychologist by profession. I don't know why they broke up, but I *do* know that they got along well enough at least once to produce a little boy; my grandson, a delightful little guy. They named him Tom after his dad so I call him 'little Tom' and I love him – a lot.

I wish seventy-three weren't so damn old. I wish I were still back working on the Taku River when my major concerns were how to get to town and how to get some beer and a date when I got there. At the time I thought I had other concerns, but they couldn't have been too serious because now I can't even remember what they were. I wish for a lot of stuff that isn't going to happen, I suppose most old guys do. Sometimes I like to look back and try to remember the details of the places where my profession has taken me. I'll try to describe some of them and the memories that have stuck with me. Although some of the comments here may be repetitious, I'll try to recall something different. The listing here is sort of in geographic order from north to south and west to east – not in chronological order.

Point Barrow and Wainwright are as far north as I got with any of the jobs I was on. I went to Barrow a long time ago because there was a brief period when the Alaska Road Commission was considering the feasibility of a road from Barrow to the little village of Wainwright. As I recall, we only stayed there for about two or three weeks, if that, and I don't think we left any stakes at all in the ground or any lasting impression on the people there either. Apparently, whoever dreamed up the project to begin with thought better of it after some reflection.

We *did* do some surveying along what I remember as a well-worn trail between the two places, but we were probably just there for the purpose of collecting topographic data. I can remember that the weather was good, so it must have been in the late summer. This was in about 1952 and after we left I never heard any more about the job. The road was never built, of course. At that time, no one ever consulted me about things like that, so I have no idea why the project was abandoned or why it was considered in the first place! I don't think anyone in Barrow wanted to drive to Wainwright, and I don't remember any private cars in either place anyway. When we explained to them why we were there, they probably thought we were nuts, but they were (and are) such polite people that it's doubtful if they ever said so. I went up there again in 1967 when I was serving as director of aviation for the State of Alaska, but there are no strong memories that stick in my mind about the place.

Proceeding southward in this brief mental journey, Kotzebue was the next place (geographically) where I spent some time. Unlike Barrow, I have several memories of Kotzebue. I'll try to relate them.

The town is sort of strung out along the edge of Kotzebue Sound (Chukchi Sea), and it's mostly private houses. I think there are a couple of businesses along the main street, but as I recall, they are in what look like houses too. There's a pretty big hotel there called the Iglooruk.[38] There is (or was) also an inn on the main street called the Whale's Something. I can't remember whether or not there are any rooms there, although there is (or

[38] 'Big House' in English.

was) an excellent lounge and restaurant. Both the Whale thing and the Iglooruk overlook Kotzebue Sound, but so does everything else in town.

Kotzebue is a regularly scheduled stop for Alaska Airlines, and there is apparently enough of a municipal administrative structure to require a city manager.

I don't think their manager while I was there had a whole lot to manage in Kotzebue, but one of them *did* come to Petersburg as city manager while I was city engineer *there*, and as far as I know, he managed things pretty well. He was a good guy, easy to get along with and I considered him a *very* good manager, mostly because he left me alone and didn't try to interfere with any of my projects. I worked on two projects in Kotzebue; a subdivision retracement in 1978, and a post-construction investigation of a utilidor project in 1976.

I also have a lot of memories of Nome, which is located on Norton Sound along the south coast of the Seward Peninsula about 150 miles south of Kotzebue. There is no road all the way from Nome to Kotzebue because the northern half would have to cross Kotzebue Sound and the cost of doing that would make such a project completely infeasible, or maybe even impossible. Even if the road *could* be built and everybody who owned vehicles in both Nome and Kotzebue drove the road both ways every day, the traffic volume still wouldn't justify the horrific construction cost, and the yearly maintenance costs would be humongous.

Nome is, or was, a good town. In about 1973 when I was last through there, the Alaskan attitude was still alive and well, the folks who lived there were still not in a hurry to get everything done *immediately*, and the time-honored Alaskan hospitality was still evident. Of course, that was about thirty-five years ago and by now the disgusting 'outside' efficiencies, attitudes and pomposity may have begun to seep in. It's difficult to keep those kinds of things out because: 1. Alaskans are traditionally reluctant to tell anyone to take their hotshot ideas and put them where 'the sun don't shine.' 2. The people who brought those sorts of things up north crept up all over, like an infestation of cockroaches (no insult to cockroaches is intended); I fear that Nome could not have escaped them permanently. 3. Fundamental changes like that typically and perhaps intentionally move in so slowly that it may be too late before they are noticed.

I traveled to Nome several times in 1967 in connection with my duties as director of aviation for the state before I got fired but I don't remember what I was doing there. In 1970, my business partner and I did a foundation bearing capacity and consolidation analysis at the Nome airport for the division. I also spent about two weeks there just relaxing with the Nome folks on the way back from a project on St. Lawrence Island.

When my partner and I were awarded the commission to conduct feasibility studies for possible water supply and distribution systems at Gambell and Savoonga on St. Lawrence Island in the Bering Sea, the controlling agency for the work was the U.S. Public Health Service (USPHS). They are, in many ways, a typical bureaucracy-bound government agency, although, thank God, in this case the engineers had somehow maintained operational control of technical matters. Perhaps a few more words on this subject are not out of line here.

In a few cases of federal agencies that have been in existence since black rocks were green, they have somehow reached a balance, however precarious, between the technical people and the administrative dragons who have infested and paralyzed so many of the less-fortunate organizations. In Alaska, because of our naïve ways, our inability (at the time) to recognize raw bureaucracy and, I like to think, our straightforward approach to most questions, the federal agency freeloaders who moved in early in the statehood conversion were able to infiltrate our simple organizations and begin redirecting our efforts from *product* to *process*; there it is again. Once accomplished, that's an open invitation to the hotshot 'Managers' to move in and bring their equally useless assistants, administrative aides, para-something or others, and assorted non-producing cohorts with them. They then waste no time in introducing policies involving meetings, endless memoranda, and irrelevant regulations. It's an old story and it's an infestation; there is no more accurate word with which to characterize this destructive process. It's easy to go on at great length about these administrative idiots and what they did to us, but I won't, at least not here. Besides, I already have.

Our St. Lawrence Island studies went well. I hope that our reports, conclusions and recommendations didn't, like so many of these studies, just end up on the shelf in some administrator's office never to be referred to again. I fear, however, that such a fate was exactly what awaited it.

While on this project we were told that, happily, the Eskimo people on St. Lawrence Island did not demand a large sum of money for their share of the benefits accruing from the Alaska Land Claims litigation. Much of the idea behind the land claims issue was to award the aboriginal people large sums of money to supposedly compensate for the land they had 'lost' to the old settlers, and the way of life that had been taken from them. I know less than nothing about the legal issues involved, but I suspect that the lawyers were the chief beneficiaries in the end. The St. Lawrence Island people, unlike most of the other groups, asked for clear and unassailable title to the entire island as primary compensation for whatever it was they had lost. This was, in my opinion, one of the most farsighted and wise decisions of the twentieth century – worthy of a Churchill or a George Washington. Although little known to the general public, it will reap benefits for their descendants far into the future, and, equally important, it demonstrates to the world that there are still people that cannot be bought off with just monetary riches.

As a result of their settlement, and the extreme climatic conditions of the area, the St. Lawrence Island Eskimo people may be able to fend off the inevitable Americanization of *their* home a lot longer than most of us – I hope so. Nonetheless, such changes must come about and the people are perceptive enough to see it. Throughout Eskimo country they have set up organizations, programs and incentives aimed at keeping the young people in the villages. It's almost always one of the topics at village council meetings, and the older people will emphatically insist that the drain (migration) of the young people away from the villages is one of the most, if not *the* most, serious threats to their ancient way of life. Who will tell them that change is truly inevitable, remind them that they have already begun to accept new technologies and advise them to 'get in step'?

I can't repeat often enough that I have found Eskimo people (at home) to be the kindest, most considerate, most giving and, paradoxically, the toughest people one could ever hope to encounter. No matter, the self-serving and greedy society that has moved, and is still moving, into Alaska will change all that soon enough. What does *Pogo* Say? "The enemy is *us*."

In terms of actual latitude, Fairbanks is further north than St. Lawrence Island; it just doesn't seem like it. There are some trees around Fairbanks, and there are also some well-drained properties where there is no permafrost. I didn't see any trees at all on St. Lawrence. Personally, I spent a lot of time in Fairbanks, almost eleven years. My first wife and I lived there from 1957 to 1967, we went to college at the nearby main campus of the University of Alaska, and we bought our first house there for $25,000.

Fairbanks is an old town, much older than the urban neophyte Anchorage. It served as a marshalling center and supply distribution point for the mining areas to the north and west that flourished during much of the nineteenth century. I think that at one time it was known as 'Barnette's cache'. He must have been a pretty influential guy because about half of everything in Fairbanks is named after him.

There was enough mining potential in the immediate vicinity to justify establishing the headquarters of the Fairbanks Exploration (FE) Company there. FE was a wholly owned subsidiary of the massive USSR&M Co. (United States Smelting, Refining & Mining) Company. The debris of the booming mining days still litters the creek valleys and meadows throughout the surrounding country. There's a lot of history there – enough to write a book if one wanted to do all the research.

Sometime after 1970, my business partner and I did a lot of development-related work around Fairbanks, mostly property surveys and subdivisions, some of which we never got paid for. A lot of people thought that Fairbanks, being closer to the North Slope than Anchorage, would really benefit when all the oil activity started. It didn't work that way. Apparently Anchorage tooted their horn enough louder than Fairbanks to draw the major headquarters offices to them, although I can't remember if the folks in Fairbanks even tried. The weather might have had something to do with it, but in any case, all the development has proven to be a mixed blessing.

Ever since its birth, Anchorage has pushed hard to be the center of activity for any and all Alaskan economic development. The effort has been largely effective and, in a manner of speaking, successful if one can measure success by the degree to which the city has transformed itself into a copy of most stateside cities. Anchorage has strongly encouraged this sort of thing since well before statehood and, when subsequent events appeared to offer promise in accelerating local development, the city was poised to jump in and lobby hard for the opportunity to help fuel such acceleration.

The people of Fairbanks have, by contrast, never displayed much enthusiasm for new development although many of the local politicians and businessmen frequently sponsored parades and celebrations at the slightest sign of potential new industry. Indeed, some of the local citizens groups would occasionally show outright hostility toward some of the larger outside corporations attempting to establish Fairbanks branches. There are a number of families in Fairbanks that have been there for six or seven generations, or maybe even more; this seemed to produce an unspoken undercurrent of resistance to change. In my role as Fairbanks city engineer and secretary of the local Planning and Zoning Commission during the 1960's, I was in a good position to observe such things.

Nonetheless, during my last visit to Fairbanks two or three years ago, it was easy to see that the city wasn't the same as it had been during the years my first wife and I lived there. At quitting time, the people who stream out of the office buildings are now wearing suits and ties and often carrying briefcases or file folders. I didn't see *any* open-collared shirts, boots or beards. The same guys seemed to be filling the downtown restaurants and coffee shops at lunchtime, carrying on animated discussions about things that apparently didn't require any drawings or samples for clarification. Maybe they were actually productively employed, but they looked suspiciously like managers and administrators to me. Ah, the loss of Fairbanks, another crack in the firmament of my own memory-shrouded *Camelot.*

Early in 1967, I was offered the job of public works director in Juneau, but when I got all set up to accept and start the job, an old friend said he wanted to hire me as director of aviation for the state; a real big-shot job. I explained things to the movers and shakers in Juneau, accepted the directorship and, after some flying back and forth between Juneau, Fairbanks and Anchorage, my first wife and I moved to Anchorage. As a result of some decidedly un-political behavior and attempts to remain primarily Alaskan oriented, I only lasted a year in the job, but that's another story told in another part of the book. My first wife and I remained in Anchorage until our divorce in 1972, and I think she remained there after that, but I don't know for how long.

Alaskans used to say Anchorage was located only fifty to seventy-five miles from Alaska. That may have been true at one time, but after statehood and the oil strike hit us, Anchorage sucked up as much as possible of the outside money and influence. This seemed to widen the distance from there to Alaska, and by some sort of political manipulation Anchorage gained more and more control over state politics, procedures and policies. Of course, one of the major outfalls of this shift in the political center of mass was the increasing influence of the Anchorage attitude, by now completely infected with the outside administrative and managerial virus. In many ways, a lot of the rest of south-central Alaska has become a sort of bureaucratic suburb of Anchorage. All one has to do now is watch television coverage of our state to see how many people in the states get the idea that everyone in Alaska lives in Anchorage. I guess we could make an analogy here. The modern Anchorage might be likened to an infected boil that has attached itself firmly to the political 'body' of the state and spread its infection throughout the entire administrative 'bloodstream'. That may seem a little too graphic, but I think most *real* Alaskans of long-term residence have pretty much the same opinions, although maybe not so extreme.

My partner and I did mostly property development projects in the Anchorage area. Just coincidentally, the time-span of our business covered the pre-oil period, the period of giddy optimism and the surprising failure of many, if not most, of the numerous over-ambitious development projects in that area. It was something of a puzzle, at least to me, why so many of those projects failed. The North Slope oil field was still furnishing lots of jobs in the development phase, and money was being spent in record amounts both there and on the pipeline to Valdez. Perhaps there was a slowdown while the line was being built since none of the oil could get to its market until the construction was completed. In any case, the rush of property seekers expected to descend on Anchorage didn't materialize in time for the hopeful developers to realize the mountainous financial return they had predicted. Whatever outside interests were bankrolling those local development projects must have gotten tired of waiting for their share of the 'great Alaskan oil boom' money and started putting the squeeze on the developers. Alaskans, in our simple ways, were being introduced to 'High Finance' – stateside big time. The lessons we learned started in Anchorage and, in the end, spread throughout the state and changed us all. As it turned out, Anchorage would indeed see its share (and a large portion of everyone else's) of the oil money, but for whatever reason there seemed to be a temporary hiatus in the money flow while waiting for Alyeska to finish the pipeline. In the midst of the resulting local financial slump, some of the old Alaskan character finally showed through like a cut and polished diamond in a gravel pit.

My partner and I lost quite a large amount of money as a result of the failed projects in Anchorage. Most of the carpet-bagging opportunist developers from outside packed up all their gear and left as soon as their projects showed signs of failing, leaving the property owners, and whoever else they owed money to, holding the bag so to speak. The Alaskan developers, unlike the outsiders, made us feel proud. Virtually without exception they took their lumps and, although it was obviously difficult, eventually paid off all their suppliers, contractors and financiers. They finally paid us too even though it took some time. Out of respect, we made it a point never to pressure them for the money. We kept sending the bills but *never* with any demanding notations. Alas, I fear that most of such people are gone now. Many of them have left the state out of disgust at the pollution of Alaskan business and legal ethics. Shamefully, some of the old-time entrepreneurs have learned and adopted the business practices brought north by the opportunists. Admittedly, a few of the near-swindlers were already in Anchorage, even before statehood. However, in those days they were usually exposed before they could do too much damage. Maybe we were better at spotting phonies then. While headquartered in Anchorage, my partner and I also did projects on Kodiak Island, near Homer, in the mountains north of Palmer, and at Lake Louise west of Glennallen.

Of all the many places that I lived and worked during my fifty plus years in Alaska, I must concede that, with the exception of Petersburg, Kodiak has (or had) probably changed least of all. I haven't been back there since about 1975 or 1976, but after living there the better part of a year I got to know the people well enough to be convinced that changing their collective attitude would be nearly impossible. Kodiak is home to a lot of crab fisherman who, as I recall, work both the Gulf of Alaska and the Bering Sea, although I've been told that boats from Dutch Harbor are just as common in the Bering Sea. There is a military base south of the City of Kodiak, but fishing has long been the main economic activity supporting the folks who live on Kodiak Island and, as far as I know, it's the only natural resource. I don't think there's much potential for any other resource development there either. I could easily be wrong since I don't look into such things as potential resources. This is not a bleak characterization. In fact, it may be a big factor in saving Kodiak and Kodiak Island from the destructive influences that flow in inexorable waves in the wake of resource exploitation and industrial expansion. As we know this has already been the tragic fate of much of the rest of Alaska and all indications are that such influences will soon dictate the dominant characteristic of the state. Just being an Alaskan is no longer anything special, but maybe being a Kodiak

Islander still is, and it may stay that way for some time simply because of the unique and refreshing attitudes of many (if not most) of the people who live there.

Happily, Kodiak, its institutions, its businesses, its image-makers, and its residents are decidedly and intentionally provincial. As a result of this characteristic, the island and its people have been able to preserve their separate identity during the sad transformations of the rest of the state. I never got the impression that the islanders were disinterested or that they didn't give a damn about the rest of the state, the nation or the world. It just seemed that they were not particularly anxious to shoulder the often-transparent concerns that dominate so much of today's news. They seemed to feel that taking care of family and community matters was enough and should be their primary area of interest. I found this attitude to be *extremely* pleasant, both to encounter and to experience.

Since Kodiak and the Island enjoy a relatively mild climate and take in some of the most spectacular and beautiful scenery in the state, I suppose that, as the Americanization of Alaska becomes overbearing, the pure pressure of an ever-increasing national population will force a significant increase in Kodiak's growth. When it comes, a major portion of the increase will undoubtedly be immigrants from down south who will bring their stateside attitudes with them. When this happens to Kodiak and the other few enclaves that still cling to their Alaskan way of life, the takeover will be complete.

Don't let it be forgot
that once there was a spot
for one brief shining moment
that was known as Camelot

–Lerner and Leow

Chapter 5: Closure

Currently, we live in Washington State. It's not really where I want to be, but the place I really *do* want to be doesn't exist anymore. So why doesn't it exist anymore? Is it just my imagination or has Alaska really changed as much as it seems to have? Assuming the changes are real, did they happen for the reasons I've outlined in the foregoing text or just as a result of overall changing times?

As I mentioned several times previously, I grew up in Juneau. The country around there hasn't changed except that much of what used to be undisturbed woods, ponds and so on near town has been stripped off and is now covered with homes, businesses and such. Of course Juneau is the capital, and I think most long-time Juneau residents knew that statehood was bound to bring in a bunch of new agencies, bureaucrats and 'Managers'. Perhaps all the changes had an even more profound effect in the areas of Alaska where people rarely even *thought* about government or government control prior to statehood. However, I doubt that even people in Juneau could have foreseen the management nightmare that ultimately swallowed the municipal government there. This has been the Juneau experience, and it's hard to say how much of it was a direct or indirect result of either statehood or the oil boom. Probably very little, I've always felt that the intrusion of the grotesquely bloated and misshapen stateside concepts of 'generic management' were responsible for at least initiating what happened to the Juneau Municipal Government's administrative structure. The past city manager and his accomplices just stepped in at the right moment to twist it to their own selfish ends.

I guess that's pretty much it, as they say. As great as it would be for Alaska to return to the way it was, I'm realistic enough to know that such a thing just isn't going to happen, no more than I'm going to wake up tomorrow morning and find that I'm twenty-five again.

Why things are the way they are and who's to blame are questions that are the province of politicians and lawyers.

What things are and how to deal with them is the legacy left for the ordinary people.

Now it's nearly over. The experiences and the emotions that seemed so fierce at the time are beginning to fade into the mist of memory. It's not as tragic as it sounds. With age comes the recognition that such things are truly transitory, and that we must be content to enjoy the bittersweet nostalgia of the happy times and the lost loves that defined our past lives. There are reminiscences and reflections to be gathered, and conclusions to be made. This final sentence admits that, a few deep disappointments notwithstanding, it has so far been a pretty good life, and I hope there's a fair amount left to go yet.

www.ingramcontent.com/pod-product-compliance
Lightning Source LLC
Chambersburg PA
CBHW020358100426
42812CB00001B/109

* 9 7 8 0 5 7 8 0 1 0 0 1 4 *